African American Theology

African American Theology

AN INTRODUCTION

Frederick L. Ware

Published by Westminster John Knox Press
Louisville, Kentucky

16 17 18 19 20 21 22 23 24 25—10 9 8 7 6 5 4 3 2 1

The publisher and the author gratefully acknowledge reuse of the author's following essays:

"Black Theology," taken from *Global Dictionary of Theology: A Resource for the Worldwide Church*, edited by William A. Dyrness and Veli-Matti Kärkkäinen. Copyright © 2008 by InterVarsity Christian Fellowship/USA. Used by permission of InterVarsity Press, P.O. Box 1400, Downers Grove, IL 60515, USA. www.ivpress.com.

"Methodologies of African American Theology," taken from *The Oxford Handbook of African American Theology*, edited by Anthony Pinn and Katie Cannon. Copyright © 2014 by Oxford University Press. Used by permission of Oxford University Press, USA (www.oup.com).

"Toward an Alternative Engagement of Black Theology with Modern Science," taken from *Black Theology: An International Journal*. Copyright © 2011.

Book design by Drew Stevens
Cover design by Allison Taylor

Library of Congress Cataloging-in-Publication Data

Ware, Frederick L., 1961–
    African American theology : an introduction / Frederick L. Ware.
        pages cm
    Includes bibliographical references and index.
    ISBN 978-0-664-23950-3 (alk. paper)
    1. Black theology.   I. Title.
    BT82.7.W36   2016
    230.089'96073—dc23

                                    2015034507

Most Westminster John Knox Press books are available at special quantity discounts when purchased in bulk by corporations, organizations, and special-interest groups. For more information, please e-mail SpecialSales@wjkbooks.com.

In memory of
my mother,
Dannie Vee Benson (1926–2009)

Contents

Preface

My experience as a student and now as a teacher parallels shifting perceptions of African American theology in the last thirty-two years. In the spring semester of 1984, while I was an undergraduate student in philosophy at Memphis State University (now the University of Memphis), I was introduced to black theology by Otis Clayton. Otis, a recent seminary graduate, was enrolled in the master's program in philosophy. We talked often and at length before and after our course in the philosophy of religion. Otis's command of the literature and coherent summaries of the debates in black theology convinced me that black theology was a field of study that I needed to know. At this same time, I was learning about black philosophy but was more intrigued with black theology because I was undertaking studies in philosophy in preparation for my later theological studies. For me, black theology seemed to deal with the economic, social, and political situation of black people in a sustained way that I had not earlier witnessed in the church. Though leaders in the church expressed deep concern and were involved in various types of ministries to address the condition of black people, they had not developed a level and intensity of theological reflection comparable to their passionate activism. While preparing this book, as fate would have it, I had the privilege, after nearly ten years since our last conversation, to speak again with Otis. By his present questions and tone, I sense his unease with recent works in black theology, especially those that purport to do theology without a professed commitment to fundamental Christian beliefs.

In spite of several notable figures leading in contemporary black and womanist theology, no one today actually masters the field. In the 1980s, when I was in college and a divinity student, I read and compiled notes on every book available on black theology and womanist theology. At that time, there was a small, manageable corpus of literature. For a while, it was possible to stay current. Now it is questionable as to whether anyone is able to read every book and article at the rate they are being published today. Some books and articles may fall into similar patterns of methodology. Still other books and articles seem to be aimed toward new trajectories. Further complicating the matter is the fact there is not always an obvious connection between the publications.

Consequently, this book in no way purports to be a comprehensive study covering every publication in African American theology. More to the truth, the book represents my reading over the last thirty years and my teaching for the past sixteen years. Though my reading is extensive, I have been selective about which publications in black and womanist theology to include for this book. This is not an admission of personal failure or professional neglect but rather a recognition of the abundant corpus of literature now available to persons who wish to explore the field of African American theology as well as a word of caution for any persons who claim immodestly to have mastery of the entire field. As the subtitle of the book implies, and the best that I am able to do, the book provides a manageable source for persons unfamiliar with the field to begin their study and a stimulus for further conversation among persons who have experimented, as I have, in the field for a considerable length of time.

Over the years the types of questions and concerns voiced by my students have motivated me to think very deeply about the structure of African American theology. Throughout my teaching African American theology, the questions and concerns by students in various settings and at various offerings of the course seem always to be the same. Their questions are rarely about content, about the literature. Their questions have been mostly about the connection of African American theology, in its forms of black theology or womanist theology, to mainstream traditions of Christian theology and the broad range of issues, in addition to liberation, that concern black Christians.

In the past sixteen years, I have offered the course in African American theology a total of eight times, half of them under the title "Black Theology" and the other half under the title "African American Theology." During the 2012–13 academic year, I had the privilege to offer the course to students in two different settings, one at Howard University School of Divinity (HUSD) and the other at the Lutheran Theological Seminary in Philadelphia (LTSP). Here I list the names of the students enrolled in my African American theology courses offered during the 2012–13 academic year: Agnes Smith Brown, Kyra Brown, Constance Cotton, Patricia El, Dedra Florence-Johnson, Timothy Gavin, Phillip Harris, Timothy Hearn, Gail Hicks, Yvonne Lembo, Linda Manson,

Meagan McLeod, Wanda Pate, Michelle Pinkney, Marcia Price, Diane
Pryor, Barbara Satchell, Edmond Sewoul, Candace Strand, Robin
Thornhill, Stephanie Wooten, and Lisa Younger. Though students in
each course that I have offered have always been engaging, this group
of scholars named above were most instrumental in thinking through
with me several of the topics covered in this introduction to African
American theology.

I interpret my experience and the general shifts in the perceptions of
African American theology—most certainly as I have observed them in
my students' quest for a conception of blackness and sense of community beyond existing polarized classifications in American society—as a
movement from the "politics of identity" to the "politics of truth." On
the one hand, the politics of identity is a trend in the humanities, inclusive of religious and theological studies, that focuses on the social locations and political leanings of scholars and the populations they study.
The politics of identity indicates the academy's poor adaptation to the
social protests of minorities and women and the slow increase of these
underrepresented groups in the student bodies and faculties of American colleges and universities. The focus on the various social locations
for theological reflection has enriched religious and theological studies;
yet with the increasing fixation on social identity, scholars rarely engage
in conversations about the principal nature of their disciplines and the
meaning of life for all humankind. On the other hand, the politics of
truth is a quest for the best possible experience of life in universal community. It is a quest that more scholars are willing to take, desiring to
gain a view of human identity and issues of social justice in the widest
possible context, global or cosmic, where efforts to understand who we
are as human beings and to find solutions to our social problems are
linked to the question of humanity's place in the universe. As a scholar
leaning toward a politics of truth, my blackness as well as other aspects
of my identity contributes to my awareness of self. This sense of self is
not, for me, an end in itself but rather a window to peer into a deeper
sense of my life, where the various disparate parts of my personhood
are united and my internal wholeness is paired with the harmony of all
that is. There is no part of me that I wish to deny. And yet there is no
single part of me that alone defines me. My aim is to be "human," to
live and to live well as the creature that I am.

Discussion about the big questions and perennial issues always begins
from some location. Howard Thurman said that in order for a person to be everywhere, they must first be somewhere. African American

theology represents one among several starting points for this large and important conversation among human beings. My study of theology is ethnic-specific, but not in an exclusive way. I intend that my study of African American theology will contribute to reflection about the discipline of theology and the religious dimensions of human existence.

In addition to the stimulus to my thinking provided by my students, other persons have been supportive of my work. To them I am thankful. In 2009, I began conversations with Donald McKim, at Westminster John Knox Press, about writing a book on African American theology. Before moving into another position with the press, Don had arranged anonymous reviews of my book proposal. These reviews helped me gain better clarity on the contribution that my project may make to the discipline of African American theology. Robert Ratcliff, who assumed the role of editor, has been very supportive and patient as I worked, sometimes at snail's pace, on the book project. My research assistants Linwood Blizzard and Rhonda Rhea were very thorough in their research. Any omissions of materials from the book are attributable to my choices. I am thankful to the Howard University librarians Carrie Hackney and Ida Jones for working closely with Linwood and Rhonda. Quintin Robertson, Director of the Urban Theological Institute, and Dean Jayakiran Sebastian extended to me the invitation to engage a wonderful group of students at the Lutheran Theological Seminary. A sabbatical leave provided by the Office of the Provost of Howard University provided the financial support I needed in order to give sustained and uninterrupted attention to the book project. I benefited greatly from many conversations with my Howard colleagues Kenyatta Gilbert and Renee Harrison about my project, from start to finish, as well as our shared concerns on various matters.

My family has always affirmed me in every project that I have undertaken. My daughter Kayla, a senior in college, often reminded me about the need for textbooks to be interesting for students like her who for the first time would be learning about African American theology. My daughter Megan, a sophomore in college and a promising researcher, devoted many hours to reviewing with me the numerous primary sources unearthed in my research. My wife, Sheila, has always been a patient listener and thoughtful interlocutor, accompanying me along my musings and asking questions of the kind to encourage me to think seriously and deeply about how to express my ideas in words understandable to nonexperts. My mother, Dannie Vee Benson, even several years after passing, remains with me in spirit, along with other members of our family, providing inspiration for many of our personal and professional accomplishments.

Reverend Arnor S. Davis, an alumnus of HUSD, passed away in August 2013. I seem now to hear his words more than ever before. He would often say, "Tell me something that I do not know. Explain to me why I should be interested and how it matters for the church." I hope that a book of this kind answers his and other readers' queries.

Introduction

In the United States, religion and ethnicity represent spaces for creativity and opportunity in the development of American culture by virtue of the unique political structure of the United States. In the language of economics, religion in the United States is an unregulated, free market.[1] The constitutional separation of church and state has allowed individuals and groups freedom in the area of religion to develop numerous belief systems and organizations for furthering their shared aims and convictions. Over the course of American history, certain religious traditions have become "mainstream," that is, widely regarded as acceptable expressions of religion. Still other religious traditions run counter to or, in some instances, complement the mainstream traditions. In either case, religion thrives through emphasis on personal religious experience and voluntary association between persons who share similar experiences and convictions.

Before the U.S. Constitution was drafted, this form of religion, emphasizing personal experience and initiative, took shape in what has been termed the Great Awakening, an important event not only in American history but also in African American history. In the fervor of revival, anyone could take the title of minister on the basis of one's inner sense of calling, which may or may not be affirmed by an existing religious organization. All persons were believed to be equal before God and granted the same privilege by the Holy Spirit to participate in religious life and ministry. "The revivalism of the Great Awakening, spread over time and space by evangelical preachers, created the conditions for large-scale conversion of [African American] slaves."[2] Jonathan Edwards and other revival preachers described the Awakening as the "dawning of a new day" and the conversion of African Americans as "showers of grace" preceding the "glorious times" of the millennium.[3] For Edwards, the revivals were a sign of the millennium, which was starting in America and would spread to other parts of the world. Revival preaching, during and after the Revolutionary War, blended with the rhetoric of patriotism to produce an association of God's work in history with politics and government. In the zeal of evangelical churches (i.e., Presbyterian, Baptist, and Methodist) to spread the gospel, strong positions were taken against slavery and visions were cast for the reform of society. The evangelical churches' challenge of the existing social order and African Americans' own adverse experience of racism and oppression provoked African Americans to propose alternative interpretations of the American nation and its mission. For African Americans, slave and free, and even many white Americans, slavery violated the fundamental principle of the American Revolution, as stated in the Declaration of Independence, that all persons are created equal by God and have God-given inalienable rights to life, liberty, and the pursuit of happiness.

Like religion, ethnicity in the United States is a form of voluntary association between individuals that flourishes without government regulation. The United States is a pluralistic society. This pluralism is not unique to the present. From its beginning, the United States has been made up of many peoples, with some groups having more or less power than other groups. In American history, not all groups of persons have equally enjoyed the rights of citizenship.

In African Americans' efforts to move from mere relationship by common racial designation based on physical appearances, their conceptions of black racial identity and black solidarity have functioned much like ethnicity, particularly with an emphasis on ancestry, heritage, religious beliefs, and moral values. In religious and secular institutions and even through government structures, African Americans have voiced their concerns and acted to address matters affecting their existence and quality of life. This inspired protest and activism is a sign of the grave spiritual crisis of the American nation, where the high moral ideals of freedom and democracy are often diminished by deep-seated injustice. Thus the black experience in the United States "reflects some of the richest dimensions of the human experience and human existence and also some of its most oppressive and wretched realities."[4] African American experience, which may also be true of other ethnic groups in the United States, exposes the beauty and cruelty of human life in America.

DEFINING AFRICAN AMERICAN THEOLOGY

African American theology is a study and interpretation of religious beliefs and practices regarded by African Americans as significant, having either positive or negative consequences for their existence and quality of life. When focused on Christian beliefs, African American theology represents an understanding of God's freedom and the good news of God's call for all humankind to enter life in genuine community, with true human identity and moral responsibility. Defined in this way, African American theology crafts meanings of freedom, a central concept in both Christianity and American culture. In the American context, African American theology shows that racism, among other forms of injustice, complicates the human predicament, and its eradication requires nothing less than an enlargement of salvation to include the liberation of persons who lack full participation in society.

The term "African American theology" is coming into more use for two reasons. First, the phrase is meant as a covering term for various theological studies dealing with the religious traditions of persons comprising the African American population. African Americans are not monolithic. Even with common ancestry, the connections with black sub-Saharan peoples, African Americans have religious, political, economic, and cultural differences. The largest percentage of African Americans are the descendants of Africans, mostly from West and Central Africa, who were enslaved in the United States. The suppression of the Atlantic Slave Trade coupled with the Domestic Slave Trade of the South had profound consequences for the growth of the native-born slave population.[5] At the time of the Civil War, with few Africans then being imported directly to the United States, the four million persons forming a majority of the American slave population were born in the United States and generations removed from their African ancestors, though condemned by law to follow their condition of servitude. Since the Immigration and Nationality Act of 1965, a substantial and rising number of Africans, with the largest contingency from Kenya, Nigeria, Ethiopia, and Ghana, have settled in the United States. Another significant wave of immigration has come from blacks in the Caribbean, mainly from Jamaica, Haiti, Trinidad and Tobago, Dominican Republic, and Barbados. Recent African and Afro-Caribbean immigrants have not assimilated into the native-born African American population, as happened when their numbers were smaller, but have instead formed communities to continue their unique religious and cultural traditions. African American theology is a phrase meant to encompass theological studies of the varieties of traditions among the numerous black peoples who make up the African American population.

Second, the phrase is used to avoid generalization and reductionism. The phrase "African American theology" allows an important distinction for "black theology" and "womanist theology" as specialized studies in contemporary systematic theology. Black theology and womanist theology are African American theology. However, not all African American theology is black theology or womanist theology. Black theology and womanist theology may be regarded as forms of liberation theology. Emerging in the 1960s and aligned with the black power movement, black theology addresses, often but not always from a Christian perspective, the oppressions rooted in racism. Beginning in the 1980s and endeavoring to be holistic, womanist theology addressed the oppressions rooted in the triad of sexism, racism, and classism. Because not all African American theologians are doing liberation theology but still attempt to bring African American contexts, interests, and sources to bear on the theological topics they study, the phrase "African American theology" aims to encompass their theological studies as well as those studies of African Americans who are intentional about doing black theology and womanist theology.

If theology may be regarded simply as the study and interpretation of religion or religious beliefs, then it is not limited to Christian beliefs.[6] Theology could involve the study of beliefs of non-Christian religions. For example, black religious humanism, which will be discussed in chapters 4 and 5, is an intellectual tradition that interfaces with Christian beliefs. Often expressed as reflection on the adequacy of Christian beliefs for black liberation, black religious humanism is an important source for critique of Christian beliefs. Also, African and African-derived religions are practiced among black peoples in the African American population. The African American emphasis on African heritage warrants examination of past and current African religions for an understanding of how these religions illuminate the history as well as the current expressions of African American thought.

In this book, the study of religion and religious beliefs is limited to Christianity, particularly to the beliefs of African American Protestant Christians who share the narrative of the experience of and struggles against chattel slavery and its impact on subsequent law, policy, and custom in the United States. Over the course of United States history, the membership of African American Christians has remained consistent, ranging from 80 to 90 percent in Christian denominations and congregations that are predominately black and Protestant. However, common Christian affirmations are not treated in this book in order to avoid unnecessary repetition of basic aspects of Christianity and, what is more important, the caricature of African American churches as a rival sect in Christianity or a separate branch of the same. It would be a flagrant error in judgment to portray African Americans as having a "black" version of each major doctrine of Christianity such as a "black Trinity," "black Christology," "black Pneumatology," "black soteriology," or "black eschatology," although there is casual and random use of these terms in some publications of black and womanist theologies. The book will not discuss an African American perspective on original sin unless there is some argument and special nuance to the concept by African Americans. The book is not a reiteration, in the whole or in part, of Christian dogma or a juxtaposition of African American theology over against Christian theology, as if African American theology represents an invention of a competing worldview. In view of the division of mainstream Christian churches and their inaction against the injustices in American society, African American churches have perceived their existence and mission as crucial to the authentic expression of Christianity, involving belief and practice. African American Christians are not representing an alternative Christianity: they are seeking to practice genuine Christianity. The book looks selectively at topics of religious significance that emphasize African Americans' contributions to Christian faith by virtue of their historical and social experiences.

LOCI THEOLOGICI AS MODERN GENRE OF SYSTEMATIC THEOLOGY

Since the Reformation of the sixteenth century, the style of systematic theology in Western Christianity has focused primarily on the identification and exposition of *loci*, which literally means "locations." Loci are regarded as the main branches or subject areas of theology or, at minimum, basic topics for discussions in theology. With each locus, there are smaller component doctrines. For example, under the locus of soteriology (salvation), there are the doctrines of justification and election.

The notion and literary genre of *loci theologici* (topics of theology) began in 1521 with the publication of Philipp Melanchthon's *Loci communes rerum theologicarum, seu hypotyposes theologicae* (Theological commonplaces, or theological hypotheses; trans. as *Commonplaces: Loci communes 1521* [2014]), which underwent several revisions until reaching its final form in his 1559 work *Loci praecipui theologici* (*The Chief Theological Topics: . . . 1559* [2010]). Melanchthon's work replaced Peter Lombard's *Sententiarum libri quatuor* (Four books of sentences, trans. as *The Sentences* [2007–10]) to become the premier theological textbook at European universities. The loci, or topics, that Melanchthon chose were inferred from his study of Paul's Letter to the Romans. He identified these loci as the topics of sin, law, and grace. According to Melanchthon, the sum total of Christian doctrine can be constructed under these topics. Melanchthon's style of theology was further popularized in John Calvin's *Institutio Christianae religionis* (Institute . . . , trans. as *Institutes of the Christian Religion* [1960]), published and updated from 1536 to 1560. His style of theology was best refined in Johann Gerhard's *Loci theologici* (Theological commonplaces), published and revised from 1610 to 1622 (trans. as *A Golden Chaine of Divine Aphorismes* [1632]). Whereas Protestant theologians like Melanchthon, Calvin, and Gerhard focused on topics supposedly at the heart of Scripture, the Catholic theologian Melchior Cano utilized the loci method to focus attention on the sources that support all argument in theology. Cano's approach appears in his work *De locis theologicis libri duodecim* (Topics of theology, twelve books), written in the 1540s but published posthumously in 1563.[7] The genius of Melanchthon and his imitators was to apply the Renaissance humanists' hermeneutics, modeled on the rhetorics of Aristotle and Cicero, to the discipline of theology.

The Reformers' construal of theology framed by loci, supposedly extrapolated from Scripture or based on incontestable authority, limits awareness of Christianity as a religion being generally meaningful and a life-altering path for human beings. In general, religions are not seeking the meaning of life but instead an experience of life. The religions, each in a unique way, are striving for a certain quality of life and propose certain beliefs and practices that will help persons to achieve that quality. By the Reformers' selected topics (loci), it is not always clear that Christianity as a religion is aimed at a particular quality of life.

While the loci method represents an established and widely used genre, it has not resulted in any uniformity in theology. There are numerous and varying lists of loci. Not only do the lists contain different loci; lists with similar loci are also arranged differently. Melanchthon's *Loci praecipui theologici* contains twenty-four loci, which include God, creation, free will, sin, law, gospel, grace, good works, Scripture, church, sacraments, predestination, kingdom of God, resurrection, prayer, human government, and Christian liberty. The loci used by Gerhard are Scripture, God and Trinity, Christ, church, and ministry. The loci used by John Calvin are God, Christ, salvation, and church. In the twentieth century, Karl Barth's multivolume work *Church Dogmatics,* designed to cover all Christian doctrines, is organized around the loci of revelation, God, creation, reconciliation, and redemption. In contrast to Barth, Paul Tillich's three-volume *Systematic Theology* is organized around the loci of reason and revelation, being and God, existence and Christ, life and the Spirit, and history and the kingdom of God. Now, in the twenty-first century, students can expect to see all or some of the following loci in theology textbooks: revelation, God, creation, human being and sin, Christ, salvation, Holy Spirit, church, and last things.

There are benefits but also limitations to the loci method. It does bring some organization to Christian theology, but not all beliefs or doctrines are treated thoroughly and evenly. For example, though Melanchthon claimed to have developed a system for the study and interpretation of the whole of Christian faith, he omitted discussion of the doctrine of the Trinity, preferring to treat the Trinity as a mystery, like other divine mysteries to be adored rather than investigated. He affirmed the incarnation and the two natures of Christ, but he did not address any metaphysical questions about how the two natures are both fully present and operative in Christ. Similarly, in the works of other systematic theologians, their treatment of topics is selective and uneven. The reader will notice that this book is likewise selective in its treatment of topics in African American theology. This acknowledgment of selectivity is important in order to show the connection with, yet also the departure of this text from, other works in systematic theology using some form of organization around a particular set of topics or themes.

The loci method is problematic when there is lack of awareness or denial of the arbitrariness of the topics. Reformist theologians claimed that the loci (topics) are derived from Scripture. Clearly, while they were using Scripture, the hermeneutics by which they derived the topics was largely influenced by the pedagogy and literary theory of the Renaissance humanists. If the topics were as obvious as the Reformers assumed, then it would stand to reason that these topics would have been recognized by earlier Christian theologians. For example, Augustine, a teacher of rhetoric, did not use the loci (topics) method for Christian theology.

Other unfortunate consequences of the loci (topic) method are the tendency of Christian theologians to treat the topics as concepts and thus regard theology mainly as the clarification of these concepts by supposedly proceeding in an objectively neutral manner. When theology is fixated on the task of clarifying topics as categories, theology becomes esoteric and disconnected from the lived experience where Christian faith is expressed and evolves. In theology, as in Western thought as a whole, scholarly study is said to take place among a "community of intellectuals [that is] raceless and shares only work-related problems of methodology, analysis, craftsmanship."[8]

Adolf von Harnack identifies encounter with God (or Jesus Christ and his gospel) as the constant in Christianity.[9] Religious faith is dynamic, arising from lived experience shaped by encounter with God. Testimony (i.e., self-reporting, witness, or narrative) is offered in response to the encounter. It is testimony and not dogma that is fundamental in the propagation of faith. Stories of individual encounters with God hold forth the possibility for other persons to encounter God. Lived experience is prior to theological reflection and must continue to inform theology; only thus can theology be a study that represents actual religious traditions. Theology best functions to enable us to remember, retell, and relive the divine encounters that empower, enlighten, and then transform us. Experience is something to which we must always return. Theology, which may begin with speculation, is enriched when it returns to and is reckoned with the experiences that give rise to our initial thoughts.

Over the history of Christianity, the majority of theological writing has not been in the genre of theological loci as common now in systematic theology. For the most part, theology has been devoted to the development of statements (i.e., answers and solutions) directed to specific issues and problems of concern to theologians and their audience at a given time. This practical approach has resulted in the production of theology through sermons, letters, pamphlets, essays, and editorials to address specific challenges or issues at particular times and under certain circumstances.

Lacking awareness of the origin and development of the loci method, theologians rarely exhibit any sense of the limitations of the loci method and how the so-called traditional topics, though far from any uniform list, constitute a coherent whole. The Protestant Reformers' insights and creativity, framed within a particular historical and cultural context, have become dogma and applied generally for theological studies. The unquestioned assumption is that genuine theology must not only proceed from loci (or topics) but also from a definite set of loci (or topics). The innovation of the Reformers has been eclipsed by an orthodoxy that actually terminates theological studies. The Reformers' insights were gained through a new approach to Scripture, which has always been important to the church, but now these Reformers are deemed the principal source of theology. Martin Luther, a professor of biblical studies, sought to ground theology in the reading of the Scriptures. If theology, as Luther argued, is founded upon the Scripture, then our reading of biblical texts must be more rigorous than his. It is impossible for us to advance theological inquiry beyond what the Reformers accomplished unless, for reading sacred texts, we make full use of the critical, analytical, and historical tools of today. Might not we gain new insight by our fresh reading of the Scriptures?

Though this book does not present African American theology through an exposition of Scripture, it does presuppose a particular and what might be a fresh reading of Scripture. A rereading of Genesis 2–3 is fundamental for a renewed and robust mythos to halt the erosion of religion in modernity. The alteration of earlier oral and written sources in Mesopotamian mythology (e.g., Enki and Ninhursag in Paradise, in *ANET* 37–41; and Gilgamesh and the Huluppu Tree in the Epic of Gilgamesh, tablet 12; and the origin of humans in the *Enuma Elish*, tablet 6) by the writers of the Hebrew Bible and the reinterpretation of the Hebrew Bible by later Christian writers (e.g., Paul's assertion that sin entered the world through Adam and Augustine's development of the doctrine of original sin) obscure meanings in the primal religions of the ancient Near East. Paul's interpretation of Jesus as the Second Adam, who removes the sin and death caused by the First Adam, and Augustine's development of the doctrine of original sin are possibly attempts (though now seen as poor ways) of constructing Christian thought on the human condition and the universality (i.e., general relevance) of the gospel of Jesus Christ. The redaction and reinterpretation of the primal myth of human origins in Genesis 2–3 shifts attention to commitment to (maybe fear of) Yahweh and the depravity of human nature and away from primal religion's interest in human agency and the relation of human beings to the realities of their physical and social environment.[10] The survival of religions, Western and non-Western, is in the creation of world community and the connection of temporal life with the eternal. In what sense, if any, can the modern person be a Christian? In response to this question, Josiah Royce has proposed that they can indeed be Christian if Christianity is focused on universal community and, true to its historical sources, identifies the moral burden of the individual (i.e., the human predicament aggravated by the misdirection of human efforts away from community) and the power of atonement (i.e., the ultimate remedy of the moral burden in actions that build and sustain community). According to Royce, focus on these basic ideas in Christianity not only keeps the church centered on its mission but also widens the church to the larger project of enabling human life, in all of this diversity, to flourish in the world.

The current challenge of Christianity (as well as other historical religions) is to provide depth, connection, identity, and purpose for human beings in the complex web of global economic and political interactions and the fragile physical environment on which human life depends. Modernity is not only hostile to religion but also, through its preoccupation with the temporal, deprives most people of an adequate understanding of soul in order to engage eternity. "Eternity is life in its fullness, and temporal existence is life striving after an infinite fullness it cannot comprehend in any finite sequence of moments."[11] Properly understanding eternity becomes crucial for personal and social transformation. If human beings are to be fulfilled, they must be challenged by notions of eternity, life in its fullness.

The previous discussion about the loci method may be summarized in the following three points. First, the loci (topic) method is a development that arose only a few centuries ago. For most of the history of Christian thought, loci (topics) have not been used. Second, there is no uniform list of topics, though some topics tend to be repeated more than others. Although Christian theologians may be intentional in their use of topics and may provide plausible rationales for their selection of topics, there still remains some arbitrariness in the use of topics. Third, the topic-specific approach is useful but does carry with it certain limitations and risks. Given these limitations and risks, the topics that I am proposing should not be regarded as absolute descriptors of the elements of African American Christian theology.

CONFIGURATION OF LOCI
FOR AFRICAN AMERICAN THEOLOGY

In chapters 5 through 13 of part 3, the loci chosen for African American theology do not follow strictly the usual listing of topics in most theology texts. These topics for African American theology have been chosen for three reasons. First, the topics are generalized and allow for study not only of Christian beliefs but also of non-Christian beliefs. This approach makes possible the study of Christianity as a religion and then as a religion in comparison to other religions. Though this book does not undertake this comparison, it lays a foundation for comparative studies at a later time.

Second, the loci have been selected to facilitate the study and interpretation of "religious speech" in African American communities. Instead of theology defined narrowly as God-talk, in this book, it is treated as religion-talk. Religious speech or religion-talk is the expression of ideas, beliefs, attitudes, and practices relative to matters of ultimate concern to persons in community. The aim of the book is to examine the specified religion in its obvious and overt forms as well as in its concealed forms, in symbols that convey African Americans' conscious awareness of their life experiences and cultural practices. Too often theology is disconnected from the academic study of religion as a pervasive phenomenon in human society. The loci selected for this textbook represent topics for the study and discussion of how "faith," which may or may not be Christian, has been expressed in African American history. The examination of Christian beliefs in this textbook should not be mistaken as the reduction of African American religion to Christianity only.

Our focus on religious speech or religion-talk has pragmatic and normative features. This focus enables us to give serious consideration to positive and negative interpretations of beliefs, in order to ascertain the nature and importance of the belief and its relevance to African Americans' lives. The languages of affirmation and negation are necessary for clarification of matters deemed to be of ultimate concern. As a normative discipline, theology does more than describe what persons

believe or how they believe differently. In theological study, there may
be stipulation of criteria governing religious speech. Determination of
"good" religious speech, in the opinion of persons who use this religious speech, encourages internal critique in addition to scholars' judg-
ments originating amid different sets of standards.

Third, the selected topics represent a schema that is alternative to
the paradigm of theology fixated on the *loci theologici* in Protestant
orthodoxy. Given the rigidity of the paradigm, important questions
on human identity in theological anthropology are ignored or not
addressed adequately because of the inordinate concentration on the
idea of original sin, in particular the notion that sin more than anything else defines who we are as human beings and our relationship to
God. Could it be that God relates and interacts with us in ways other
than our having sinned or not sinned?

Though the topics of this book are not inherently or, even by some
accounts, remotely "theological" in the so-called traditional (post-
sixteenth-century) sense, the topics may still be correlated with the
usual loci in most Christian theology texts. An approximate correlation
is as follows:

Loci in Traditional Theology (after 16th c.)	In *African American Theology*
Prolegomena	chapters 1–4
Revelation	chapters 4 & 7
God	chapters 5 & 8
Creation	chapter 12
Human beings	chapters 6 & 7
Christ	chapter 9
Salvation	chapter 9
Holy Spirit	chapter 7
Church	chapters 10 & 13
Last things	chapter 11

FREEDOM AS AN OVERARCHING THEME

Freedom may be utilized as an overarching theme to unify and illuminate the loci (topics) of chapters 5 through 13. Why this emphasis on
freedom? Freedom is a central category of African American experience. It is also an important concept in American culture.

Freedom in African American experience is shaped through four contexts: (1) constitutional secularism, (2) the nonregulation of religion, (3) resistance to oppression, and (4) Christian conceptions of egalitarianism and liberty. The American Republic was formed without an established church. However, the new republic was predominately Christian. The democratic ideals of individual liberty and equality of persons, framed in the Constitution, are patently similar to Christian conceptions of spiritual egalitarianism and freedom in Christ or the Holy Spirit. Yet the United States Constitution maintains a separation between church and state, which contributes to an interesting dynamic for the expression and influence of religion in the public square.

The First Amendment to the Constitution, in reference to religion, contains important clauses affecting religion. The two most obvious clauses relevant to religion are known as the Establishment Clause and the Free Exercise Clause. The Establishment Clause prohibits the government from creating and supporting an official religion for the nation. The Free Exercise Clause prevents the government from curtailing the expressions of religion arising from persons' choice. Also, in the First Amendment, the Free Speech Clause and Peaceful Assembly Clause have major consequences for the practice of religion in the United States. These latter clauses guarantee that religious speech is unregulated by government and that persons who engage in religious speech may gather and organize according to their shared interests. If religion in the United States appears, however, to be regulated, it is because of self-imposed restrictions. The various associations that persons form are governed by principles that they voluntarily accept.

The rights of citizenship as defined by the Constitution were not, from the beginning of the United States, granted en masse to black people. In order to bolster the number of white Southern elected representatives in the Congress, blacks were counted as three-fifths of a person.[12] This provision in the Constitution was crucial for white Southerners because black slaves outnumbered whites in their states. For example, in 1860, before the outbreak of the Civil War, the black population, slave and free, accounted for nearly 59 percent of the total population in South Carolina. The relatively small percentage of free blacks, in the North and the South, lived under extreme restrictions and the fear of capture into slavery.

The concept of citizenship (or civil) rights and the meaning of freedom has been shaped by black protest and activism directed at specific injustices. In 1794, Absalom Jones and Richard Allen wrote a pamphlet, *A Narrative to the Proceedings of the Black People during the Late Awful Calamity in Philadelphia*, to counter a white press that accused blacks of robbing the homes and businesses of whites fleeing the city when the yellow fever struck. Step-by-step Jones and Allen refute the white journalist's argument and shift the focus to what they saw as the real problem in Philadelphia: slavery and numerous other political and economic barriers that deprived blacks of greater contribution to the city. Jones and Allen's pamphlet marked the beginning of a black protest rhetoric that utilizes media communications and argues the worthiness and right of blacks to enjoy greater participation in American life. More recently, since the 1960s, freedom has meant very tangible things such as access to and enjoyment of public accommodations, such as education, transportation, customer service, and housing. The famed 1963 Birmingham Civil Rights Campaign had as its goal the accomplishment of four demands: (1) the desegregation of all amenities within department stores such as lunch counters, restrooms, fitting rooms, and drinking fountains; (2) the upgrading of employment opportunities, including the hiring of Negro sales clerks; (3) the dismissal of all charges against persons involved in peaceful protests; and (4) the formation of a biracial committee to establish and monitor the integration of public schools, parks, libraries, swimming pools, and other facilities used by the public. Thus, what freedom means at any given time is influenced by what African Americans have seen as obstacles to be overcome or rights and privileges to be secured.

Spiritual egalitarianism and Christian liberty have contributed substantially to African American thought on freedom. Spiritual egalitarianism is the belief that all persons are equal and infinitely valued in the sight of God. It is a belief that is reinforced by other Christian concepts such as the priesthood of all believers, emphasizing that all Christians have direct access to God; freedom from the power and various manifestations of sin; and the work of the Holy Spirit, who acts impartially in bestowing spiritual gifts and callings. Christian liberty, freedom from sin, is especially impactful when sin is defined broadly to encompass not only personal moral failure but also systemic evils rooted in social structures. When denied civil rights and equal protection of the law, African Americans found ground for equality in Christianity. Though not an official religion of the United States, Christianity is prevalent in the United States. Adhering to the same religion as enslavers and oppressors, African Americans could cite fundamental tenets of this shared religion that contradicted the injustices in American life.

The future of African American theology, in particular black and womanist theologies focused on liberation, requires further investigation of the concept of freedom in Christianity. While the Christian idea of freedom has resonated with African Americans in their economic, social, and political struggles, the concept is minimally useful due to the obfuscation of wisdom traditions overwritten by Judaism and Christianity during the Axial Age. Karl Jaspers coined the term Axial Age to refer to the period in human civilization when major cultural ideas were constructed and around which new institutions and traditions were formed.[13] For example, the Hebrews reworked earlier Mesopotamian mythology on origins to construct a narrative of Israel's beginning. This reworking of ancient mythology, such as found in Genesis 2–3, was altered even further in the theologies of Paul and Augustine.

Why is early mythology so important? We now have our exegetical tools for source criticism and the connection of these prebiblical traditions to the earliest human beings, as they tried to understand themselves and their place in the world. Thus we stand to gain from study and reflection on these wisdom traditions, which provide context for and contrast to the now-loaded terminology of Christian theological anthropology. As stated before in this introduction, the experiment begun by the Reformers is to read Scripture. If persons dare to take up that task of reading, then new insights may emerge.

In Christianity, the concept of freedom is disassociated from its meanings in primal religion. The recovery and revitalization of mythos is needed in order to articulate a credible narrative that deepens consciousness of the global realities of humankind and the tasks of seeking meaning and fulfillment in this new global context. In addition to the study of primal religions, the natural sciences offer stories (i.e., empirical facts arranged in narrative form) that describe the contexts of humans in nature and therefore hold clues on how, from our religious traditions, we may plausibly speak about the meaning of human life in the universe.[14] In *Race and the Cosmos*, Barbara Holmes suggests that African Americans' view of themselves in nature (what we see and observe in space) may disclose grander meanings of human existence than the conceptions of life narrowed by the ideologies emerging from social and political struggles in American life.[15] In a subsequent work titled *Liberation and the Cosmos*, Holmes defines freedom as the ability and condition necessary for human fulfillment and flourishing in the cosmos.[16]

Charles H. Long, a historian of religions, speculates that the great contemporary crisis, if resolved, has the potential for launching another axial transformation in the global reality of humankind. The migration of peoples from Europe, starting in the fifteenth century, has formed a complex web of organization and interaction. This migration altered the identities of Europeans as well as the identities of the peoples whom they encountered. All these identities are linked with interpretations of the past and visions of the future. In the modern period of global contact, the world religions, including Christianity, have failed to present a grand narrative or overarching mythos to provoke human introspection and inspire action toward building universal community. This failure of religion is due to internal institutional problems and external assaults of modernity.

Freedom is best regarded as a deep symbol of the fundamental reality of human existence. We are not merely persons in a body politic but also persons in the universe. The quest for freedom in sociopolitical terms is symbolic of a deeper quest for human fulfillment, as we consider our overall context of existence in the cosmos. If consciousness is "embodied agency," then what religious teachings and mythos will enable us to grasp this truth about ourselves and gain the wisdom required to live successfully in light of this truth? Free creative action is intrinsic to human beings. Freedom is essential to human beings. However, for those persons who experience oppression, resistance may consume much of their labor to the degree that liberation is mistaken as the goal of human being. More to the truth, liberation is a means to another end. The desired end is universal community—a new reality beyond the conflicting identities among humans in social arrangements that fall short of the highest ideal of culture. The ultimate aim of the culture is human survival and fulfillment. The focus of culture is (or should be) a crucial question: How do we structure, discipline, and deepen subjectivity for the survival and fulfillment of the individual and the group? Religion is key to answering this question. Through religion, humans learn and practice freedom by imitating God (or the gods).[17]

Focused now on Christian beliefs, *African American Theology: An Introduction* depicts African American theology, in a positive sense, as an authentic representation of God's freedom and the good news of God's call for all humankind to enter life in genuine community, with true human identity and moral responsibility. Defined in this way, African American theology crafts meanings of freedom, a central concept in both Christianity and American culture. In the American context, African American theology shows that racism complicates the human predicament: the eradication of racism requires nothing less than an enlargement of salvation to include the liberation of persons who lack full participation in society.

DESIGN OF THE BOOK'S PARTS AND CHAPTERS

In parts 1 and 2, information on history and methodology are presented before exploring the thoughts of African American Christians on the topics in part 3. Part 1 presents chapter 1, a historical overview of black theology. Part 2 consists of chapters 2–4, which deal with matters in methodology. Part 3, with chapters 5–13, discusses themes and issues in African American religious life. Parts 1–2 are background studies for the third part. After part 1 focuses on expressions of black theology in both Christian and non-Christian religious traditions in the United States, parts 2 and 3 focus on black theology in Christian religious traditions.

There are three important features of the chapters. Most chapters end with a summary of the main ideas discussed in the chapter. Following the summary is a set of questions for reflection and discussion. Last, to round out the chapter, is a bibliography with suggestions for further reading.

The reader does not need to accept my choice of loci (topics) for African American theology or my presupposition of freedom as a unifying theme and deep symbol of the human quest for fulfillment. The design of the chapters is not intended as a defense or support of my approach and presuppositions. In the preface and introduction, my aim is merely to inform the reader of my motivation and bias as both relate to this textbook. Because numerous books explain the basic doctrines of Christianity, this textbook omits discussion of several fundamental Christian beliefs so as to avoid undue repetition. Instead, my concern has been to suggest topics around which attention may be focused on African Americans' unique contributions to Christian theology. The key word is "contribution." I am reluctant to treat African American theology as some kind of special branch of Christianity or a complete system of thought juxtaposed to other significant traditions of Christianity. If African American theology in African American Christian churches aspires to be an articulation of the Christian religion, it will be much like other Christian theologies. African American theology contributes a limited set of emphases within the larger framework of Christianity. Using a select number of topics, this textbook shows the implications of African American theology for the practice of Christianity in the United States.

PART 1

History

1
History and Historical Study

APPEARANCE AFRICAN THEOLOGY

THE IMPORTANCE OF HISTORY AND HISTORICAL STUDIES IN THEOLOGY

History may be regarded as an established or common narrative representing knowledge of something that has happened and is therefore a matter without controversy. However, history is always told from a certain perspective, which makes for disagreement and contention. Human societies are characterized by internal differences. For the persons in a society who do not have the benefit of cultural dominance, their story rarely, maybe never, gets told. For the persons in a society who possess more power, that is, greater advantages than normal, a narrative is created that supports and furthers their interests. Privileged groups interpret as they will the events of the past, or they may even choose certain events to suppress and rid from cultural memory. Even groups that lack or have less privilege may seek to support their own interests through the creation of alternative accounts of the past that may also involve selective memory of events. As people from various quarters of society engage in the practice of creating history, differing stories will be told that sometimes conflict and at other times harmonize but are always indicative of contrasting perspectives on the substance and meaning of the past. Nonetheless, history remains important. This chapter addresses the matter of history's relevance in African American theology through reflection on the questions of why history is important for theology generally, what is the history (the origin and development) of African American theology, and what kinds of methods of historical interpretation are used in African American theology.

THE IMPORTANCE OF HISTORY AND HISTORICAL
STUDIES IN THEOLOGY

History and historical studies are important in theology for three reasons. First, historical study shows the origins of beliefs and practices and their development over time. Historical study is most advantageous because it enables one to see roughly when a belief or practice began, how that belief or practice has changed over a given period of time, and how that belief or practice compares or contrasts with other beliefs and practices from different periods. Gaining a historical understanding of religious belief and practice may be liberating. Through historical study, people are no longer tied and restricted to a belief or practice when it can be shown clearly that a belief or practice is temporal, that is, situated in time and probably not intended for or capable of perpetuity. If the beginning of the belief or practice is identified, then very likely suggestions may be made for its possible end. Historical study has the potential of endowing persons with greater control over their beliefs and practices and enabling them to decide how or whether they will continue believing or acting in a particular manner.

Have you ever noticed persons in a church or religious setting behaving in a certain way either without any explanation or maybe with an explanation that is not convincing? Maybe the practice is something that they do not want to do but feel obligated to continue. If they can be shown how the practice began and persuaded thereof, then they may take the liberty of either modifying or rejecting the practice. Many Christian congregations in the United States meet for worship at eleven o'clock on Sunday morning. There is no clear Scriptural mandate for worship at that hour on Sunday. From the earliest period of Christianity, there have been differences of opinion on which day, Saturday or Sunday, is the principal day for worship. What would happen if persons were shown and persuaded of how this time-specific worship began and how earlier generations of Christians associated worship with either the Sabbath or the Lord's Day? They probably would not be wedded to the eleven o'clock hour anymore. They may decide to worship instead at eight o'clock on Sunday morning. They may even go further to ask, "Why worship on Sunday?" They may choose to worship, as many American Christians do, on Saturday and other days of the week.

Second, history and historical study is important for theology in light of the prominent role of tradition in theology and the church.

Tradition is a principal source for theological reflection. The sources used by theologians for theological interpretation are Scripture, tradition, experience, reason, and culture. More will be said about these sources in chapter 2. For now, our focus is on tradition.

Tradition is something that is passed from one generation to the next. Christian communities aware of their possession of heritage utilize tradition for maintaining connection and continuity between themselves and previous groups in the history of Christianity. These communities may also be intentional about preserving and passing on their beliefs and stories to future generations.

Tradition is the *content* as well as the *process* by which something is handed down from one generation to the next (or from some persons to other persons). As process, tradition is the practice of and the mediums used for handing something over from one generation to another. As content, tradition is the very thing that is handed down. Tradition includes historic creeds; confessions; catechisms; denominational beliefs and practices; rituals; customary ways of speaking, acting, believing, thinking, and worshiping; and "classic" theological texts. Though all forms of tradition are vital for theology, in academic study greater emphasis seems to be on the writings of theologians. The works of past theologians are records of their thought and reflection. The existence of their works reminds us that the matters that concern us at present were addressed during earlier times in Christianity. In our contemporary theological work, we do not need to produce from thin air or reinvent the Christian faith every time we are beset with an issue or problem. Tradition provides us with a resource from which to begin our thinking. If we look to the past, search in the tradition, we may find insights made by others who wrestled with the same or similar issues or problems that we face today. Their insights may be a stimulus for our coming to deeper understandings and better expressions of the Christian faith.

In addition to the appreciation of tradition itself as history, historical study may be made of tradition. Historical study of tradition may involve the construction and preservation of the church's narrative. In addition, historical study may involve examination of forces at play in the creation of what Christians regard as tradition.

Third, history is important because it functions as a grand narrative. The term *grand narrative* refers to the story that integrates various events, movements, and ideas to the degree that the mass of data they represent is in a manageable and accessible format. A grand narrative makes it possible to think about phenomena that, without succinct summary, cannot be comprehended. Imagine, for example, your review of one thousand years. Over this thousand-year period, many events have transpired. Many things would have happened in human life. There have been big events and small events. Some events may be primarily of a social or political nature. Other events may be occurrences in our physical environment on and beyond Earth. How do you make sense of all that has happened? You tell a story. The story ties these events together, though not always perfectly. Still, the past is no longer murky or overwhelming. The story, this grand narrative, has now made all of this data a single object in our consciousness. The story makes us aware of something that has happened and the many things connected with this phenomenon.

THE ORIGINS OF AFRICAN AMERICAN THEOLOGY

Since history lacks seamlessness and is therefore characterized by both continuity and discontinuity, the origin of African American theology may be explained in terms of four phenomena, any of which may account for the rise of this form of theology as well as current undertakings in it: (1) resistance to discrimination and oppression; (2) the body-soul problem, (3) religious humanism, and (4) black ethnic identity. Neither phenomenon needs to be identified or restricted to a particular year or period, although we may study the phenomena for its development over a specified period of time. Singularly or in combination, these phenomena provide sufficient explanation of African American theology.

When persons are responding to discrimination and oppression singularly or in its plurality as it impacts African Americans and frames their response, positively or negatively, in relation to religion, they are doing African American theology. Discrimination refers to prejudice and unfair treatment on account of one's race alone or one's race in combination with gender, sexual orientation, and class. Oppression refers to cruel, harsh treatment by the hand of the persons who benefit from inequality and injustice. Slavery and segregation characterize periods and well-known forms of oppression in American history. However, the phenomena of oppression are not limited to slavery and segregation. Oppression exists in other forms such as sexism, classism, ethnocentrism, and heterosexism.

The body-soul problem is a concept clarified by Riggins Earl.[1] He says that African American theology emerges from an effort to resolve this body-soul problem. Earl uses the period of slavery to show how the problem is posed; however, the problem may and has arisen in later periods. The body is identified with that which is physical and belongs to the material world. The soul is identified with that which is spiritual and mental and belongs to or points to another realm. Body and soul are separate aspects of the persons. When soul and body are brought together, the soul is valued over the body. The Western dualism of body and soul has tragic consequences when applied to oppressed people. For the oppressed, body and soul are related in the bizarre combination of either soulless body or bodiless soul. As soulless bodies, the oppressed are regarded as inferior persons, not human or less than human, whose only value is in the commodification of their bodies, for example, in the goods produced by their labor or the uses of their bodies from which other persons derive the greater benefit. Thus they have no value in their souls but only in whatever can be gained or taken from their body. As bodiless souls, the oppressed are treated humanely but not justly. They are regarded as human in their souls, but the injustices to which their bodies are exposed remain in force. For example, kindhearted Christian masters wanted their slaves to hear the Word of God and convert to Christianity so that their souls would be saved, but these Christian masters would not free their slaves from bondage. According to Earl, African American theology emerges from the desire of the oppressed to be whole. The oppressed do not want to live as fragmented human persons. The wonderful aspects of their souls must be reconciled with the beauty in their bodies. The affirmation expressive of this desire of wholeness is "I am my body." By this affirmation, the oppressed are saying that all of the good and splendor in the human soul is located in the physical body. Both the soul and the body must be equally valued.

Religious humanism challenges the compatibility of Christianity, mainly the belief in all-powerful and morally perfect God, with the continued suffering of African American people. Black religious humanists are responding "philosophically" to the situation of African Americans by raising doubts and proposing alternatives to Christian theological explanations of human suffering. These religious humanists may or may not be Christian but, in either case, are critically assessing Christian beliefs in terms of the capacity of these beliefs to square with the realities of African American experience.

Black racial identity, a construction of ethnicity, reveals beliefs about human existence that are "religious" in substance. Though race has been discredited as a scientific classification of human beings and descriptor of human ability and behavior, it remains one among several markers of personal and group identity, albeit a mode of self- and group identity that greatly impacts human relationships and self-awareness. The fact that we are conscious is taken for granted and relatively unexplored in religious studies and theology. Being *conscious* means awareness of being a self, remembering experiences and thoughts occurring in oneself, constructing identities of self, and situating the self in time— past, present, and future. Though race neither encompasses fully nor exhausts totally the meaning of human life, the religious significance of racial consciousness (i.e., awareness of the self as having a particular ethnic identity or belonging to a particular social group) is to be found in its contribution to the saga, the long and ongoing story, of the human quest for a fulfilled existence. Racial identity or racial consciousness is a primary symbol for understanding one's place in the world and apprehension and discovery of the sacredness (ultimacy or "depth") of the forms through which one's culture is manifest. By providing grounding and integration of one's consciousness (awareness) of and as a self, race is a medium for understanding one's place in and connections to the world and gaining insight into the nature of the physical, social, and cultural environment where one lives.

Racial consciousness gives rise to not one but multiple conceptions of identity. There is not a singular African American identity. Among African Americans presently and in the past, there are several conceptions of ethnic identity. Change in the use of racial designations, for example, from "African," "Negro," "Colored," and "Black" to "African American," is indicative of shifts in ethnic identity in response to fluctuating social and political realities. Common to these racial designations is the sense of race, not as a biological classification of human persons but as a social construct that influences notions of belonging and that traces relations, for better or worse, between groups. While race has been shown to be invalid as a scientific concept for human biological classification, race persists as a social reality that structures past and present social relationships and forms a context of meanings in the struggle and quest to be human.

That race is utilized for discerning one's place and the processes going into the formation of one's world gives to it a religious quality. Racial consciousness holds implications for the conduct and structure of religious life. Key to defining and practicing religion is discernment of one's place in the world. Racial consciousness is a symbol for religion, that is, a medium for understanding one's place in the world. Race provides grounding and integration of one's consciousness (awareness) of and as a self. As one among other markers of human identity, race does not fully exhaust consciousness. It does, however, supply insight with respect to understanding one's connection to the world as well as the nature of this world forged by the interactions between groups.

The above explanation of the origin of African American theology—in terms of the four phenomena: resistance to discrimination and oppression, the body-soul problem, religious humanism, and black ethnic identity—is a *genealogical* account.[2] Genealogy is used here in a metaphorical sense to describe an approach to the study of history and culture. In its literal sense, genealogy is a way of telling and writing family history. Persons may be identified as belonging in the family tree, but without much detail about each person's life. There are only bits and pieces, a few stories here and there, for identification and connection between persons in the tree. Without question, certain persons are responsible for my existence; their existence explains my existence. I emerge from them but do not have knowledge of all details about their lives, nor do I know fully the previous generations that account for their existence. Applied to African American theology, the genealogical method identifies significant points (phenomena) in American culture presently and in the past that somehow influence the construction of African American theology. The vagueness is cleared up by further investigation of the phenomena and their connections. There are points, and there are connections between the points. We can do further study in order to determine and trace the series of connections between the points. For now, the genealogical method establishes which points (phenomena) in the historical tree of African American theology are sufficient explanations of its origin and nature.

CONTEMPORARY BLACK THEOLOGY AND WOMANIST THEOLOGY

In African American theology, black theology and womanist theology are areas of specialization that have well-established meanings, cores of concerns, and unique patterns of historical development. According to James H. Cone, black theology emerges from three major contexts:

the civil rights movement, the black power movement, and the publication of Joseph Washington's controversial *Black Religion* (1964).
According to Washington, although black religion parallels evangelical
Protestant Christianity and American democratic ideals emerging from
the Bible, black religion has no genuine concern in Christian worship,
liturgy, or doctrine but displays its genius in how it utilizes, even dis-
torts, Christianity for political ends.[3] Washington claims that Negro
churches are "religious communities" and not "Christian churches."
Washington's thesis and recommendation were not in sync with the
mood and sense of mission of the black church. The Theological
Commission of the National Committee of Negro Churchmen (later
renamed the National Conference of Black Churchmen) insisted that
African American churches are indeed Christian, that the civil rights
and black power movements are compatible with Christianity, and that
there is theology in the black church.

Out of these three contexts, black theology came to be (and in some
instances is still thought of) as "an interpretation of the [Christian] faith
in the light of black history and culture and completely separate from
white religion [and perspectives adopted by conservative blacks]."[4] In
the early stage of black theology, it exhibited both strengths and weaknesses. One of its weaknesses was its neglect of women's experience and
failure to address the injustice of sexism.

Black theology's neglect of black women's experience and insights
represented an area of opportunity for African American women theologians to explore. According to Monica A. Coleman, womanist theology emerges from the intersection of American feminism and black
women's experience and is developing in three waves.[5] The first wave,
beginning in the 1970s and 1980s, is evident in black women PhD
students who insist upon and defend the legitimacy of scholarship
focusing on black women's experience. The second wave is the normal-
izing (determining standards and foci of) womanist religious discourse.
During the second wave, womanist theology is mainly Christian and
focused in the United States. The current third wave engages previous
womanist thought yet also departs from it. It is global, focused on justice, liberation, survival, and quality of life around the world. Also, it is
not narrowly focused on Christianity but now examines non-Christian
traditions and religion in other social and institutional manifestations.
It engages the works and thinkers outside of black religious scholarship.
The third wave of womanist theology is being done by persons who are
not black women, though still focused on black women's experiences.

CONTRASTING HISTORIES AND CHARACTERIZATIONS
OF AFRICAN AMERICAN THEOLOGY

In addition to accounts of the origins of black and womanist theologies, other historical accounts have been constructed to explain the development of these specializations in theology and their connections to earlier expressions of African American theology. These histories usually describe the development of African American theology by using the language of "stages." According to Gayraud Wilmore's historical analysis, contemporary black theology has evolved in three distinct stages. To Wilmore's theory of the three-stage evolution of black theology, Dwight Hopkins adds a fourth stage, the emergence of what he calls a "second generation" of scholars and pastors. Anthony Pinn constructs a five-stage historical analysis of black theology.

Wilmore identifies the first of the three stages as the emergence of black theology from the civil rights and black power movements. While the civil rights movement was the initial context for origin of the contemporary black theological movement, black power ideology has had the greater influence upon the development of contemporary black theology. The second stage of the contemporary black theological movement is its entry into academic settings. According to Wilmore, this second stage begins with the participation of black seminary professors in the Theological Commission of the National Conference of Black Churchmen. The third stage of the contemporary black theological movement is characterized by academic black theologians' designation of the black church as their principal audience and by these theologians' interest in global issues in relationship to African American communities in the United States.

Dwight Hopkins adds a fourth stage to Wilmore's theory of the three-stage evolution of black theology. Hopkins contends that black theology is now in a fourth stage, begun in the mid-1980s by what he calls a "second generation" of scholars and pastors. Second-generation black theologians focus on strengthening ties between scholarship, ministry, and social activism. These theologians are creating new academic guilds, examining previously neglected primary sources and utilizing them in their constructions of black theology, and proposing models for the involvement of black scholars in the ongoing life of African American churches and communities. According to Hopkins, black womanist thinkers are a part of this second generation.

By concentrating on the theme of radicalism, Wilmore connects contemporary black theology to earlier movements in African American theology. He identifies radicalism—the quest for economic, social, and political change—as the most distinctive feature of African American religious thought. According to Wilmore, this tendency toward radicalism is not restricted to African American Christian churches. He also says that African American religious life, Christian and otherwise, is not reducible to radicalism. Yet radicalism is "the most distinctive, persistent, and valuable part of the religious heritage of African Americans in the United States."[6]

Anthony Pinn constructs a five-stage historical analysis of black theology. For Pinn, black theology is progressive and cumulative. The first and longest stage starts near the beginning of the slave trade. The second stage begins during the civil rights movement in the 1960s. The third stage is a globalization of black theology through cross-cultural dialogue with liberation theologies of other peoples. The fourth stage is open and frank discussions about gender and sexuality. The fifth and present stage is the expanding range and scope of black theological sources for the interpretation of the black experience.

These histories exhibit two common features. First, they have in common an emphasis on the present. With the exception of Wilmore's attempt to create a grand narrative of black theology based upon the theme of black radicalism, these histories mostly focus on the present. The greater attention to history has been telling the story of how contemporary black theology and womanist theology began. They tend to read back into previous periods the emphases of the contemporary period, as if there is a seamless connection between the present and the past.

The second feature held in common by these histories is their "linear" treatment of history. By use of the metaphors of "stages," "generations," and "waves," the history of African American theology is depicted as sequential and supersessionist. The use of numerical sequencing implies multiple cohorts or units. If there is a first or second stage, generation, or wave, then there will be a third, fourth, and further stages. It is not altogether certain that a latter development always represents an improvement upon the previous stage. New is not necessarily better.

In my own account of the origins and development of African American theology, I have used the metaphor of genealogy for historical interpretation. Genealogy is history but of a special kind. Ideally, persons would like to know their past in full detail. With a genealogy, the person has a few names and limited details, if any, of their ancestors. That the person exists is without question. The genealogy does not prove the person's existence; it is an appendage to what the person knows about their own present. In most cases, it is not possible to construct seamless, linear histories with detailed information about the continuities between various social and cultural phenomena. Hence, a genealogy may provide a complement to the collection of known facts about the present circumstances, that is, known better than we know the past.

African American theology is varied and diverse. I have defined African American theology as the study and interpretation, positive or negative, of any religion (or religious beliefs) in relationship to the experience of blackness.[7] With regard to offering some form of historical interpretation, I have come to rely more on genealogy, on citing sufficient reasons to account for or explain the practice of African American theology. In my genealogy, African American theology may be explained in terms of the resistance of black people to slavery, segregation, and other forms of oppression, the body-soul problem (i.e., blacks regarded as and resisting their depiction as soulless bodies or bodiless souls), black religious humanism, and the shifts in the constructions of black ethnic identity that warrant a rethinking of how religion or religious beliefs may be related to new experiences of blackness.

BLACK HISTORY AND CRITICAL HISTORIOGRAPHY

African American history, as an academic discipline and profession, poses challenges for interpreting African American religion, especially with regard to the questions raised about African American theologians' use of collective memory, which forms the foundation for popular notions of black history.[8] Collective memory—known also as social memory, historical memory, and cultural memory—represents a social group's (or scholar's) attempt to define the present situation through objects and events in the past. From a heuristic point of view, collective memory is extremely valuable: it makes the past intelligible and accessible for present thought and action. Collective memory is a reconstruction of the past, whatever of it is yet available for present reflection. Although collective memory involves the past, it is not founded on the past. The remembered past always comes to the present as broken, as fragmented, in bits and pieces. Collective memory is grounded in the present, particularly in present social interests and conceptions of identity. While facts from the past can influence present conceptions of identity and inform persons of certain things they should be concerned about, the sense of urgency experienced in the present can cause them to be selective in appropriating facts from the past. Persons in the present can omit, overlook, or downplay past facts for the purpose of achieving current interests and promoting a desired image of themselves. Meanings more endemic to the present may be imposed on the past, leading to a distortion of the past rather than an accurate representation of it.

The problem of collective memory and its contribution to the lack of rigor in scholarship of African American history and culture has been acknowledged by Black Catholic theologians, not by Black Protestant theologians. In 1996, a gathering of Black Catholic educators and theologians was at the Institute for Black Catholic Studies. Cyprian Davis, a Black Catholic historian and theologian, and Eva Regina Martin, nun and director of the Institute for Black Catholic Studies, presented perspectives on the challenges to Black Catholic Studies posed by collective memory, mainly popular notions of history and the ideologies that fuel its formulation.[9]

Collective memory has its place in human life; it is a fact, a feature of social life. All groups engage in some active form of reconstructing their pasts. At issue is whether collective memory can serve as a reliable *method* of theological interpretation resulting in *justified true* claims that meet prevalent standards of knowledge in the university setting. The inadequacy of collective memory in academic theology and religious studies can be illustrated by conflicting interpretations of the ring shout, a form of religious dance prevalent among African Americans in the American South in the nineteenth century and, based on recent observations, lasting into the twentieth century. The illustration that follows is not a special or rare case of collective memory; concerns about collective memory arise in the course of other scholarly investigations of how the African American past is constructed.[10]

That the ring shout existed and, in some nostalgic performances, continues to exist is indisputable. In terms of its performance, the ring shout has remained consistent over time. Of greater interest are the radically different responses of nineteenth- and twentieth-century black intellectuals to the ring shout. Because it is impossible to go into exhaustive detail about all black intellectual responses, the following discussion will cover a select few in order to highlight contrasting perspectives.

Outside observers first described the ring shout in the mid-nineteenth century. The "shouters" are the persons who perform the dance. They or onlookers may sing, usually spirituals. The shouters form a circle, moving in counterclockwise rotation. The torso leans in the direction of forward motion. The arms are relaxed, with elbows slightly bent. As they proceed around the circle, the feet are moved in a shuffling motion, in pace with the song. Care is taken not to raise feet too high off the ground. The ring shout was widespread in the American South. It was performed in worship settings, on Sundays or other days of religious significance. The shout could last for many hours, with tired shouters being replaced by rested ones, to continue the dance. The once widespread dance is kept alive by small groups such as the popular McIntosh County Shouters of Bolden, Georgia, who perform not only for worship purposes but also for the nostalgic reason of preserving a practice nearly extinct.

Daniel Alexander Payne, bishop in the African Methodist Episcopal Church and a missionary among former slaves in the South, represents the nineteenth-century black intellectual response to the ring shout. In Payne's *Recollections of Seventy Years* (1888), he describes his encounters with the ring shout. Payne had great disdain for the ring shout, seeking to discourage its practice wherever he encountered it. He referred to it as "heathenish," "ignorant," and a "disgrace" to the race. Payne did not esteem the shout as an African cultural practice worthy of preservation. His interest in African civilization was in demonstrating the fact that black Americans' history began before chattel slavery and included outstanding achievements. Payne was guided by a concept of ethnic identity aimed at counteracting negative images of blacks and forging solidarity among newly emancipated slaves. Like other black leaders in the Post-Reconstruction era, especially those associated with the literary societies organized by the black middle class, Payne Christianized human history and interpreted world events through American history. Ancient civilizations, including African ones, contribute to American history. The Emancipation, an event in American history, represented a new age where blacks would take their place among other races in the world. This process of taking their place requires readjustment in behavior. Conforming to mainline Protestant thought, Payne tended to view rationality and ethical behavior as essential to Christian life.

Judging from Payne's biography, his objection to the ring shout is not the fact or likelihood of its being African but rather its deviation from his understanding of Christian doctrine and practice. He shows deference for a conservative and dogmatic evangelical Protestant opposition against religious, recreational, and social dance. This tendency has not eliminated dance from American life, but it has forcibly removed dance from worship settings.

Sterling Stuckey and Albert Raboteau, both historians of African American religion and culture, represent the twentieth-century black consciousness that is now prevalent in African American studies. In classic texts in contemporary black religious studies, Albert Raboteau's *Slave Religion* (1978) and Sterling Stuckey's *Slave Culture* (1987), the ring shout is labeled as "African" in a positive way. Raboteau and Stuckey identify the use of call-and-response singing, polyrhythms, shuffling-feet movements of the dancers, the circle formation—all as indications of the African origins of the ring shout. Stuckey's *Slave Culture* and especially his forthcoming book titled *Ring Shout* construe the ring shout as a form of cultural mnemonics, a ritual that preserves vital knowledge for reconstructing African identity and beliefs that flourished, then and even today, wherever the ring shout is performed. Raboteau and Stuckey's works are grounded in a conception of ethnic identity that defines blackness over against whiteness and other racial and ethnic designations. There is an intense desire to show the African influence to the exclusion of all other cultural influences of other peoples in black American life. The works of Raboteau, Stuckey, and other scholars following their example function as a necessary corrective to gross omissions in traditional Western cultural studies, not to mention their lift to the pride of black Americans wounded by the untruth of blacks' not having a past or a culture.

Black intellectual responses in both centuries overlook the ring shout's connection with revivalism in America and the ring shout's association with the religious and social circle dances of European Americans and southeastern Native Americans (i.e., Creek, Choctaw, Chickasaw, Cherokee, and Seminole). The United States has always been a nation made up of many peoples and a nation engaged in conflict and cooperation with other nations. The history of the American South is not a simple dichotomy of white and black but a history that is inclusive of Native Americans, Europeans, Africans, Mulattoes, and Mixed-Bloods. There is documentation of circle dances performed among Indians in the southeastern states before their mass relocation by the United States government, beginning with the Indian Removal Act of 1830.[11] More than any other group, the Shakers popularized circle dances in religious services, starting during the Great Awakening in the late eighteenth century.[12] Culture is fluid, not static. In contact between different peoples, borrowing and blending often occurs. Sometimes human societies that have never had contact with each other will develop similar ideas and practices.

The contrast between nineteenth- and twentieth-century interpretations of the ring shout are best explained in terms of the conception of ethnic identity prevalent in each historical period. In African American history, there have been shifts in black ethnic identity. The several changes in African Americans' preferred racial designation, over time, is indicative of these shifts. It seems futile to argue for or against any particular racial designation or conception of ethnic identity. The point to be made here is this: however persons view themselves in the present will affect the way they interpret the past and their cultural heritage.

In any religion there is continuity and discontinuity. African American religion is no exception. As easily as one may find some beliefs and practices that appear unchanged over time, one may also find points at which consistency in other beliefs and practices ceases and breaks as the flow of tradition occur. Innovations in thought have been categorized as both insightful and distortive. More often, the introduction of new patterns in religious thought and action represent ways to make a religion intelligible and credible to persons in each generation. Where connection is demonstrated between present and previous forms of religious expression, historical study enables one to discern the interruptions in the transmission of belief and practice from earlier periods to the present time.

History and historical studies are important in theology in general and for African American theology in particular. First, historical study shows the origins of beliefs and practices and their development over time. Second, history and historical study is important for theology in light of the prominent role of tradition in theology and the church. Last, history is important because it functions as a grand narrative that, like a conceptual framework, integrates various data on the beliefs, practices, and perspectives in African American churches.

African American history, as an academic discipline and profession, poses challenges for the interpretation of African American religion, in particular questions raised about African American theologians' use of collective memory, which forms the foundation for popular notions of history. The prospects and problems of collective memory in academic theology and religious studies can be illustrated by conflicting interpretations of the ring shout, a form of religious dance prevalent among African Americans in the American South in the nineteenth century and, based on recent observations, lasting into the twentieth century. Contrasting interpretations of the ring shout are linked to the prevalent conception of black ethnic identity in each historical period. Different identities contribute to different renderings of history and religious heritage. Collective memory is an inherent feature of social life that at times proves to be valuable in many ways, yet it functions imperfectly as an instrument for achieving knowledge, that is, if knowledge is thought to have an objective quality beyond personal and political interests.

African American theology is theology of the kind that pays attention to history. We expect history to answer some questions: How do events of the past influence today's realities? How do our present beliefs and practices either conform to or depart from enduring values in our cultural heritage? How is history, the way it is presently told, open to question with respect to its extent of inclusion of the experiences and thoughts of the poor and oppressed? Also, history deals with questions about important events of the past that have been forgotten or, if remembered, are minimized and suppressed in present cultural debate. In utilizing history as a source and methodological approach, African American theology must be attentive to the social processes that influence perceptions and constructions of the past, for different identities contribute to the formation of different memories of the past.

Questions for Discussion

1. What do the terms "black" and "African American" mean?
2. What insights are gained by use of the concepts "black" and "African American" in the study and interpretation of religion in the United States?
3. How does the association of African American theology generally with liberation theology, systematic theology, or constructive theology affect, positively or negatively, how African American theology is done?
4. What does African American *critical historiography* contribute to African American theology in comparison to the benefits gained from collective memory?

Suggested Reading

Chapman, Mark L. *Christianity on Trial: African-American Religious Thought before and after Black Power.* Maryknoll, NY: Orbis Books, 1996.

Cone, James H. *For My People: Black Theology and the Black Church.* Maryknoll, NY: Orbis Books, 1984.

Hopkins, Dwight N. *Introducing Black Theology of Liberation.* Maryknoll, NY: Orbis Books, 1999.

Maffly-Kipp, Laurie F. *Setting Down the Sacred Past: African-American Race Histories.* Cambridge, MA: Belknap Press of Harvard University Press, 2010.

Mitchem, Stephanie Y. *Introducing Womanist Theology.* Maryknoll, NY: Orbis Books, 2002.

Wilmore, Gayraud S. *Black Religion and Black Radicalism: An Interpretation of the Religious History of African Americans.* 3rd ed., revised and enlarged. Maryknoll, NY: Orbis Books, 1998.

Wright, William D. *Black History and Black Identity: A Call for a New Historiography.* ABC-CLIO, 2002.

———. *Critical Reflections on Black History.* Westport, CT: Praeger, 2002.

PART 2

Methodology

2

Sources

This chapter is designed to answer certain questions: What are the sources of African American theology? Where are these sources found? This chapter identifies the foundational Christian sources and black cultural forms through which black theology is expressed and the documents vital for persons studying and doing (constructing) African American theology. Another question to ask is this: Where do we begin? To be more exact, where do we begin in terms of managing the information overload? Many primary sources, more than what most persons may imagine, are available. In African American studies and in its earlier naming as "Black Studies" and "Negro Studies," the discipline has gone from a scarcity of resources to an abundance of primary source material. With respect to managing the data for African American theology, we begin with a discussion of the customary sources of theology and then move on to a definition of black religion and identification of the cultural expressions by which it is conveyed, criteria for the selection of sources from black religion, and an exploration of various places where these sources are held and therefore accessible.

CUSTOMARY SOURCES OF THEOLOGY

The principal sources from which Christian theologians study and interpret faith are Scripture, tradition, experience, reason, and

41

culture. Scripture, as a source, generally refers to "sacred writing," which is believed to have or be an authority (of divine origin and instructive and final in matters of faith) and believed also to be found in a canon, in a defined body (collection) of writings. However, the formation of canon in Christianity has not been a simple process or a decision reached by unanimous consent. There are multiple collections. Alongside the canon that was revised during the Protestant Reformation are other sacred texts, such as the Apocrypha (works accepted by Catholics and Orthodox Christians but not by Protestants), the Pseudepigrapha (Jewish writings not included in the Septuagint version of the Old Testament), and the *Gospel of Thomas* and other gnostic writings.

Tradition refers to the content as well as the process by which something is handed down from one generation to the next (or from some persons to other persons). Hence tradition includes historic creeds; confessions; catechisms; denominational beliefs and practices; rituals; customary ways of speaking, acting, believing, thinking, and worshiping; and "classic" theological texts. Tradition may also refer to "legacy," "historical connectedness," and "doctrinal and interpretive compliance." Continuity in Christian faith may be interpreted in terms of (1) historical, empirical connectedness; (2) ecclesiastical connectedness; and (3) analogical connectedness, which is established by associations inferred by the same or similar language and concepts and associations inferred by observance and practice of the same or similar rituals. If discontinuity is acknowledged as a fact in Christianity, and if Christianity is perceived contextually and normally to be inclusive of various communities that are unconnected historically and ecclesiastically, then there may be multiple points of entry into the Christian religion. African American churches (and the same could be said of other denominations and congregations) may be authentically Christian without having the burden of seamlessly tracing their origins back to early Christianity.

Experience refers to events that persons live through and the resultant perceptions that are organized into a form of knowledge or skill. In theology, experience may refer to individual and communal experiences, social events, or secular and religious history.

There is no "common" or generic human experience through which each person passes. The world is marked by diversity. People have many experiences. A task and challenge of theologians is to demonstrate the relevance and articulate the message of transformation for a variety of situations in the world today.

Experience and history are related sources: history may be regarded as a subcategory of experience. Some of the meanings of "history" are the following: (1) the past considered as a whole, (2) narrative or story of past events, (3) study of the past, (4) something done that is memorable (worth remembering and celebrating) and influences the present or future, (5) the changes and development of a thing over time, and (6) events in space-time (space and time in the world). Also, history as a form of tradition (as discussed in chap. 1) and history as record and/or recollection of past events, religious and secular, is a source for theology.

Reason is the capacity of the human mind to obtain truth as well as the resulting knowledge gained through the exercise of the human mind. Thus reason is inclusive of common sense or conventional wisdom, logic, philosophy, empirical observation, or the natural and social sciences and other fields of knowledge.

Though culture is rarely regarded as a source, it nonetheless represents a major influence in religious thinking. Culture is a group's total way of life, through language and education passed from generation to generation. Hence culture is the sum total of ideas, values, language, knowledge, customs, material products and artistic creations (such as food, clothing, buildings, machines, books/literature, music, etc.), social relationships, institutions and organizations of a group of people—all transmitted from generation to generation. Human survival and quality of life are determined by the adaptive capacity of culture. Of interest to the theologian are a people's shared ideas, values and beliefs of a society expressed in art, music, film, drama, literature, patterns of social organization, rituals for birth and burial, and other mediums.

If one is going to do theological work, at some point it will be necessary to engage primary material. This primary material is drawn from the lived experience of believers as well as the texts and traditions created to express and preserve their thought. These texts and traditions include not only the writings of notable theologians in Christian history but also the hymns, testimonies, liturgy, and so forth of various gatherings of believers. There exist both "official" published doctrines of churches and "actual" doctrines that persons live by. A good theologian will give attention to both. Early into the contemporary black theology movement, emphasis was placed on the lived faith experiences of black people in what became known as black religion.

BLACK RELIGION AS PRINCIPAL SUBJECT MATTER

Theology does not create religion (or religious beliefs) but rather interprets religion (or religious belief) as it is expressed and practiced in communities of persons.[1] While African American theologians may be members of African American churches and communities, they are not the creators of the beliefs held in common in these churches and communities. Theologians may participate with other believers in constructing beliefs, that is, in formulating new beliefs or revising existing beliefs. However, the faith given to the church or community is not authored solely by any one theologian. The theologian always begins the task with what already is. For African American theology, this given faith is black religion.

Joseph Washington, Charles Long, Gayraud Wilmore, Cecil Cone, and Anthony Pinn have proposed contrasting definitions of black religion. Washington's, Long's, Wilmore's, and Cone's definitions were worked out during the early period of black theology. Joseph Washington defines black religion as a folk religion and quest for freedom and equality. Charles Long defines black religion as a view of reality discerned through the use of symbols that interpret black experience. Gayraud Wilmore defines black religion as the belief in freedom and the radicalism employed in obtaining that freedom. Cecil Cone defines black religion as a syncretism of African religions, Negro slave religion, and biblical Christianity, grounded in belief in the Almighty and Sovereign God. More recently, Anthony Pinn defines black religion as the quest for complex subjectivity and transformation of consciousness that enables persons to seek human fulfillment and resists the dehumanizing affects of fixed and false identities.[2]

In 1964, the publication of Joseph Washington's *Black Religion: The Negro and Christianity in the United States* received mixed reviews and was met with controversy; yet it proved to be influential in promoting the idea of a black religion distinguishable from institutional religions in America. According to Washington, this black religion is essentially black people's folk religion, grounded in their quest for freedom and equality. Washington claimed that black churches are not Christian churches but instead are political associations splintered from white churches and therefore devoid of liturgy or theology of the kind present in white churches. He argued that white churches are true churches because they are historically connected and contiguous with Christianity originating in the Middle East and spreading to Europe. His claim was convincing to persons who saw, even in predominantly black schools, no African American professional theologians who focused solely on research, reflection, and writing on issues and concerns of black churches. The Theological Commission of the National Conference of Black Churchmen, composed of African American clergy and scholars in religion and theology, aimed at putting black theology into print and thereby refuting Washington's criticism of black churches.

In varying ways, Charles Long, Cecil Cone, and Gayraud Wilmore emphasized the necessity of rooting black theology in the black religious experience, that is, in the unique response of black people to the sacred. Common to Long, Cone, and Wilmore is the assertion that black religion is of African origins, related to but not identical to Christianity and related to but not identical to black power and other black protest movements. Black religion is a phenomenon that is inclusive of black persons' vision of themselves in the image and likeness of God and thus having value, worth, relevance, and responsibility as human beings.[3] They suggest that there is "something more" to black religion than political strategizing or assent to a set of faith propositions or reflection framed by the customary sources of theology. Black religion is a primary source: material extracted from black people's lived experience.

According to Charles Long, black religion consists of "experiences of opacity," centered on a view of reality discerned through black people's sufferings. As a historian of religion, Long takes the position that religion is conveyed through symbols. He identifies three primary symbols for (or ways of) seeing and studying black religion: (1) Africa as a historical reality and religious image for black people's origins and authentication of black movements in the United States, (2) race as a symbol for sense of place and context for black people's creating alternatives to mainstream American religion and culture, and (3) the experience and symbol of God as a transforming presence and power source of value.

In contrast to Long, Cecil Cone and Gayraud Wilmore identified black people's fundamental assertion of faith as the foundation of black religion. Cone is critical of Joseph Washington's *Black Religion* (1964) and *Politics of God* (1969), where he describes black religion as the quest for freedom, justice, and equality; Cecil Cone says that this sort of

approach to black theology finds nothing in black religious experience
that stands apart from political protest. By contrast, Cone declared that
black people's belief in the Almighty and Sovereign God is the focus of
black religion. Wilmore claimed that black people's belief in freedom
and their radicalism employed in obtaining it are the focus of black religion. Wilmore and Cecil Cone agree that African Americans' struggles
for freedom and equality in American society and their longings for
survival and quality of life are inspired, to a large part, by their faith in
and encounters with God.

Cecil Cone's *Identity Crisis in Black Theology* (1975) began an
exchange of ideas about the sources and norm of black theology.
According to Cone, due to the lack of priority black theologians have
given to the black religious experience and the various cultural forms
used for expression of this experience, these theologians are embroiled
in a crisis of identity. Black theology is improperly aligned with the
academic paradigm of predominately white seminaries and with the
black power motif of African American political activists.[4] Rather than
conducting black theology from the starting point of either the dominant paradigm of rationality in American theological schools or the
ideology of black power, Cone contends that black religion must be the
point of departure for black theology.[5] He envisages that the way out
of crisis and a necessary step forward is for black theologians to clarify
what black religion is.[6]

I am inclined to agree with Anthony Pinn that black religion should
be defined in terms of subjectivity or consciousness. However, my perspective on black religion as complex subjectivity parts from Pinn's
atheistic materialism. Pinn's suspicion of metaphysics leads him to
restrict the notion of subjectivity to the physical body. He examines
subjectivity through its expression in narrative, practices of embodiment, and display and depictions of the body in the cultural arts.

I define *black religion* as "the beliefs and practices resulting from
the use of racial consciousness, as a primary symbol, for understanding one's place in the world and apprehension and discovery of the
sacredness (or import) of the forms through which one's culture is
manifest." I regard subjectivity or consciousness as "embodied agency"
in the webs of language, society, and culture that form our world
and sense of reality. My position is influenced by emergence theory,
wherein consciousness is said to arise from matter, the "stuff" of the
universe, but possesses properties very different from the material and
forces that gave rise to it. Experience, thinking, feeling, and spirit are

embedded in physical bodies but are not merely reducible to what we know empirically about our physical bodies and the things produced from our physical activity.

Black religion is defined appropriately in terms of the influence of the reality and experience of race on the formation and shape of human consciousness. By *race*, I am referring to "social constructions," not biological or physical features. Race is but one among several markers of personal and group identity, albeit a mode of self- and group identity that greatly impacts human relationships. By *consciousness*, I mean that a person is aware of being a self, aware of experiences and thoughts occurring in the self, constructing identities of self, and situating the self in time—past, present, and future. Though race neither encompasses fully nor exhausts totally the meaning of human life, the religious significance of racial consciousness (i.e., awareness of the self as having a particular racial identity or belonging to a particular social group) is to be found in its contribution to the saga, the long and ongoing story, of the human quest for a fulfilled existence. By providing grounding and integration of one's awareness of and as a self, race is a medium for understanding one's place in and connections to the world and gaining insight into the nature of the physical, social, and cultural environment where one lives.

Black religion is a heuristic concept that facilitates investigation and learning. As a heuristic concept, black religion is an abstraction created from and supervening on the concrete expressions of religion in African American culture. Here the term "concrete expression" refers to the ways in which persons actually express themselves religiously within their respective communities. Also as a heuristic concept, black religion is related to African American religious institutions (organizations and traditions), not as an essence or prototype or goal but as a category for perception and evaluation of phenomena that disclose the religious dimension of life in African American communities.

BLACK RELIGION AND THE DEPTH OF BLACK CULTURE

According to Cecil Cone, sermons, prayers, testimonies, and slave narratives are repositories of black religion and thereby among the best sources for constructing black theology.[7] Since the publication of Cone's book, black theologians have suggested and turned to many other sources, such as religious and secular songs (spirituals and blues, gospel, hip-hop, and rap), folktales, speeches and writings of African American public figures and protest leaders, black women's experience and spirituality, and the folk religion of poor African Americans, the black underclass, from the period of their enslavement and onward to their current plight in the deteriorating inner cities of the United States.

According to Long, the meaning of religion is not restricted to any particular historical movement or social institution. He defines religion as "orientation in the ultimate sense, that is, how one comes to terms with the ultimate significance of one's place in the world."[8] Religion is a way of relating and reconciling oneself to things and matters of ultimacy. It is a dimension of culture that focuses on those aspects of experience that are permeated with a quality of sacredness, setting them apart from ordinary cultural objects. Commenting on the cultural objects by which he has examined religious meanings, in addition to Christian symbols, Long says, "I have been as interested in other forms of religion in the history of black communities—as those forms are contained in their folklore, music, style of life, and so on. Some tensions have existed between these forms of orientation and those of the Christian churches, but some of these extra-church orientations have had great critical and creative power. They have often touched deeper religious issues regarding the true situation of black communities than those of the church leaders of their time."[9] A cultural form, an expression of cultural life, that bears religious meaning can be found at any level of human consciousness. Thus black religion is revealed in objects, practices, and beliefs with "depth," that is, with the capacity to direct attention to matters of ultimate importance, interrelate varied experiences, provoke reflection on meanings of human existence, and inspire the quest for fulfillment in life. This way of defining religion in general and black religion in particular enables intensive and comprehensive examination of various cultural forms, though disparate and not drawn explicitly from a society's established or recognized religious institutions.

Long's approach aims for "depth," a metaphor cited by Paul Tillich in his definition of religion. According to Tillich, "Religion is not a special function of man's spiritual life, but it is the dimension of depth in all of its functions."[10] So, religion represents that which pervades and connects various experiences, which if viewed superficially may appear to be unrelated. For Tillich, religion is intricately woven into the fabric of human consciousness. Through its use of symbols and reflection on symbols, the self penetrates through the form and objects of its consciousness to the ground of the reality upon which it is based. Tillich says, "The self is the medium of the unconditional apprehension of reality, and as medium it participates in the certainty of what it mediates. Still, it participates only as a medium; it is not that which upholds, but rather that which is upheld."[11] Sense of self is constitutive of and a basis for certainty of external reality. Consciousness comes to realization through culture. The products of our culture, when interrelated by deep symbols, are tools for human self-understanding.

According to Long, the power of Africa, race, and God, as deep symbols, is indicative in the types of questions that each is able to generate for thought and reflection.[12] With Africa as central focus, the sorts of questions asked are these: From where did I come? May I return? When and where does my history begin? What is my past? *Africa*, as symbol, reminds black persons that they came to the Americas from another place. Their history began before enslavement in the Americas. Through the prism of race, other sorts of questions are asked: Who am I? What is my place in the world? What is the history and experience at which I am the center? Race as a social construct (for identification and group belonging) is part and parcel of and continues to impact the structuring of human life and relationships in the world. Questions revolving around God as symbol also appear: What or who is the source of my value? To what or whom may I compare myself? Can I be other than what I am? What can or will I become? God symbolizes and inspires the quest for something other than what is possible in the existing social order.

CRITERIA FOR THE SELECTION OF SOURCES

Black religion, as a wide range and variety of sources, can seem to be an overwhelming mass of information. There is nothing obvious about a source that would cause the theologian to use it. Also there is no inherent meaning or value of the cultural expression by virtue of its genre or style. Not every sermon merits consideration. There is nothing that makes a spiritual or gospel song better than a blues, rap, or hip-hop song, and vice versa. Any cultural expression may have the potential for generating reflection and self-understanding. In any genre of expression, one may find positive and negative messages as well as sound or unsound formulations of thought and belief connected to adaptive or maladaptive behaviors.

In addition to the theologian's context, personal interests, and commitments, four criteria may influence their selection of a source for the study and interpretation of black religion. The first criterion, already discussed at length, is the depth of the source. Here the term *depth* refers to the capacity of the source to raise awareness of the self, the relation of self to others, and certain aspects of the culture affecting the survival and quality of life for both the self and community. The theologian is not looking indiscriminately at cultural expressions/artifacts but watching for expressions/artifacts that have the capacity to function as "religious symbols," as expressions/artifacts that have the quality of "depth," to raise awareness of self and the foundations in culture on which the self and other selves persist. A second criterion is the potential of the source to represent the belief of the community whose faith is of concern to the theologian. A third criterion is the source's necessary relation to the tradition of the faith community, either as an original or earlier expression of that faith tradition or as a recent or current expression developed to interpret, question, extend, or apply that tradition in new ways. The fourth criterion is freedom. As the penultimate of human fulfillment, freedom is the norm to which the sources and resources, as well as African American experience generally, is subjected. This norm, rooted in African American experience, determines which sources and resources will be used and how they will be used for reflection. By the norm of freedom, African American theology is tested, criticized, and revised.

Though African American experience is a source of African American theology, it stands in a special relationship with other sources. The sources are transmitted and received through the medium of experience. For example, what the text means—and here text could be a written document or an oral tradition or ritual practice—is inseparable from the experience of the persons who are in possession of the text. Experience, as medium, receives and does not produce the source; yet experience "colors" the presentation of the source and determines how it will be interpreted. The norm is the criterion (or set of criteria) for assessment of both experience and other sources. In African American theology, as Christian theology, the meaning of freedom is constructed through faith in Jesus Christ and an awareness of who he is and the life and living made possible by Christ. "The hermeneutical principle for an exegesis of the Scriptures [and the same can be said of other sources] is the revelation of God in Christ as the Liberator of the oppressed from social oppression and to political struggle, wherein the poor recognize that their fight against poverty and injustice is not only consistent with the gospel but is the gospel of Jesus Christ."[13] In other words, the norm is the new humanity in Jesus as the Black Christ, variously portrayed by African American theologians. These depictions will be discussed in chapter 9 (below). For now, it can be said that belief in Jesus as the Black Christ is based on biblical, communal, and personal conceptions of black liberation theism, which privileges both black experience and liberation. Jesus and God as well are in solidarity with oppressed African Americans and will liberate them. Liberation, then, is of infinite and unquestionable value, and black experience becomes a part of sacred history.

Black religion may be the principal source of African American theology, but it is not the only source of African American theology. African American theologians have consulted a variety of sources. For example, they have utilized the theories, literature, and findings from academic disciplines other than theology. They have also used philosophical traditions such as pragmatism, humanism, and process metaphysics. Willie Jennings, J. Kameron Carter, and Brian Bantum have turned to the use of "orthodox" Christian sources, that is, to patristic and dogmatic texts in Christian history and theology, showing that with these sources it is possible to construct a liberation perspective.[14] Some black theologians thought that was possible only through the use of "black sources" or "black religion," but these three are illustrating how the theme of liberation, social justice, and reconciliation may be developed by the use of ancient Christian sources. Notwithstanding such efforts, it seems that if any interpretation is to pass as African American theology, it must be able to establish which aspects of blackness it is addressing in relation to other theological sources, and it does this by documentation of blackness in the forms of black religion through which it is expressed.

MINING FOR BLACK RELIGION IN ETHNOGRAPHIC STUDY, LIBRARIES, AND ARCHIVES

Given that black religion is *lived*, ethnographic research along with quantitative analysis are suitable methods for the study of black religion. Religion, of any kind, is first and foremost something that is expressed in lived experience. Ethnographic study, with special sensitivity to how and through which means persons express themselves religiously, is a disciplined and respected academic approach for collecting data on a religious community. Several African American theologians are members of African American churches and communities. As members or participants in African American churches and communities, African American theologians have access to a lot of primary source material: the words and practices that are the expression and representation of the people's beliefs, values, concerns, stories, and hopes. By observation and participation in these churches and communities, African American theologians have access to a substantial portion of the subject matter at the center of their scholarly concerns. Instead of engaging in a kind of apologetics, defending the beliefs and practices of their church or community at all costs and contradictions, African American theologians seek to not only describe the faith statements and ritual and ethical practices but also the aesthetics (system of values and norms) by which these beliefs and practices are evaluated by persons in these churches and communities. In addition to the resources drawn from participant observation, African American theologians have at their disposal several intellectual and analytical tools of the academic guilds to which they belong. In ethnographic study and quantitative analysis, African American theologians are aiming for a level of sophistication in theological interpretation that does not view the people being studied as "exotic" or "infantile" (simpleminded) but rather recognizes them as persons who operate often within a complex pattern of ideas, meanings, and relations.

In addition to the data drawn from ethnographic study, African American theologians may, in a number of other places, find the foundational Christian sources and the black cultural forms through which African American theology is expressed. These resources for theological study include libraries, archives, oral history collections, church and denominational publications and records, and online digital collections and searchable databases. In the United States, African American theologians may gain access to various libraries, some operated by government agencies (federal, state, and municipal) and others by colleges and universities. In any case, libraries are an excellent source for the theologians' search for books, articles, special collections, research centers, and databases. Among the exemplary libraries are the Schomburg Center for Research in Black Culture (New York Public Library), Moorland-Spingarn Research Center (Howard University), Robert Wood Library and Archives (Clark Atlanta University), Fisk University Library and Archives, W. E. B. Du Bois Institute for

Afro-American Research (Harvard University), John Hope Franklin Research Center (Duke University), Smithsonian Institution, and the Library of Congress. The holdings of these and several other libraries may be searched by using online catalogs. The African American Odyssey Collection of the Library of Congress, which may be accessed through an online catalog, is a survey that highlights the rare books, government documents, manuscripts, music, films, newspapers, flyers, advertisements for runaway and captured slaves, notices of auctions and sales of slaves, photographs, and sound recordings in the Library of Congress's numerous African American collections. The Smithsonian Institution maintains several special collections, recordings, and photographs pertaining to African American history. The Schomburg and Moorland-Spingarn, premier research centers, have within their holdings a variety of materials, such as rare books, manuscripts, sheet and recorded music, paintings and other works of art, photographs, films, video and sound recordings, newspapers, periodicals, diaries, and letters that document many aspects of African American life and thought. The records of the Black Theology Project, from 1976 to 1987, are kept by the Schomburg Center.

Archives are another important resource for primary source material. These archives may be governmental (federal, state, county, and municipal) or denominational. Often denominational and local historical societies maintain some of the same types of documents held at archives. The U.S. National Archives maintains records on American Slavery and the International Slave Trade; this information is fully accessible to online researchers during the month of February. The National Archives also publishes a journal titled *Prologue* that contains many articles and guides for research in African American studies. The Amistad Research Center is the oldest and largest independent archive that documents the history and experience of African Americans in manuscripts, books, articles, photographs, audio and video recordings, and searchable databases.

Although in many cases it is still necessary to make visits to libraries and archives, researchers are able to access large amounts of information online via the Internet. Many historical materials have been digitized. The African American History Digital Library links black history information in libraries across the United States. Some libraries make available to their patrons the Black Studies Center and Accessible Archives databases produced by Chadwyck-Healey, Inc., one of the largest independent archives in the United States. These two databases encompass Chadwyck-Healey's core collections of primary sources and secondary sources, mostly Historical Black Newspapers and other Black Periodicals, from the eighteenth century to the nineteenth century. Chadwyck-Healey also maintains an African American Biographical Database, covering the same period, that contains photographs, a variety of illustrations, and many biographies. Alexander Street Press has produced the Black Thought and Culture database for research. The Documenting the American South Project or DocSouth (University of North Carolina, Chapel Hill) makes available to online researchers its Church in the Southern Black Community digital collection, which covers the period of the 1740s to 1940s via images, photographs, slave narratives, biographies, and rare books. Materials in DocSouth may be searched by religious topics such as baptism, biblical interpretation (for/against slavery), conjure/magic, conversion, funeral practices, heaven/life after death, beliefs about Jesus Christ, marriage, morality and Christian living, prayer and worship, revivals, Sabbath observance, shouting and other religious experiences, and spirituals. The Association of Religion Data Archive maintains a collection of surveys, polls, reports, articles, and other data contributed by research organizations such as the Pew Research Center, Baylor Religion Surveys, Public Religion Research Institute, and U.S. Congregational Life Survey.

African American churches and denominations are an important resource. Local churches and denominations maintain archives and other records to which researchers may be allowed access. Important documents and artifacts are kept at denominational headquarters and publishing houses. The Episcopal Church in the United States maintains an online archive that documents the history and contributions of African Americans in the Episcopal Church. Historic Black Christian denominational publications include *The Christian Recorder* (A. M. E. Church), which began in 1852 and is the oldest continuous African American church periodical and theological journal; *The Christian Index* (C. M. E. Church), from 1867 to the present; *The Star of Zion* (A. M. E. Zion Church), 1876–present; the *A. M. E. Zion Quarterly Review*, 1895–present; the *National Baptist Voice* (National Baptist Convention, U.S.A., Inc.), 1915–present; and *The Whole Truth* (Church of God in Christ), 1907–present. Black Christian denominations regularly publish educational literature and manuals for their members and clergy. In the educational literature, hymnals, discipline books, ministers manuals, and convention proceedings and minutes, researchers will often find information on the history and doctrines of the denomination. In addition to the publications of churches and denominations, Black (Negro) newspapers are a good source for church news, printed sermons, reports of regular church activities, special events, and regional and denominational meetings.

Questions for Discussion

1. What is the *essence* of black religion, that is, the unique property or special feature that sets black religion apart from other things?
2. Which sources and academic disciplines other than black religion might African American theologians use in order to interpret and assess the beliefs and practices of African American churches and communities?
3. How does the priority of black religion (or black sources) influence the selection of other kinds of sources for African American theological interpretation?
4. In what way does a definition of black religion and a stipulation of criteria for the selection of primary source material in black religion enable or complicate the tasks of African American theology?
5. Is there any truth that can be understood and communicated beyond a person's social context or unique experience of life?

Suggested Reading

Cone, Cecil W. *The Identity Crisis in Black Theology.* Nashville: African Methodist Episcopal Church, 1975.

Cummings, George C. L., and Dwight N. Hopkins, eds. *Cut Loose Your Stammering Tongue: Black Theology in the Slave Narratives.* Maryknoll, NY: Orbis Books, 1991.

Hopkins, Dwight N. *Shoes That Fit Our Feet: Sources for a Constructive Black Theology.* Maryknoll, NY: Orbis Books, 1993.

Smythe, Victor N., and Howard Dodson, eds. *African-American Religion: Research Problems and Resources for the 1990s.* New York: New York Public Library, 1992.

3
Methods

With respect to methodology, African American theology is quite varied and diverse. Many approaches are taken in order to construct theological interpretations. However, one thing seems to be common: the centrality of African American (or black) experience and acknowledgment that the work of theology consists of the manifold tasks of describing, analyzing, evaluating, explaining, and when necessary, revising or rejecting religious beliefs. African American theology begins with an examination of religious knowledge that emerges from the historical and social experiences of peoples of black African descent in the United States and ends with a test of the validity of their religious beliefs, restated or amended, in social situations endangering their humanity, freedom, survival, and quality of life. This circle of interpretation is accomplished through correlation and the use of symbols and themes that structure racial consciousness, religious and cultural sources that illuminate insights of black experience, and contemporary research paradigms for the development of black constructive theology.

THE METHOD OF CORRELATION

Early into the contemporary black theological movement, James H. Cone identified correlation as a fundamental method of African American theology.[1] In following this method, African American theology is constructed by relating the corpus of Christian theology to the black experience. Cone's *Black Theology of Liberation* (1970) weaves an interpretation of black experience into the traditional schema of Christian theology. In Cone's early attempts to construct black theology, he utilized the writings of major Christian theologians such as Karl Barth, Paul Tillich, Dietrich Bonhoeffer, and Rudolf Bultmann. Yet his correlation of these theologians' works to black experience yielded interpretations of Christian doctrines radically different from those espoused by these theologians.

M. Shawn Copeland goes further to describe how the method of correlation, in a broad sense, unfolds in African American theology. According to Copeland, the method unfolds through the tasks of critique and retrieval, social analysis, and construction.[2] Critique and retrieval involve assessment of cultural practices and careful historical study to identify and employ sources that facilitate critical reflection on culture. Social analysis involves studies of society and social institutions. Construction refers to constructive theology, that is, reflection and writing that restate, in present language and in light of current situations, Christian doctrines. The purpose of constructive theology is to relate the Christian faith to the contemporary situation in ways that are understandable and relevant for persons today. Jamie T. Phelps similarly claims that the three major tasks of any liberation theology are critique, retrieval, and construction.[3] Phelps credits Jacqueline Grant for first, as far back as 1984, describing this schema of tasks.

Presently, in African American theology, correlation is applied within a complex web of connections between religion and experience. Correlation is not a simple matter since there are multiple expressions of African American religion and many conceptions of blackness. The notion that correlation involves the task of relating blackness to the corpus of Christian theology must be modified to include a broader range of intellectual and religious traditions. The religious life of African Americans is not limited to Christianity or Christian thought. While the dominant tradition among African Americans is evangelical Protestant Christianity, African Americans have expressed themselves religiously in a number of ways. Other important religious traditions for correlation to blackness include Roman Catholic and Orthodox conceptions of Christianity, Islam, Judaism, African-derived religions (i.e., Santeria and vodou), eclectic spiritualist traditions, Hinduism, and Buddhism.

Not only must the meaning of religion be expanded to include non-Christian religions; the meaning of religion must also encompass secular worldviews and pervasive cultural beliefs. Religion provides orientation, guides for behavior, and a core of symbols and beliefs that is foundational to, of ultimate importance or basic for, explaining and understanding all else in human experience. Modern science, political economy, and political ideology now have the quality of religion in that they present comprehensive views or conceptions of the world, define persons and peoples, and suggest how they should act and the kind of future that humankind has to look forward to.

Like religion, blackness is a malleable category. There are many conceptions of blackness, not just one. Blackness has never been defined definitively, once and for all times. According to W. E. B. Du Bois, the history of blacks in America is fraught with images that are not always of their own making. For several generations of African Americans, their goal has been to reconcile conflicting images into "a better and truer self."[4] Toward defining this better and truer self, blackness may be, and more often is, characterized by experiences of oppression, humiliation, discrimination, political disenfranchisement, and economic injustice. When these negative aspects of black people's experience are of chief concern, African American theology takes on a liberation orientation with the aim of transforming the conditions that adversely affect black people's lives. However, blackness may also refer to those positive aspects, the "beauty and joy," of African American life that express deeply held values and mores enabling African Americans' fulfillment as human beings.[5]

A compelling argument for enlarging the concept of blackness is found in Victor Anderson's *Beyond Ontological Blackness: An Essay on African American Religious and Cultural Criticism* (1995). Anderson coins the term "ontological blackness," based upon James Cone's use of the term "symbolic blackness" and the metaphysical underpinnings of this terminology. Symbolic or ontological blackness dominates contemporary black theology. According to Anderson, this conception of blackness is defined over against and in opposition to whiteness. This is a form of black ethnic identity that needs whiteness and victimization by whites in order to understand and assert itself. Anderson argues that blackness can and should be defined independently of any antagonistic relationship to whiteness. He proposes a form of cultural pluralism that acknowledges and appreciates difference without extolling or devaluing any ethnic group. Anderson, in his *Creative Exchange: A Constructive Theology of African American Religious Experience* (2008), cites Edward Farley's theory of "deep symbols" and says that race may be understood as a "deep symbol," a word of power that constrains, guides, and becomes a focus of human behavior.[6] Within the context of cultural pluralism, Anderson thus situates a conception of postmodern blackness where race becomes one symbol among many for discernment of place and the history and experience at which the racialized self is the center.

Correlation is an ongoing process of African American theology. Identity as well as religion are not fixed and therefore are subject to change. As a people change, so will their religion. Blackness is constantly undergoing redefinition and renegotiation. African American religious preferences are capable of shifting. As long as race and religion circumscribe American reality, black theology will continue and will proceed by using the method of correlation.

Alistair Kee's critique of black theology is a call, though not welcome as such, for African American theology to achieve a new correlation suitable for the present moment in African American history.[7] Kee points out that contemporary black theology emerged simultaneously with and developed its paradigm around clarification of the religious symbolism of the black power movement. He claims that black theology, in its present form, is therefore antiquated. Now that times have changed, which is indicative of the new social and political landscape in the United States following the Civil Rights and Black Power movements of the 1960s, another paradigm (conceptual and methodological) is necessary for the current and future development of black theology. Anthony Pinn has characterized Kee's critique as a superficial analysis and evasion of the realities of race and racism in the world today.[8] Since the publication of Kee's book and Pinn's response to Kee's thesis, the American nation has witnessed and experienced its first elected two-term president, Barack Obama, who is African American. The sustained growth but precarious status of the black middle class and the ongoing plight of the black poor during the Obama presidency has raised new questions about the current state of race, racism, and black leadership in America. While few African American theologians have responded to Kee's call, they are keenly aware that the present moment in African American history is significantly different from the conditions at the center of concern in the black protest movements of the 1960s.[9]

DEEP SYMBOLS AND RECURRING THEMES

In addition to correlation, the use of symbols and themes is vital for the construction of African American theology. Symbols may be either nonlinguistic (physical objects) or linguistic (words, phrases, and ideas). In either case, symbols focus attention on self, society, and culture. Linguistic symbols are highlighted in this treatment. Themes are concepts that, when expressed in propositional form, are presumed true. Thus themes are foundational propositions for constructing interpretations. Symbols and themes function as "reality-detectors," tools for enabling self-understanding, discernment of meanings in the contexts through which persons live, and relating to that which is ultimate and transcendent so that life is never restricted solely to what life happens to be at any given time. Symbols and themes are not mutually exclusive: there is much connection, intersection, and overlap between the two. Though symbols and themes are used and repeated frequently, they are subject to reformulation (modification and renegotiation) as new events and challenges emerge in African American experience, which itself is never static.

In African American religions, there are many symbols. Given the dominance of evangelical Protestant Christianity, there is a pervasiveness of biblical motifs, metaphors drawn from Christian language, and the dogmas of Trinity and Christology in African American communities.[10] However, the primary symbols, first identified by Charles H. Long, are God, race, Africa, and freedom. They are "deep symbols," words of power that constrain, guide, and become a focus of thought and action.[11] Freedom functions both as symbol (that which represents ultimacy and transcendence) and theme (something claimed to be of great value). Race, as symbol, is now expanded to include emphases of gender and sexuality.

God is a symbol for transcendence and ultimacy.[12] Several questions revolve around God as symbol: What or who is the source of my value? To what or whom may I compare myself? Can I be other than what I am? What can (or will) I become?

The meaning of God is not limited to a particular doctrinal system of theism, African or Western. God is the Other. God is the One who is apart from the world. Charles Long describes Africans' encounter with God as an existential crisis finding resolution in a new locus of value. He says, "To whom does one pray from the bowels of a slave ship? to the gods of Africa? to the gods of the masters of the slave vessels? to the gods of an unknown and foreign land of enslavement? To whom does one pray? From the perspective of religious experience, this was the beginning of African American religion and culture. In the forced silence of oppression, in the half-articulate moans of desperation, in the rebellions against enslavement—from this cataclysm another world emerged."[13] God represents an altogether different reality. God is something, somewhere, or someone other than what is. Belief in God emerges from racial consciousness marked by an awareness of the power and sacredness of life (being itself) that is not restricted by the existing social order.[14] While subscribing to traditional Christian theism, African Americans have depicted God as ultimate and the locus of value over against American mores, particularly those customs, policies, and laws detrimental to African Americans' well-being. For example, at the conclusion of Henry McNeal Turner's detailed analysis of the Supreme Court's decision to overturn the Civil Rights Act of 1875, he declares faith in God, the One who is ultimate and thus another source of truth and justice.[15] For both Maria Stewart and Martin Luther King Jr., God is the source of authority and courage in the struggle for freedom and justice.[16] In a rather different approach to theistic faith, womanists like Zora Hurston and Alice Walker view God as the power that pervades nature, the unity that underlies as well as the spirit that animates each living thing.[17]

Race is a symbol for discernment of place. Thus race is used for fixing social location and for detecting and assessing the processes, historical and social, going into the formation of the world wherein African Americans live. Through the prism of race, various questions are asked, such as these: Who am I? What is my place in the world? What is the history and experience at which I am the center?

According to Charles Long, African Americans' sense of place is perceived, for the most part, as an "involuntary presence," a condition resulting from a history of forced migration and exploitation.[18] However, in addition to the idea of involuntary presence, race may refer to color caste, minority status, ancestry, subculture, and group belonging and solidarity. The use of race is clearly beyond discussions about physical characteristics and biological classification.

Africa is a symbol for representation and reflection on origins.[19] With Africa as central focus, pertinent questions are asked: From where did I come? May I return? Where do I belong? When and where does my history begin? What is my past? What is my cultural heritage?

Africa is both a historical reality and a mythological place. It is a historical fact that the ancestors of black Americans came from the

African continent. Unfortunately, documents for precise tracing of African American ancestry are scarce and, when available, limited in coverage for most African Americans. Even DNA analysis showing the specific geographical areas and ethnic groups from which enslaved Africans came seldom leads to direct connections to named ancestors. Though popularized by the novel and film *Roots*, Alex Haley's discovery of his ancestor Kunta Kinte is rare in African Americans' genealogical research. In most cases, a general sense of belonging may be all that is possible. Africa is a point of origin lost in obscurity. Still, the general designation of "African" reminds these persons that their progenitors came to the Americas from another place. Their history began before their enslavement in the Americas. The extant logs of slave ships chronicle the transport of persons from Africa to the Americas. In addition, the writings of Olaudah Equiano (Gustavus Vassa), Venture Smith (Broteer Furro), Phillis Wheatley, and Omar Ibn Said are notable recollections on life in Africa. Even when African American opinion has been mixed about African colonization (and back-to-Africa movements), African Americans have never denied their origins from Africa.[20]

Africa is not only a place of origins; it is also a place of destiny. African American folklore treasures numerous stories about persons who, when dreaming or when expressing hopes about their status upon death, have flown back to Africa.[21] Far from being artifacts of an age past, these stories continue to influence the production of black culture. Toni Morrison structures the ending of her popular novel *Song of Solomon* (1977) by using this folktale about some Africans who claimed that they could fly back to Africa. Today, African Americans are using more than dreams to get to Africa; they are using airplanes. Since the 1960s, African American travel and tourism to Africa has increased dramatically, becoming a multimillion-dollar industry. During slavery and after emancipation, in colonization and later back-to-Africa movements, Africa was perceived as a natural location for black people to settle. Then as well as now, there in Africa, it was believed that black Americans will find a sense of belonging, economic opportunity, and meaningful involvement in the evangelization and moral and cultural uplift of the indigenous African population.

Africa is a resource for the development of black culture in the United States. Since the 1970s, the dramatic increase of African immigrant communities in the United States has contributed as well to African American awareness and appreciation of African religion and culture. African American theology exhibits increasing interest and use of African religion and culture for theological interpretation.

Freedom is a symbol of the fulfilled life. When expressed in propositional form, in the statement that freedom is something of great (ultimate) value, freedom functions as a theme. The importance of freedom to African Americans is expressed best in the following spiritual:

> Oh, freedom! Oh, freedom! Oh, freedom all over me!
>   Before I'd be a slave,
>   I'll be buried in my grave,
> And go home to my Lord and be free.

The spiritual makes clear that a life without freedom is not worth living. Death is preferable to a life of oppression. Worse than death is the mode of existence marked by bondage, injustice, and nonfulfillment.

Recurring themes, stated propositionally, include the following: (1) African American Christianity is an authentic expression of Christianity. (2) African American people are special (distinct, having qualities not found in other peoples). (3) Community (black solidarity) is vital for liberation, survival, and quality of life. (4) Education (literacy and knowledge) is a route to freedom.[22] These themes are found in a variety of sources. A dichotomy between "true Christianity" and American Christianity (white religion) and the association of African American Christianity with true Christianity is found in works like David Walker's *Appeal* and Frederick Douglass's *Narrative* and speeches.[23] In Frances Ellen Watkins Harper's speech on "Duty to Dependent Races," she identifies the problem with American Christianity: its impotence against injustice and not following the example of Jesus Christ.[24] In Francis Grimke's thanksgiving sermon at the close of World War I, he is hopeful that a better form of Christianity, more faithful to the teachings of Jesus, will emerge in America.[25] Black inferiority is refuted in Benjamin Banneker's personal letter to Thomas Jefferson.[26] In Maria Stewart's address to the Afric-American Female Intelligence Society of Boston (1832), she describes blacks as a special people with a glorious past and potential for great contribution to human civilization.[27] The importance of community (black solidarity) for liberation is emphasized in Frederick Douglass's newspaper, *The North Star*, where he wrote: "We are one, . . . our cause is one, and . . . we must help each other, if we should succeed."[28] In essays and speeches by Sarah Mapps Douglass, Maria Stewart, Anna Julia Cooper, Mary Church Terrell, W. E. B. Du Bois, and Frances Ellen

Watkins Harper, education is proclaimed as what will enable blacks to fill their place in American society.[29]

A recent restatement of African American Christian faith as true Christianity is found in Diana L. Hayes's work. She says, "Black faith is indeed by itself the real Christianity, for it is, in its revolutionary, radically liberating form, the true bearer of the gospel, the good news, of Jesus Christ. This means that in the Roman Catholic Church, we must all become ontologically black, in our very being, in our innermost selves."[30] To be "ontologically black" means that persons must comprehend Christian faith from the experience of black people and join God and Christ in their solidarity with black people. African American theologians have defined the concept of blackness and related that concept to God and Christ. Several African American theologians have claimed that God and/or Christ are black. For the majority of African American theologians, the blackness of God and Christ means that God and Christ are in solidarity with black people. All African American theologians seek to correlate the gospel with the situation of black people. African American theologians have claimed that blackness is a medium of divine revelation and a deep symbol for theological reflection. Though speaking to a Roman Catholic audience, Hayes's claim may be applied also to black Christians in Protestant churches.

Through the above themes and other propositions, African American theology is construed as an alternative to dominant interpretations of Christianity in the United States. In contrast to the dominant forms of Christianity and Christian theology, usually emerging from churches of white Americans, African American theology assigns priority to addressing the suffering of black people, highly values and links freedom with equality and justice, and emphasizes the role of the church in the transformation of society.

SOURCES AND RESOURCES

African American theologians are at a consensus about "black religion" as the proper subject matter of African American theology. For the most part, black religion has meant the use of black sources, oral and written, or adoption of a perspective that emphasizes African American experience, and the functional capacity of black religious organizations for cultural critique and social change. Since the mid-1970s, through debate initiated by Cecil Cone's *The Identity Crisis in Black Theology*

(1975), the literature in African American theology is enriched greatly by the use of black sources.

Three methodological questions are raised about the treatment of black religion: (1) What are the sources by which African American religious beliefs are conveyed to the theologian and religion scholar? (2) How are these sources and other resources for theology mediated through and subjected to the norm in African American experience? (3) How are these sources distinguishable from the theological constructions produced through the use of these sources?

Many sources have been identified as bearers of religious belief. These sources include the following: songs, sermons, ways of reading the Bible, speeches, essays, poems, art, narratives, church and community histories, folktales, and institutional practices and customary ways of behaving. In the black hermeneutical school (BHS), sources include revelation (God's self-disclosure in history, black experience, the Bible, and Jesus Christ), the Bible, black experience, spirituality, history and culture, and reason (when compatible with revelation). In the black philosophical school (BPS), sources include reason (humanism and other philosophies), black experience, spirituality, history and culture, the Bible, Christian tradition, and other customary sources of theology (when compatible with reason). In the human sciences school (HSS), sources include black religion (as a complex phenomenon), black experience, history and culture, reason, the Bible, Christian tradition, and other customary sources of theology (when compatible with reason).

Besides conveying ideas and beliefs, black sources contain methods of reflection on African American experience, religious beliefs, and practices, or even critique and rejection of the same. For example, in Langston Hughes's story of his experience as a teenager at a revival service, he both describes and critiques the idea of conversion as salvation.[31] Hughes's narrative conveys important information about religious ritual in African American churches, ritual of the kind he knew, but also shows the inadequacy of routinized ecstatic experience for authentic personal transformation.

The turn to black sources should not be construed as a turn to legitimization, which Victor Anderson claims is the case.[32] According to Anderson, legitimization amounts to attempts to make theology appear to be "black" by using black sources but without any rigorous critical scrutiny of these sources. Still, the turn to black sources is appropriate for two sets of reasons: acknowledgment of (1) the general yet major role of these cultural expressions in religion and (2) the essential role of cultural forms for memory, recall, and introspection. A common form of cultural expression like narrative should not be equated with legitimization because, in African American culture, not all narratives are essentially Christian or support Christian categories and themes.[33] Not all narratives are essentially about liberation or have an ethic of liberation.[34] Narrative is a fundamental cultural product, which can be said also about other black sources. In systematic theology, experience is the medium for receiving, understanding, and analyzing sources of any kind. Black sources are "markers" and "snapshots" of African American experience.

Black cultural expressions, like African Americans themselves, have not evolved in a vacuum. African Americans are citizens of the Western world. Their theologians have utilized a wide variety of resources that are not solely unique to African Americans but are deemed valuable for understanding and illuminating various aspects and insights derived from African American experience. In addition to using various academic disciplines and reliable information sources, African American theologians employ a number of intellectual traditions ranging from commonsense realism, humanism, existentialism, pragmatism, and personalism to process metaphysics.

PARADIGMS IN CONTEMPORARY BLACK AND WOMANIST THEOLOGIES

In African American theology, several paradigms function as research programs, models, perspectives, and theoretical frameworks for constructing African American theology. In contemporary black theology, there are three principal schools of thought: the black hermeneutical school, the black philosophical school, and the human sciences school. These schools of thought are described and examined in Frederick Ware's *Methodologies of Black Theology* (2008).

The schools of thought have developed as a result of individual and collaborative work. The black hermeneutical school (BHS), which first emerged in clergy and seminary settings, is devoted to a quest for a "black hermeneutic"—a method of biblical and theological interpretation that recovers and is accurate in representing the earliest expression of Christian faith and the struggles for liberation among African Americans in the United States. Thinkers in the BHS include Katie Cannon, Albert Cleage, Cecil Cone, James Cone, Kelly Brown Douglas, James

Evans, Jacquelyn Grant, Dwight Hopkins, Major Jones, Olin Moyd, J. Deotis Roberts, Delores Williams, and Gayraud Wilmore. The BHS has been and continues to be the most prolific and popular of the three schools of academic black theology.

The black philosophical school (BPS) was formed by the entry of philosophers of religion into and the use of philosophy in the field of black theology. Thinkers in the BPS include William Jones, Anthony Pinn, Alice Walker, Cornel West, and Henry Young.

The human sciences school (HSS) encompasses the kinds of cultural studies of black theology conducted by historians of religion, theologians of culture, sociologists of religion, religious studies scholars, and other intellectuals adhering to prevalent canons of scholarship in college and university settings. Thinkers in the HSS include Charles Long, Cheryl Townsend Gilkes, C. Eric Lincoln, Henry Mitchell, Charles Shelby Rooks, and Theophus Smith. While the works of African American women may be classified within these schools of thought, the special emphases and themes of womanist theology warrant separate examination of womanist approaches as a unique vantage point for African American theology.

Womanist theology is characterized by an intentional holism on several levels. On one level, womanist theology appreciates the insights and contributions of African American women regardless of the terms used for self-identification. Although African American women in religious and theological studies will refer to themselves as "womanists," some prefer to be called "black feminists."[35] In addition to embracing differing women's identities, womanist theology, on another level, aims for a comprehensive analysis of oppression. African American's resistance to racism and sexism is related to opposition to classism, homophobia, and human destruction of the environment. Inspired by the writings and works of notable African American women of faith— such as Jarena Lee, Harriet Tubman, Sojourner Truth, Amanda Berry Smith, Anna Julia Cooper, Maria W. Stewart, Mary Church Terrell, Ida B. Wells, Mary McLeod Bethune, and Fannie Lou Hamer—contemporary womanist theology seeks quality of life and liberation for both women and men. Womanist theologians link their work and movement to the struggles of other persons and groups seeking liberation and fulfillment. According to Anna Julia Cooper, as "black" and "Christian," African Americans cannot be indifferent about the condition of African American women.[36] The uplift of African Americans, as a whole, depends on the uplift of black women. No adequate analysis

may be made of African American experience without giving attention to the experience and status of black women and other minority groups within African American communities. Through all this,
womanist theology is conducted on a level of harmonizing scholarship
and advocacy. Womanist theology develops from the use of interconnecting emphases: valuing women's experience and wisdom, identifying and preserving sources on women's experience, and disseminating
theology through teaching and publication in both academic and community settings.

Delores S. Williams claims that the methodology of womanist theology, as a specialty distinguished from black theology, is determined
by four parameters.[37] These parameters are emphases on the principal source and tasks of womanist theology. The first parameter or
emphasis is what Williams calls womanist theology's multidialogical
intent, which is black women's involvement in dialogue and activism
in social, political, and religious communities. The second parameter
or emphasis is what Williams calls the liturgical intent of womanist
theology as involving witness to and celebration of Christ's prophetic
message. The third parameter or emphasis is what Williams calls the
didactic intent of womanist theology, which involves teaching wisdom
and sharing insights. The fourth parameter or emphasis is women's
experience: the use of female imagery, women's stories, and gendered
language in theology.

Theological interpretation in the three named schools (BHS, BPS,
and HSS) proceeds along a trajectory set by the priority assigned to
blackness and liberation. In the BHS, the new humanity in Jesus as
the Black Christ (based on biblical, communal, and personal conceptions of black liberation theism) privileges both black experience and
liberation. Black liberation theism is the belief that God (and Jesus) is
in solidarity with oppressed African Americans and will liberate them.
Liberation then is of infinite and unquestionable value, and black experience becomes a part of sacred history. In BPS, human freedom (based
on secular humanism or humanocentric theism) privileges liberation
but not black experience. Humanocentric theism emphasizes human
freedom and responsibility in dealing with problems (such as racism,
war, and poverty) traditionally thought to be only under God's control
and thus requiring God's supernatural intervention for their solution.
Apart from God's will, liberation is valuable simply because oppressed
people need and want it. In HSS, human consciousness (based on
phenomenological study and other disciplines for the discovery of

structures of mind that enable awareness and action) does not privilege black experience or liberation. However, blackness and liberation are perceived as aspects of African American life that no responsible scholar should ignore.

BLACK EXPERIENCE AND THE NORM OF FREEDOM

All sources are mediated through experience, and both these sources and experience are subjected to the norm of freedom. In African American theology, as is true in other forms of theology, experience is the medium for receiving, understanding, and analyzing sources of any kind. Black sources are "markers" and "snapshots" of African American experience. The norm of freedom, however it is defined, determines which sources and resources will be used and how they will be used for reflection. In African American theology, the norm (freedom) may be grounded in either a christocentric or theocentric conception of faith.[38] African American humanists would argue that neither form of grounding is necessary in order to justify freedom.[39]

The broad categories of sources from which the theologian draws data for the study and interpretation of Christian faith are Scripture, tradition, reason, experience, and culture. When the theologian's focus is narrowed to Christianity in African American churches and communities, the sources may be said to be drawn from "black religion." In this regard, "black religion" often functions as a covering term for the variety of sources, past and present, found in, or deemed necessary for interpreting religious life in African American churches and communities.

Though experience is a source of theology, it stands in a special relationship with other sources. The sources are transmitted and received through the medium of experience. For example, what a text means—and here a text could be a written document or an oral tradition or ritual practice—is inseparable from the experience of the persons who are in possession of the text. Experience, as medium, receives and does not produce the source; yet experience colors the presentation of the source and determines how it will be interpreted.

The norm is the criterion (or set of criteria) for assessment of both experience and other sources. Each school (BHS, BPS, and HSS) has a norm for assessing experience, other sources, and the adequacy of their theological interpretations. In the black hermeneutical school, the norm is the New Humanity in Jesus as the Black Christ. Jesus and God are in solidarity with oppressed African Americans and will liberate them. Liberation is of infinite and unquestionable value, as black experience has its own internal logic and becomes a part of sacred history. In the black philosophical school, the norm is human freedom based on secular humanism or humanocentric theism that privileges liberation but not black experience. Apart from God's will, liberation is valuable because oppressed people need and want it. In the human science school, the focus on human consciousness is normative and based on phenomenological study and other disciplines for the discovery of the structures of mind that enable awareness and action. This focus does not privilege black experience or liberation. However, blackness and liberation are regarded as aspects of African American life that are impossible to deny.

Although experience, as medium, receives and does not produce the source, experience does color the presentation of the source and determines how it will be interpreted.[40] The norm is the criterion (or set of criteria) for assessment of both experience and other sources. In Christian theology, the norm is Jesus Christ, the life and living made possible by Jesus Christ.[41]

Freedom (as the penultimate of human fulfillment) is the norm to which the sources and resources as well as African American experience generally is subjected. This norm determines which sources and resources will be used and how they will be used for reflection. By this norm, African American theology is tested, criticized, and revised. Framed within the context of Christianity, freedom becomes that "soul-stuff," emerging from God's self-disclosure in the black experience as that by which blacks are drawn into a new humanity, where they are fully human and transformed for life in God's reign.

In spite of the plurality of method and interpretation in African American religious thought, there is a continuing reluctance of scholars, white and black, to address African American theology in its rich diversity and complexity. The great temptation, which is hard to resist, is to simplify African American theology by identifying one person or one type of construal as representative of African American theology. The vibrancy of African American theology seems to be dependent on the holism commended by womanist theology. The gift of womanist theology and African American theology's future is cohesion without conformity, solidarity without exclusion.

Questions for Discussion

1. Given the shifts and changes in American society since the 1960s, what sort of paradigm (conceptual and methodological) is needed for the present construction and relevancy of African American theology?
2. Is there a qualitative distinction between black men's experience and black women's experience such that the use of either experiential source will result in different theological interpretations?
3. What is the relation between African American theology and black experience? Must a person be African American or have some type of black experience in order to successfully do (study and interpret) African American religious beliefs and practices?
4. Are postmodern blackness, humanocentric theism, and intentional holism the best alternatives and way forward for African American theology?

Suggested Reading

Cannon, Katie G., Alison P. Gise Johnson, and Angela D. Sims. "Living It Out: Womanist Works in Word." *Journal of Feminist Studies in Religion* 21, no. 2 (Fall 2005): 135–46.

Cone, James H. *A Black Theology of Liberation.* Twentieth Anniversary Edition. Maryknoll, NY: Orbis Books, 1990.

Floyd-Thomas, Stacey M., ed. *Deeper Shades of Purple: Womanism in Religion and Society.* New York: New York University Press, 2006.

Neal, Ronald B. "Beyond Fundamentalism: Reconstructing African American Religious Thought." *Journal of Race, Ethnicity, and Religion* 1, no. 8 (July 2010): 1–37.

Ware, Frederick L. *Methodologies of Black Theology.* Eugene, OR: Wipf & Stock, 2008.

4

Epistemology

In this chapter, African American theology is examined as a form of knowledge, mainly as an academic discipline comparable to other disciplines in the university and theological curriculum.[1] African American theology constitutes a subject area and form of knowledge in four ways. First, in addition to faith and revelation, African American theologians utilize reason in the form of several philosophical traditions that happen to be used also by scholars in other areas of study. Second, African American theology is epistemically public.[2] That is to say, African American theology is intelligible and defensible outside of the confessional contexts from which it emerges and has relevance and application beyond black churches. Third, African American theology has an established canon. Through its disciplinary development over the past four decades, especially in theological schools and academic guilds, certain written works are regarded as primary or exemplary. The recognition of these works may be attributable to the status of the authors with major repute in theological education and, in the case of lesser-known authors, the conformity of their published works with the styles and methods prominent among African American theologians. Fourth and closely related to the third way, African American theology is a form of knowledge based upon the social practices and publishing operations that produce and market materials identified as African American theology. Over the past several decades, African American theology has recognized authorities or experts that any aspiring author in the field must engage, in one way or another, in order to achieve publication.

FAITH, REVELATION, AND REASON

Across the three schools of academic black theology, there are various strategies for relating faith and revelation to reason.[3] In the BHS (black hermeneutical school), though, priority is given to faith and revelation, and reason is regarded as an acceptable source, especially when it is compatible with revelation and faith. The BHS derives its criteria of truth from nonfoundationalist (e.g., biblical, communal, and personal) conceptions of Christian faith. In the BHS, Christian faith has its own internal logic and does not require a foundation or grounding in anything else. In James Cone's *God of the Oppressed*, he claims that black theology is committed to truth, but not truth understood primarily as an abstract, philosophical concept. Cone says that black theologians are committed to the truth revealed in Jesus Christ, the truth that liberation is the work of God in the world. Blackness is ontological and symbolic and therefore revelatory.

In the BPS (black philosophical school), reason (humanism and other philosophies) is prominent, but the Bible, Christian tradition, and religious experience are regarded as significant for their compatibility with claims drawn from the use of reason. Whereas the conceptions of Christian faith in the black hermeneutical school are nonfoundationalist and require no justification beyond the believing community's valued sources of revelation, the conceptions of Christian faith in the black philosophical school are foundationalist and grounded in systems of thought regarded as reliable underpinnings for religious belief. For the BPS, conceptions of Christian faith are rooted in humanism and other philosophies, such as pragmatism, process metaphysics, and analytic philosophy. In the BPS, the conceptions of God are compatible with William Jones's notion of humanocentric theism.

In the HSS (human sciences school), religion, as conveyed through experience and various cultural expressions, is the primary subject matter for theological reflection and interpretation.[4] The study of religion does not depend upon or require of its researchers, teachers, or students any specific religious belief or affiliation, political commitment, race, culture, or gender; therefore theologians in the HSS as well as those in the BPS hold various faith and nonbelief perspectives. Like theologians in the black philosophical schools, theologians in the human sciences school supplement the justification of religion with systems of thought not found in believing communities. Several theologians in the HSS hold foundationalist conceptions of Christian faith rooted in phenomenology.[5] More will be said about phenomenology and other systems of philosophy in the discussion below.

One area of challenge for African American theologians is in the verification of their claims to truth. Especially problematic for bolstering religious claims and theological assertions are appeals to experience, usually subjective religious and social experience, and appeals to eschatology, sometime in the future. Must all persons be black, in a literal physical sense or symbolic sense, in order to understand African American theology? Are events in sacred history—such as the exodus, Jesus' crucifixion, or resurrection—adequate justification of claims made by theologians that non-Christians ought to accept? The concepts of ontological blackness and eschatological verification have been critiqued by Victor Anderson and William R. Jones, respectively.

According to Victor Anderson, ontological blackness is defined over against and in opposition to whiteness. In a positive sense, ontological blackness is the notion that blackness is a symbol for discernment of God's action in the world. Aside from racial designation, blackness represents the persons whom God favors and is seeking to liberate from oppression.[6] In a negative sense, according to Anderson, ontological blackness is a form of black ethnic identity that needs whiteness and victimization by whites in order to understand and assert itself. Anderson argues that blackness can be defined independently of any antagonistic relationship to whiteness. He proposes a form of cultural pluralism wherein blackness is one among several ways that persons identify themselves, but not at the expense of devaluing any other racial or ethnic group. I have argued that although blackness, physical or symbolic, is not an absolute requirement of scholars participating in the study and interpretation of African American religion, blackness could possibly enhance dialogue, creativity, and interpretation in African American theology.[7] When theology is open for scholarly participation from interested persons of all backgrounds, academic theology proceeds along several paths that, to one degree or another, contribute to the presentation of theology to various audiences among the intelligent public.

William R. Jones argues that, in the case of eschatological verification, the postulation of a future state as verification of belief is insufficient evidence.[8] Reasonable belief requires something in the present, something empirical. Criticism of belief is not possible if verification is constantly postponed into a remote, inaccessible future. Reliance on eschatological verification leads to irrationalism. Jones contends that black liberation theism leads to a position that is ridiculous for oppressed black people to accept. In Jones's opinion, citing biblical motifs of God's supposed acts of liberation and verification of black liberation theism in the postulation of a future eschaton does not constitute sufficient evidence. Biblical motifs are not direct acts of divine liberation in the history of African Americans. Eschatological verification does not add to our certainty but instead begs the question of why God is delaying liberation. In stating that God is a white racist, Jones means that God does not identify with and is hostile or unsympathetic toward black people. This hostility, lack of sympathy, or indifference on the part of God is what Jones calls "divine racism."

James Cone's response to Jones's criticism is to situate black humanism as a marginal tradition within African American culture and insists upon the logical integrity of black Christian faith. Cone contends that this marginal tradition lacks the kind of authority that Jones assigns to it. According to Cone, the majority of black Christians believe in the Bible. He adds that the Bible contains a certain conception of suffering. In the Old Testament, suffering is a consequence of divine election. In the New Testament, the story of Jesus' death and resurrection identifies God with the oppressed and is God's decisive liberative act against oppression. Cone goes on to say that suffering challenges but does not negate black faith. He maintains that black faith has a logic of its own wherein it finds its warrant or justification in sources other than Jones's "white" Western philosophical orientation. Cone admits that he is dissatisfied with his response to Jones' critique because his rebuttal merely voices his confessional context. He senses that speech only from one's faith perspective subtly implies that black theology is publicly indefensible. I think his intuition, here, is correct.

Cone's and Jones's works reveal the racial ideology that compromises theological scholarship. Racial ideology, as Cornel West and Michael Dyson describe it, moves back and forth from establishing some racial identity (isolating an essence that authenticates blackness) to minimizing or downplaying diversity among black people, and then to subordinating or suppressing marginal groups, dissenting voices, or differing interests among black people.[9] Clearly this type of reasoning is in Jones's and Cone's works. Each claims to have an authentically "black" position. Jones acknowledges that black religious humanism is a marginal tradition, yet he seeks to make it normative. Cone acknowledges the existence of this humanistic tradition but insists that it should remain a marginal tradition. Common to Jones and Cone is an exclusive preoccupation with racism and liberation, as if these are the essential religious concerns of all African Americans. Jones and Cone both claim that all intellectual effort worthy of the name of black theology must be for the promotion of liberation. Interests in topics other than racism and liberation are subordinated to and sacrificed for the cause of liberation. Jones and Cone, in effect, minimize the diversity among African Americans.

PHILOSOPHICAL TRADITIONS IN AFRICAN AMERICAN THEOLOGY

A philosophical tradition exists where there is a distinct set of ideas or themes held to be of major concern, a unique approach to raising and answering questions, and an oral or written body of wisdom passed on over time. Although philosophy may be appropriated for theology, philosophy has its origin beyond the community of faith that the theologian seeks to address. Philosophy, in the Western conception, is characterized by the quest to understand without appeal to any deity or religious authority and relying instead on the faculty of reason. Still, philosophy may be appropriated by people of faith. The philosophical traditions used in African American theology include commonsense realism, humanism, pragmatism, personalism, process metaphysics, phenomenology, postmodernism, and analytic philosophy.

Commonsense Realism

Commonsense realism is the tradition that emerges from the intuitive grasp and immediate perception of the way that the world is and how all or most of life conforms to this view of the world. Historical examples of commonsense realism include Sojourner Truth's (Isabella Baumfree's) speeches and John Jasper's sermons, both of which owe their origin to the genre of sayings and proverbs in African American folklore.[10] In Sojourner Truth's oft-cited 1851 speech "Ain't I a Woman?," she reasons from the proverb of a pint for the woman and a quart for the man that women, regardless of their perceived or actual differences from men, are entitled to have their "measure full."[11] By full, she is referring to each woman having one vote, as does each man. Also, in her speech, she uses Scripture and the absurdities in her as well as other persons' social experiences to argue for women's equality. She reports that women are said to be the weaker sex, but she, as anyone can see, is very muscular and has worked harder and endured greater pain than most men. Sojourner Truth goes on to declare that if sin entered the world by a woman, Eve, then good can also be brought into the world by a woman. The power of women is not only in turning the world upside down but also in setting it right-side up. Christ came into the world by a woman, Mary, and no man had anything to do with the conception and birth of Christ. Frederick Douglass's impression was that Sojourner Truth, who never learned to read and write, was a wise woman who spoke in the language of the common people.[12]

In John Jasper's "The Sun Do Move," a sermon that he reportedly preached more than 250 times, he defends a traditional evangelical Protestant view of God based on a literal interpretation of the Bible that rejects the modern scientific claim that the earth revolves around the sun (cf. chap. 12 below).[13] Jasper argues that the earth is stationary and that the sun moves. He notes that, in the Bible, the earth is said to have four corners. Anything that has four corners is square. Anything with four corners cannot be circular. A square is flat. So the earth, having four corners, is flat and not round. The sun moves in the sky but, according to Jasper, the earth remains still. Jasper's argument, in effect, assumes that the way in which the sun appears to us is how it truly exists.

Humanism

Humanism is the tradition in African American thought, be it in folk wisdom or formal philosophy, that raises questions about not only injustices in American society but also the soundness (or lack thereof) of various prevalent religious beliefs. Persons in African American theology associated with humanism include William Jones and Anthony Pinn.[14] Although Alice Walker is not a theologian, her womanism, a type of humanism, has been influential among black womanist theologians.[15] According to Jones, in African American religion and culture, humanism is a minority but contrasting tradition that provides an alternative to black Christian theism. Jones offers four theses in order to define and clarify humanism in African American religion and culture: (1) Black humanism originates in slaves' rejection of Christianity. (2) Black humanism is a philosophical perspective and not an ongoing institution like the black church. (3) Black humanism is the affirmation of radical freedom and personal responsibility as the essence of human life. (4) Black humanism is an unexplored and potentially rewarding option for black liberation theology in light of its contribution toward a more plausible interpretation of black suffering.[16] Jones goes further to point out two basic affirmations that lie at the heart of humanism: (1) freedom is the essence of human being, and (2) human choice carries with it an authority as great as or greater than that derived from faith, reason, science, or method.[17]

In order to demonstrate how humanism leads to both positive and negative interpretations of Christian faith and as well to situate his atheism within the humanist tradition, Anthony Pinn makes a distinction between weak humanism and strong humanism.[18] On the one hand, weak humanism does not call into question or deny the existence of God. It emphasizes self-awareness, the interrelatedness of human beings, and the God-given powers in human beings for effecting personal and social change. On the other hand, strong humanism denies the existence of God. Humans are solely responsible for their actions and future. The powers, if any, in human beings are the mere consequence of their biological and cultural evolution, a process that requires no supernatural explanation. The inspiration for personal and social change grows out of human beings' own desire for survival and fulfillment. By Pinn's admission, he is a strong humanist and atheist.[19]

Motivated by a quest for truth and justice, Pinn has settled on atheism as the best alternative to either black liberation theism or humanocentric theism. Though an atheist, Pinn is not within the camp of the new atheists, who are hostile to and seek to eradicate religion from society. Pinn acknowledges the good of religion as a system of belief that provides persons with an orientation toward life, although in his view some of their faith claims are not plausible.

Pragmatism

Pragmatism is the tradition in African American thought that finds the truth of ideas and beliefs in their practical application for solving human problems. African American theologians associated with this philosophical tradition include Cornel West and Victor Anderson. According to West, pragmatism as a philosophical movement aimed at achieving democracy is best comprehended in the triad of voluntarism, fallibilism, and experimentalism.[20] Voluntarism is the emphasis of pragmatists on human will, human power, and human action for resolving economic, social, political, and intellectual problems. Fallibilism means that every claim is open to criticism and revision. Experimentalism is the view that experience and the knowledge gained from it are governed by a process of trial and error. In addition, competing ideas and courses of action are adjudicated by determinations on which ones work best in experience. Cornel West bases his radical pragmatism on philosophers such as Ralph Waldo Emerson, William James, John Dewey, Reinhold Niebuhr, W. E. B. Du Bois, and Richard Rorty.

In contrast to Cornel West, Victor Anderson focuses on the works of pragmatist theologians such as Shailer Matthews, Gerald Birney Smith, George Burman Foster, and Henry Nelson Wieman.[21] Anderson consequently names his pragmatism as "pragmatic theology." He is very intentional about using theological language. His theology is pragmatic in that it emphasizes the use of theological language for enriching life in democratic society. As he frames it, his pragmatic theology seeks to make "public life spiritually meaningful, morally livable, and culturally flourishing."[22] Theological language concentrates on transcendence and grace. It sees in God the ideal potentiality to which humans can aspire, in spite of the evil and suffering in human existence. Thus theological language's vision of the ideal becomes a basis for critiquing customary modes of behavior in society, especially where these patterns of living limit moral fulfillment and human flourishing.

Personalism

Personalism is a form of idealism in metaphysics that identifies the concept of person and the society of persons interacting with the Supreme Person (God) as the fundamental feature of reality and foundation for ethics. African American theologians associated with this philosophical tradition include Martin Luther King Jr. and J. Deotis Roberts.[23] Personalism began and underwent development at Boston University. As a doctoral student at and eventual graduate from Boston University, Martin Luther King is directly connected to the Boston personalist tradition. By King's own admission, personalism was the philosophical framework for his theology.[24] Personalism is evident in King's belief that God is personal, that each human life is sacred and has dignity, that moral laws are embedded in the structure of the physical universe, and that we have a moral obligation to resist evil.[25] J. Deotis Roberts's exposure to personalism was through his doctoral studies at the University of Edinburgh. Personalism is evident in his emphasis on the sanctity and dignity of each person, God's capacity for personal relationship, human freedom and responsibility, and the person as a complex self in a community of persons.[26]

Phenomenology

Phenomenology is a philosophical tradition that informs sociological and history of religions approaches to the study of African American religion and culture. According to Edmund Husserl, a German philosopher who coined the term, phenomenology is rigorous, holistic study that includes self-introspection of our attitudes about the objects of our study as well as our examination of the objects themselves. African American theologians and religion scholars associated with this philosophical tradition are Henry Mitchell, Charles H. Long, C. Eric Lincoln, Theophus Smith, Anthony Pinn, and Cheryl Gilkes. For these scholars, observable behaviors, personal narratives, self-reports, and any other cultural expression capable of bearing religious meanings may stand as prime data in the study of religion. They have a shared interest in studying religion in whatever forms and situations it is expressed. In the various phenomenological approaches, African American religion is studied for the ways it operates matter-of-factly and is understood actually in the lives of its adherents, rather than any appeal to ahistorical notions of black religion. This way of studying religion may aid theologians in curtailing their bias for and imposition of theological apologetics onto forms of religious life that are not explicitly Christian.

Analytic Philosophy

Analytic philosophy is a tradition that is characterized by the study of language and use of logic for solving problems. It is the dominant tradition of philosophy in the United States and Britain. The influence of the analytic tradition is evident in Frederick Ware's *Methodologies of Black Theology*. As a graduate of Memphis State University, Ware's philosophical training was principally in analytic philosophy.[27] This philosophy concentrates on logic and the devices and operations of language for the resolution of philosophical problems. In *Methodologies of Black Theology*, taking cues from Richard Rorty's critique of rational commensuration—the practice of forcing various discourses under one rubric in order to deny or obscure their legitimacy and independence—Ware offers a reading of contemporary black theology to show three separate and valid approaches to constructing black theology. Instead of interpreting the arguments of black theologians as one-upmanship or aimed at a singular truth, Ware interprets their differences as efforts toward clarifying unique approaches and areas of discourse on the subject matter of African American religion and culture.

Process Metaphysics

Process metaphysics is a theory of reality developed by Alfred North Whitehead, whose aim was to produce a system of metaphysics that takes seriously the current paradigm of science. Charles Hartshorne pioneered the theological movement known as process theology, which adapts process metaphysics to Christian theology. The current evolutionary-complexity paradigm, rooted in the theories of Charles Darwin and of Albert Einstein, posits the idea of cosmic and biological evolution. The universe and living beings, even God, if God is thought to exist, are evolving. The evolutionary-complexity paradigm replaces the orderliness of the Newtonian-mechanistic view with relativity, chaos, and complexity theories. African American theologians such Henry Young, Theodore Walker, and Monica Coleman have adopted process metaphysics as a theoretical framework for their constructive theology and liberation ethics.[28]

In process metaphysics, Henry Young sees a justification for cultural pluralism. According to Young, Whitehead's organic pluralism, the interrelation of all things in a universe that is in flux, has implications for theology. No relations between entities, even those among racial and ethnic groups, are fixed, static, or permanent. Everything is subject to change. For Young, in Whitehead's metaphysics, black liberation is possible and achievable. The condition of blacks can change and improve for the better.

Theodore Walker argues that a creative synthesis of process metaphysics and black liberation theology makes process metaphysics ethically relevant and makes black liberation theology more astute in its articulation of physical and social reality.[29] According to Walker, the social identities, economic structures, and political orders of the modern world are the result and legacy of the transatlantic slave trade. A postmodern theology would therefore need to include a critique of power and an ethic of liberation. Black theology provides the needed analysis of the social-historical context of enslaved Africans. Process metaphysics provides the needed analysis of basic presuppositions about God and human beings in the universe. Together, black theology and process metaphysic form what Walker calls a "black neoclassical social ethics." The all-embracing God of process metaphysics is black theology's God of the oppressed. God struggles creatively and persuasively against oppression, an unnecessary and impermanent feature of the world.

According to Monica Coleman, process thought has three positive features when it is combined with womanist theology.[30] First, process thought tests the truths asserted in experience and literary imaginings of the possibilities in human life. Womanist theology that uses black women's science fiction and other literature "offers process theology a deeper commitment to Whitehead's airplane metaphor for testing truth. Black women's science fiction is yet another field in which the plane of process must land."[31] Whitehead likens philosophical speculation to an airplane. Like the plane that leaves the ground, human thought travels far beyond the immediate context that initially provokes and concerns human thought. Also like the plane that must land, since it cannot stay in the air indefinitely, human thought must return to the situation that first held its attention. Second, process theology is enlarged to a consideration of religious pluralism when it takes up black womanist interest in African traditional religions. Womanist theologian's preoccupation is not with Christianity alone. Third, process theology can provide hope through womanist visions of possibilities for improvement through human response to God's invitations for change.

Karen Baker-Fletcher is a womanist theologian who has been influenced by process theology but has chosen open theism as the framework for her theology.[32] While like process theologians, who believe that the future is open, Baker-Fletcher does not think that the outcome of history is completely unknowable. Life is on the side of good: good will triumph over evil. It is good, not evil, that defines life. The ultimate experience and real meaning of life is in our relationship with God. God is community as it comes into realization in the universe. In community, we find God who is the source of power and courage to overcome evil.

Postmodernism

Though not a recent development per se, postmodernism is now coming into greater use among African American theologians and religion scholars. The terms *postmodernism* or *postmodernity* may mean (1) modernity, that is, the present period in Western culture, initiated by the Enlightenment; (2) critique and rejection of ideas that characterized the Enlightenment or modernity; and (3) new theories and methods for scholarship that replace those of the Enlightenment or modernity. At an earlier time, the term postmodern seems to have been used as a synonym for *countermodern* and *contemporary*, especially in contrast to previous scholarship referred to as modern or traditional Western thought. Notable postmodern thinkers from whom African American theologians and religion scholars are drawing insights include Judith Butler, Jacques Derrida, Michel Foucault, and Richard Rorty.

Kelly Brown Douglas's *Sexuality and the Black Church*, for example, is illustrative of the influence of postmodern thought, mainly that of Michel Foucault. Douglas appropriates Foucault's theory of power, particularly his idea of how modern society achieves dominance over individuals through control of human sexuality, in order to describe the form of oppression experienced by African Americans. She says that the "violation of black sexuality by White culture is about nothing less than preserving White power in an interlocking system of racist, classist, sexist and heterosexist oppression."[33] According to Douglas, Foucault's work is essential for understanding the various mediums through which power is exercised, especially on the level of the bodies of individuals. Foucault names "bio-power" as the technique used today for dominance and control. Based on Foucault's history of sexuality and analysis of power, Kelly Brown Douglas asserts that white racism is connected to the control and disdain of black people's bodies.[34]

THE SOCIOLOGY AND PRODUCTION
OF KNOWLEDGE

It is not by rational thought alone that we come to know; the process of knowing has a social dimension.[35] The theologian not only functions as an individual but also, and most importantly, as a member of a group. Certain theologians and the groups to which they belong are regarded as professional in the sense of being skilled and qualified to speak and write on matters of faith and practice. As authorities, these experts and guilds, by their own deployment of reason and prevalent rules for inquiry and rules of inference, determine what terms and concepts will mean as well as the boundaries and content that will define an area of knowledge.

African American theologians participate in several academic guilds. Principal organizations for scholarly collaboration between African American theologians are the Society for the Study of Black Religion (SSBR) and the American Academy of Religion (AAR). The AAR meets annually with the Society for Biblical Literature (SBL). These two organizations represent the largest group of scholars in religion in the United States. Smaller organizations meet prior to or concurrently with the AAR and SBL. The Black Religious Scholars Group (BRSG) is one of these smaller organizations that meets at the beginning of the AAR/SBL meeting. The BRSG has recently launched an initiative titled The Womanist Institute for Church and Society. Significant forums for black and womanist theology are AAR program units such as the Black Theology Group, the Theology of Martin Luther King Jr. Group, and Womanist Approaches to Religion and Society Group. Through the Ecumenical Association of Third World Theologians (EATWOT) and the Transatlantic Roundtable on Religion and Race, African American theologians are able to dialogue and work with scholars and activists from various nations.

In publishing, there are certain channels of production and distribution that enable the works of African American theologians to reach reading audiences. Their book-length works are disseminated by scholarly and university presses. Peer-reviewed journals are another medium for dissemination of African American theologians' essays. In addition to essays, academic journals also contain valuable reviews and notes on books published by or of significance for African American theologians. Production and distribution of African American theologians' writings furthers the discipline and educates readers in the ideas, values, and methods of African American theology. A large number of African American theological books have been published by Orbis Books, Fortress Press, Oxford University Press, and New York University Press. In addition to publication in what are regarded as mainstream journals, scores of African American theological essays are published in the *Journal of Religious Thought*; *Journal of the Interdenominational Theological Center*; *Black Theology: An International Journal*; and *Journal of Africana Religions*.

STAGES OF DISCIPLINARY DEVELOPMENT

William Jones's characterization of black theology, as basically a form of discourse on theodicy and enlarged through the normal pattern of disciplinary development, lends credence to the view that African American theology is a valid area of knowledge. Jones identifies legitimation, critical expansion, and systematic construction as the fundamental stages in the development of academic disciplines and argues that there is documentation of these stages in African American theology.[36] In the phase of legitimation, scholars establish the boundaries or "turf" of their field and the unique set of sources needed for addressing the questions germane to their field. According to Jones, African American theologians have established their field of study in two ways. First, they have crafted arguments against "white Christianity" or "white theology" as the standard or definitive representation of Christianity. Second, and closely related to the first approach, they have argued that the exclusion of the thought and experiences of black peoples warrants the revision of Christian doctrines formulated without the benefit of wisdom and insights from black Christians. In the phase of critical expansion, seminal works are published and become the texts that not only establish certain scholars as pioneers and chief authorities but also determine the areas where others may make recognized contributions to the field. Jones cites J. Deotis Roberts's and later scholars' reactions to James Cone's first publications, which were the first book-length writings in black theology, as illustrating this critical expansion stage in black theology. In the phase of systematic construction, the personal and intuitive insights of scholars expressed in the first and second phases are replaced by the identification and investigation of the basic problem that constitutes their field of study. The publications in this third stage are less concerned with personal views and more focused on the conceptual problems of the discipline. According to Jones, African American theology is well into this third stage: African Americans are slowly making explicit the ontological, anthropological, and ethical categories presupposed in the first and second stages. Jones considers his own work to be within the third stage. He argues that the basic category of black theology is theodicy and offers a conception of God that best explains the sufferings of black people. Systematic construction remains a challenge. Several persons lecture, teach, and publish in black and womanist theologies without training in the methods and literature of theology. It seems that race, interest, and advocacy are regarded as qualifications for black and womanist theology.

Questions for Discussion

1. Since African American theology is in the *academy*, and African American theology is in the *church*, and both strands are connected to oral traditions in African American culture, how might they be integrated into a single perspective?
2. How is knowledge acquired through black experience recognizable as the revelation of God and not something else?

Suggested Reading

Earl, Riggins R. "Black Theology and the Year 2000: Three Basic Ethical Challenges." In *Black Theology: A Documentary History*, vol. 2, *1980–1992*, edited by Gayraud Wilmore and James Cone, 54–58. Maryknoll, NY: Orbis Books, 1993.

Jones, William R. "Toward an Interim Assessment of Black Theology." *Christian Century* 89 (May 21, 1975): 513–17.

Coleman, Monica A. *Ain't I a Womanist Too? Third-Wave Womanist Religious Thought*. Minneapolis: Fortress Press, 2013.

Floyd-Thomas, Stacey M., ed. *Deeper Shades of Purple: Womanism in Religion and Society*. New York: New York University Press, 2006.

Cannon, Katie G., and Anthony B. Pinn, eds. *The Oxford Handbook of African American Theology*. New York: Oxford University Press, 2014.

PART 3

Themes and Issues

5
God

This chapter explores thought and doctrine on the topic of God. Though Christian doctrine is essential for a study of the concept of God in African American churches, this chapter will examine some themes not treated normally or frequently in traditional Christian teachings on God. In addition to an examination of the existence and attributes of God and the conceptualization of God as Trinity, this chapter will address the origins of monotheistic belief in African American religion and cultures, African American Oneness doctrine as critique of and alternative to Trinitarian dogma, the tensions between black liberation theism and humanocentric theism, and African American speculative thought on the nature of the reality to which "God" as a symbol points.

THE NEGRO'S GOD

Benjamin E. Mays's *The Negro's God*, published in 1938, is the earliest and to date the most extensive study on African American thought about God. Mays examined what he called "Negro literature," which was of two kinds: "mass" and "classical." In his use of the terms, mass literature refers to sermons, prayers, spirituals and Sunday school publications that are the chief medium for communicating ideas among "ordinary" African American Christians.

Then classical literature refers to the slave narrative, biographies and autobiographies, public speeches, novels, poetry, academic (social-scientific) writings in circulation among the most educated African Americans. Mays investigated how the thought about God developed historically in each type of literature. Within three broad periods of time, Mays traced the recurring themes or attitudes expressed about God. For the period of 1760 to 1865, he observed that both the mass and classical literature—except for the otherworldliness of the spirituals—expressed thought about God as compensator yet focused on social and economic reform. Mays uses the term "compensatory" to stress African Americans' belief that God will avenge and compensate them for their earthly sufferings. In the period of 1865 to 1914, thought about God in the classical literature turned "constructive," shifting to a greater emphasis on social and economic reform. By the period of 1914 to 1937, there was a radical divergence between thinking in the two types of literature. In the mass literature, there is a shift to concerns about piety and personal security. In the classical literature, there is an increasing emphasis on constructive aspects, thought about God shaped around social and economic reform. Yet thought in this period is not totally optimistic. For the classical literature, after 1914, there is an ever-growing skepticism and disbelief in God as a useful instrument for social change.

Mays's thesis is that African Americans' ideas about God arise out of the social crises that they have experienced.[1] He offered his work as a criticism of the caricature of African American Christian faith pervading American popular culture through the musical and film titled *Green Pastures*. This production opened on Broadway in 1930 and debuted in film in 1936. The play and film, in all-black cast, presents a vision of "Negro Heaven," showing black angels playing softball; smoking, frying, and eating fish; and reluctantly tending to the wishes of a black God, who stumbles upon the idea of the incarnation and atonement as the best solution for dealing with wayward humans, all of whom in the play and film are black. Mays's focus is on written sources to the exclusion of the rich repository of oral expressions that convey important meanings that African Americans have about God; yet his study is and remains of enduring value. Mays's *The Negro's God* is an example, one way, and a standard of studying black religious belief with intellectual rigor and integrity.

ORIGINS OF AFRICAN AMERICAN MONOTHEISM

Whereas Benjamin Mays accounted for belief in God only in terms of social crises of some extreme kind, later African American religious scholars and theologians have argued that the origins of African American monotheistic belief are in African traditional religions, the crisis of chattel slavery, the Christian Bible, and church doctrine.[2] African traditional religions, though polytheistic, have a concept of God as Supreme Being. As Supreme Being, God is the creator and sustainer of life. No lesser gods or deities rival God. God is almighty and sovereign, all-powerful, all-knowing, and continually and simultaneously present throughout the universe.

Charles Long argues that African American belief in God emerges from enslaved Africans' encounter with a radical otherness.[3] God is the Other. God is the One who is apart from the world. According to Long, it is in the harshness of life—the horror of the Middle Passage (journey to the Americas) and the brutalities of chattel slavery—that enslaved Africans and their progeny found God. Since the humanity of the African was not affirmed in America, they found affirmation of their humanity in a transcendent reality: God. Thus God became their symbol for transcendence, value, and ultimacy.

Another explanation for African American theistic belief, based on Charles Long's study of the high god in West African religions, is that the slave experience resulted in the transfer of the powers of various lesser deities to the transcendent Christian God, a Supreme Being beyond and critical of American slaveholding society.[4] The transcendent Christian God was untainted by and possessing power over slaveholding society. Before their contact with Europeans, Africans were already theists, believing that divine reality is personal and apprehended through the analogy of being. Long tries to point out the shifts and changes in theistic thought before Africans' contact with Europeans. In this early period of cultural history, Africans' thinking about divine reality had undergone profound changes: belief in a high god emerged in agrarian societies dominated by women; then there was a shift to belief in the remoteness of the high god and an increasing veneration of lesser deities, corresponding to the rise of innovations in agriculture where males dominate. In the hoe culture, a form of agriculture characterized by the use of hand methods and simple manual tools, women do most of the work with men sometimes assisting them. The high god, usually associated with the sky, is prominent in the female dominated hoe culture. With the invention of the plough, a large tool requiring the use of other machinery and intensive animal and human labor, men rose to dominance and veneration of the lesser deities increased. At the time of Africans' capture and transport to America, the ultimate powers of the universe are shared among the lesser deities. In a new culture where there is only one God, enslaved Africans projected onto this God the powers of the lesser deities.

THE EXISTENCE AND ATTRIBUTES OF GOD

According to Benjamin Mays, once African Americans confessed faith in the Christian God, rarely and only recently have they doubted God's existence. Mays's perspective is confirmed by recent statistical research.[5] In the Pew Research Center's U.S. Religious Landscape Survey, 99 percent of blacks believe in God, with 71 percent convinced that God is personal, 19 percent saying that God is an impersonal force, and 7 percent unsure. Ninety percent are absolutely certain that God exists. Mays argues that African Americans' need of God has been too great for them to speculate about God's existence.[6] Nevertheless, throughout African American history, there are moments—and these moments are documented in Negro literature—when God's existence and concern for humanity have been called into question. For the most part, African Americans have aligned their conception of God with that of traditional Christian theism.[7] God, usually depicted as a male deity, is powerful and perfect, yet also personal, concerned, responding to prayer, and acting justly and compassionately on behalf of those persons who believe in God. During slavery and especially after World War I, African Americans were frustrated with the concept of God and doubted God's existence. Mays cited black literature (from the Harlem Renaissance) to illustrate African American doubt about God's existence and benevolence. Sometimes God causes or allows bad things to happen in order to get someone's attention, to correct their behavior, or even to punish them.

According to Mays, African Americans' arguments for God's existence or nonexistence are primarily moral and pragmatic.[8] Mays bemoans that nearly any religious belief is regarded as true if it uplifts, consoles, or produces in its adherents some sense of contentment, even when there is no sufficient evidence to warrant such belief. God is the ground and source of justice, compensating all losses and undeserved sufferings of those who believe in God.

Cecil Cone points out that although the existence of God is debated on moral grounds, God's existence, for persons of faith, is confirmed in their experiences of God. He stated that the question of God's existence, though phrased in a variety of ways, is rooted historically in enslaved Africans' perplexity in trying to reconcile the Christian conceptions of God with the absurdity and brutality of chattel slavery.[9] The resolution of their dilemma, according to Cone, was not in a definitive theological or philosophical argument but rather in religious experience. These religious experiences that supply believers with certitude include the events perceived as encounters with God, spiritual conversion marked by profound change in one's life and new sense of purpose, and the spirit of freedom.[10] God is thus encountered as the radically different Other, the source of justice, courage, and hope.

According to Henry H. Mitchell, growing out of African American experience is a core of beliefs that God is sovereign over creation, just, morally perfect, gracious, and involved in human life.[11] God is also free, self-determining, possessing complete liberty from restriction in pursuit of God's intentions. Major emphasis is placed on God's power to make change.[12] God is Waymaker, creative, transformative power. God creates (out of nothing) or makes (from existing things) ways, that is, alternatives and opportunities for persons who have either few or no options for survival and fulfillment. The way made, or even God's own self, is an opening or passage to new and better modes of life. God makes possible life's furtherance and fulfillment, no matter the kinds of economic, social, and political conditions under which persons must live.

The concept of God as Waymaker is not derived from either Scripture alone or experience alone. The concept emerges from an interpretation involving a back-and-forth between Scripture and experience. African American believers' encounter with God influences the way they read Scripture. They find in the Bible confirmation of how God acts in their experiences. Their further reading of the Bible builds anticipation of God's acting in their lives in ways similar to what God does in the stories of various Bible characters. The depiction of God as Waymaker is expressed in the Spiritual "Mary, Don't You Weep." The Spiritual combines the stories of the Exodus (Exod. 14) and Jesus' raising Lazarus from the dead (John 11:1–46). The Spiritual's rationale is: if God parted the waters of the Red Sea and enabled the Hebrews to escape Pharaoh's army, God will also make possible our deliverance from sorrow and death. The Spiritual is a song of comfort to all believers who grieve, like Lazarus' sisters Mary and Martha, and reminds them of God's power to make a way out of no way.

According to Mitchell, there are ten core beliefs (basic affirmations) in African American religion and culture. The first six are affirmations about God.[13] The remaining four affirmations, which will be dealt with in chapter 6 (below), are affirmations about ourselves and our experience of life and relationship with God. Mitchell lists six basic affirmations about God: (1) God is in charge and will provide for and work everything for the good of those who love God. (2) God is just, fair, and impartial. (3) God, whose power is ultimate, has no rivals. (4) God knows everything, inclusive of our suffering and how much we can bear it. (5) God is good and has created a world and made the life in it fundamentally good. (6) God, who is generous, forgives and lovingly accepts persons.

Mitchell says that African Americans, since the time of chattel slavery, have believed in the justice and righteousness of God. This conviction includes belief in "the goodness of God, the goodness of all creation, and the goodness of life itself."[14] In summary, God is sovereign over creation, just, morally perfect, gracious, transcendent, and involved in human life. God is "the personal creative force underlying all reality," but God "is not equated with that created reality."[15] God is independent of the created order by virtue of God's being "Supreme Person" and "ultimate personal category of being-itself."[16]

TRINITARIANISM AND ONENESS

In African American churches, persons have affirmed both Trinitarian and Oneness conceptualizations of God. In traditional Trinitarian thought, God is believed to be one substance (*ousia*) in three persons (*hypostases*). God exists simultaneously and externally in three persons: the Father (Creator), the Son (Jesus Christ), and the Holy Spirit (Advocate and Enabler). The term "persons" should not be confused with the common modern usage of the word in referring to an "individual." In its usage as a technical, theological term, "person" means fundamental feature or "aspect" of the being and reality of God. When speaking of the Trinity, Christians are referring to the Economic Trinity (the role of each member of the Trinity in God's interaction with the world and

Jones states that there is no justification for black liberation theism given the continued suffering of black people and the lack of indisputable proof that God is in solidarity with black people and that God will liberate them.

Jones's counterargument is as follows:

1. If God were black, then God would liberate black people from oppression.
2. God has not liberated (or is not likely to liberate) black people from oppression.
3. It follows then that God is not black.
4. Therefore, God is a white racist.

In stating that God is a white racist, Jones means that God can be more easily aligned with whites than blacks. God's delay or inaction works in the interests of whites, not blacks. According to Jones, black liberation theism is incoherent and irrational. There is no justification for believing that African Americans will be liberated by God's intervention.

Jones's counterargument should not be interpreted as a total rejection of belief in God. His purpose is to show that black liberation theism is not the best way to conceptualize God. Jones recommends that African American theologians committed to belief in God must adopt an alternative form of theism, what Jones calls "humanocentric theism."

Jones's humanocentric theism is a conception of God that accords higher priority on human agency and responsibility for improving social conditions.[25] Although we may be inspired by and partner with God, liberation is mainly the work of humans. Jones's argument does not prove that humanism is the only plausible alternative for black theology. His argument against black liberation theism and the subsequent objections raised against his humanocentric theism only relativizes the various forms of theism in African American religious thought. This relativity may suggest that human experience and yearning does not end in a symbol (a cultural form) but reaches for the ultimate (the God beyond God).

The constructive and compensatory patterns in African American Christian thought identified by Benjamin Mays correspond to the conceptions of divine-human relationship labeled as black liberation theism and humanocentric theism. To repeat: by compensatory, Mays refers to the ideas of God that together depict God as One who compensates persons for their sufferings, a requital desired now yet mostly expected in the next life. The change in persons' circumstances depends on God's miraculous intervention. By constructive ideas, Mays refers to those ideas that together depict God as One who inspires and partners with persons to change their situation. Rather than seeking solace in the interventionist God and hope of life in another world, persons with constructive ideas utilize religion (inclusive of their faith in God) for addressing and solving, while in this life, the problems of concern to them. Mays stresses the importance of understanding social context for proper discernment of motivations in humans' choice of an orientation toward God.

Black liberation theism and its alternative humanocentric theism follow the constructive pattern of ideas identified by Benjamin Mays. In black liberation theism, God partners with human beings in order to free them as God is free, although God assumes the major responsibility for their liberation. Black liberation theism is basically a conception of traditional Christian theism modified by assertions that God is in solidarity with black people. Humanocentric theism, which tends toward secular humanism, is a conception of God that accords higher priority to human agency and human responsibility for improving social conditions. In humanocentric theism, liberation is the work of humans and not God, notwithstanding the inspiration and lures that God provides for this human work.

James Cone responds to William R. Jones's evidentialist objection to black liberation theism.[26] He argues that there must be some evidence to support black Christian theism, the belief that God is in solidarity with black people and is liberating (or will liberate) them. Jones says there must be a decisive event of liberation in the history of black people. In response, Cone says that this decisive event of liberation is the resurrection of Jesus Christ. Cone espouses a kind of fideism, contending that theologians operate under a system of logic that differs from other forms of rational discourse. Cone's response begs the question of the relation and relevance of salvation (or biblical) history to African American history. How are the two distinct and yet the same or overlapping? From Cone's perspective as a black Christian theologian, suffering and philosophical critique do indeed challenge black Christian faith, but neither negates it.

William R. Jones's influential critique of black liberation theism has not resulted in an overwhelming acceptance of humanocentric theism. The few African American theologians who espouse some form of humanocentric theism base their conceptions of God on frameworks

other than secular humanism, as Jones did for his humanocentric theism. To repeat: Jones's argument against black liberation theism and
the responding objections raised against his humanocentric theism
only relativize the various forms of theism. This relativity may suggest
that human experience and yearning does not end in a symbol (a cultural form) but reaches for the ultimate (the God beyond God).

THE QUEST FOR GOD BEYOND GOD

Over the range of variations in African American Christian thought,
God is depicted as a supremely good being, separated from and independent of the world, all-powerful, all-knowing, and the Creator and
Sustainer of the universe. Several attempts have been made to move
beyond this conception of God, especially to discard the insinuation
that God is a being among other beings in the world and the simplistic
answers to evil and suffering in the world. The aim of these attempts is
not to discredit or discontinue the use of God-talk. The goal is rather
to suggest what the nature of the reality is and which purposes "God,"
as a symbol, points to. The quest for God beyond the symbol God is
an attempt to reach or comprehend an aspect of reality beyond the
normal understanding that most persons have of God. The quest for
God beyond God has found unique expression in African American
religious thought.

Karen Baker-Fletcher prefers to label her concept of God as "open
theism."[27] She describes her theology as (1) Christian (Wesleyan and
charismatic evangelical), (2) relational and integrative, and (3) womanist.[28] As an open theist, she argues that God is personal and respon-
sive to the prayers, decisions, and actions of human beings.[29] While
she believes that the future is open, she does not think that the outcome of history is completely unknowable. God knows what the
future will be. Life is on the side of good; and good, not evil, is fundamental to life.[30] God, the life and quality of relationship in God, is
normative.[31] God is community actualized in the universe.[32] God is
the source of power and courage to overcome evil.[33] God's grace is the
power and courage given in the face of evil.[34] As spirit, God moves
in and through creation in the dance of the Trinity. The immanent
Trinity is the antecedent nature of God.[35] Dance is a metaphor for
creative, renewing, liberating, and healing activity that overcomes evil,
temporal perishing, and death.[36]

Womanists like Zora Hurston and Alice Walker view God as the power (i.e., spirit or energy) that pervades nature.[37] God is the unity that underlies as well as the spirit that animates each living thing that embodies God. Thus God is identical to nature. In Hurston's autobiography *Dust Tracks on a Road* (1942), she claims not to be religious. Abandoning most of the Christian dogma that she learned about God, Hurston espouses belief in a spiritual presence pervading the universe. She does not pray to God. She accepts life for what it is and assumes responsibility for changing it. Hurston does not hope for life after death; she expects only to fuse with the energy and matter that is the one eternal reality of the universe.

According to Charles Long, in African American religious thought, God is a symbol for transcendence and ultimacy.[38] Certain questions revolve around God as symbol: What or who is the source of my value? To what or whom may I compare myself? Can I be other than what I am? What can or will I become? Transcendence involves construction of alternative meanings, postulating or gaining insight of new realities, and transformation of self and even society by adherence to these intuited meanings and values. Transcendence may be construed as a longing for God or quest for a vision of new possibility. In either case, the self encounters a reality that holds the potential for radical change.

Victor Anderson, an African American theologian and ethicist, says that God is a symbol of creative exchange and the world.[39] By creative exchange, he means harmony, wholeness, integration. He subscribes to a view of panentheism: God contains the world within Godself but God transcends or is more than the mere sum of all objects making up the world. Anderson's choice of panentheism is not motivated purely for reasons metaphysical and epistemological but for reasons existential. According to Anderson, God is the source and model of harmony for diversity. God absorbs different, conflicting aspects of the world for the benefit of each living thing. God envelops all within the world—the grotesque and the beautiful, ambiguity and certitude, death and fulfillment. God's capacity to bring harmony, wholeness, and integration in human society is best described as beloved community. Anderson contends that African Americans, as well as other groups of persons, are not indiscriminately seeking a new or alternative community but rather are seeking this beloved community that is pointed out by the symbol of God.

Dwight Hopkins names God as the spirit of liberation. He says, "God, in constructive black theology, is the spirit of total liberation for us."[40] According to Hopkins, God, working in partnership with humans, is the "I AM" who protects, assists, and fortifies with courage the poor who seek to be free.[41] As spirit and the "I AM," God is gender inclusive.[42] Yet God is not indistinct or beyond the ability of humans to understand. Hopkins says that God is revealed in nature, that is, in the equal worth of all living things and the provisions for their continued existence; in the beauty among persons who love each other; in the race and ethnicity of the oppressed, who are ontological symbols of God's presence in the world; and in the liberating power of the language that God gives to the oppressed.[43]

In African American religious thought, God is often depicted as the Waymaker. As Waymaker, God creates a way out of nothing or makes a way from existing circumstances—providing an opportunity or alternative for persons to move forward in life when they reach what appears to be an impasse. The way provided by God is a better option for persons faced with few or no options. The way provided by God, if acted upon, leads to the person's survival or the greatest possible fulfillment of life at that moment of crisis. The Waymaker is a conception of God that identifies God's being and act as creative, transformative power. However, it is not by power alone that God is Waymaker. Goodness is as basic to this conception of God as is power. In addition to having power, God is personal, loving, caring, moral, gracious, and just. God makes a way because God is both good and power.

Whether theism is conceived traditionally or in other nuanced ways, theism matters for several reasons. First, theism is a *locus for value*, especially apart from the codifications of morality and law in a society. Theism becomes a basis for social, political, economic, and cultural critique of systems that threaten the most vulnerable in human society. Second, theism is a *model of personhood and agency*. Theism amplifies the admirable qualities of humans. God is the ideal person of will, power, and moral integrity that humans aspire to be. Third, theism fosters a special *quality of relationship between contingent being and necessary being*. Theism makes possible a closeness to and understanding of the Ground of Being that is otherwise impossible if viewed as something abstract and totally foreign to us. Fourth, theism lends itself to the human experience of *self-transcendence*. Through encounter with the supremely perfect Other, the human person is able to transcend limiting or false conceptions of their identity. Self-transcendence is a change in the self that becomes foundational for new constructions of identity, apprehension of one's purpose, and successful engagement with other selves in one's social and cultural environments. Last, theism leads to *the exposure of idolatry*. Theism is a way of symbolizing the Ground of Being or Ultimate Reality but begs the question of whether it or any other symbolization of the real, sacred, or holy is adequate. By its own assertion of who or what is God, theism heightens awareness of the images and symbols that inadequately or falsely represent the Ground of Being/ Ultimate Reality or the same images and symbols that are used to legitimate (sanction) questionable acts, customs, laws, or policies. It is fair to ask, even of the various constructions of Christian theism, whether a symbolization of God points adequately to the divine reality.

THE GIFT OF GOD'S REVELATION
IN THE BLACK EXPERIENCE

According to Benjamin Mays, several important aspects of God that are noteworthy for all peoples are revealed in African American experience, particularly in the struggle for justice. Mays says that African Americans are on a "special errand" for God, to prove that people of different ethnicities can and must coexist peacefully in the world.[44] God makes no superior races or ethnic groups. God is impartial, but not so in situations of injustice. God takes sides, yet not to favor one group of people over another. God takes sides in order to tip the scales toward justice, an outcome that will fulfill the lives of all persons.

At the beginning of the Civil Rights Movement, the young Martin Luther King Jr. turned to God the Waymaker when he felt afraid, weak, and at a loss for understanding the existence and reality of sin and evil, in spite of his having extensive studies in philosophy and theology.[45] It was at this time that King came to know God in a more meaningful way. He came to know firsthand that God, as Waymaker, is personal, just, and the source of justice, courage, and hope. As a young man on his knees and praying to God, King could hear God saying: "Martin Luther, stand up for righteousness, stand up justice, stand up for truth. And lo I will be with you, even unto the ends of earth." This encounter with God would become King's definitive and foundational experience of God for the remainder of his life. Like King, many African Americans bear witness to the Waymaker, who enables life, in its personal and social dimensions, to flourish. The presence and perpetuation of justice in human society is God's creative act in partnership with humans.

Questions for Discussion

1. How is the doctrine of the Trinity relevant to and capable of illuminating aspects of African American life?
2. How does race, ethnicity, and gendered language contribute to our understanding of God's attributes and activity?
3. What evidence in African American experience is there for or against the belief that God is Waymaker?
4. How might the concept of God as Waymaker be correlated and harmonized with other conceptions of God, such as Creator and Liberator?

Suggested Reading

Baker-Fletcher, Karen. *Dancing with God: The Trinity from a Womanist Perspective*. St. Louis: Chalice Press, 2007.

Jones, Major J. *The Color of God: The Concept of God in Afro-American Thought*. Macon, GA: Mercer University Press, 1987.

Jones, William R. *Is God a White Racist? A Preamble to Black Theology*. Garden City, NY: Anchor Press, 1973. Reprint, Boston: Beacon Press, 1998.

Mays, Benjamin E. *The Negro's God as Reflected in His Literature*. Boston, MA: Chapman & Grimes, 1938.

6
Human Being

Deep questions about life and personhood are related to and explored through the experiences of various peoples. These questions have been raised and intensified by the mass movements of people. From the fifteenth century onward, in a period that may be called the Global Age, there have been increasing interactions between human societies and cultures that were either previously isolated from one another or had little significant contact with one another. For most human communities, the known world was actually a very small geographical region compared to our present map and knowledge of the planet Earth. This Global Age was initiated by the migration of Europeans, which brought them into contact, sometimes peaceful but more often violent, with other peoples. In the case of Africans, this new escalation of contact proved to be disastrous. The resulting imbalance of power that favored Europeans enabled them to construct and perpetuate a classification of peoples that would label the African as being less than human or not human at all. The African's essential value would not be as a human being but as a chattel slave, the cheapest labor for developing the sparsely populated Western Hemisphere.

In the case of African Americans, the meaning of human life is associated with this tragic experience of Africans entering the New World as slaves. As a nation that emerged from European settlement and the resistance of these new settlers against their European monarch, the United States poses a unique crisis for human beings. The United

States is a plural but unequal society, with certain groups, over the course of its history, overrepresented in the lowest social and economic classes. The historical experience of African Americans is often told as a story of the struggle for recognition as human and for full participation in a nation built from their exploitation.

This chapter emphasizes the human being and the value, meaning, and fulfillment of humanity in relation to God, especially with regard to the existential crisis narrated in African American history. The topics covered in this chapter are explaining the crisis-ridden status of Africans in the New World in terms of the body-soul dualism in Western thought; clarifying and applying the concept of the image of God to the black experience; exposing the use of race as a symbol for discernment of place in history and the cosmos; claiming freedom as an essential property of human beings and showing how the misuse of freedom constitutes sinfulness and therefore is the major dilemma of human beings; and recognizing the possibility of the transformation and fulfillment of the human person through encounter with God.

BODY-SOUL DUALISM IN THE BLACK EXPERIENCE

Enslaved Africans were dehumanized. In the United States, the African's value was only as property. The African's language, customs, religion, and art were deemed by slave masters to be of no value. Chattel slavery, that is, the practice of "owning" a person or that person's labor as if their entire life were under the control of whoever owns their work, erased African names and disrupted family and kinship structures. Masters held legal right to name blacks and to even decide with whom they would procreate. In chattel slavery, race became the basis for determining which rights or privileges persons would have or not have at all. One's humanity, which was often questioned or denied, was of no consequence in deciding one's status before the law. Not only was the African's identity as an African in crisis, but the African's essential humanity also was and is in crisis. The slave system, designed for the exploitation of black labor, placed black people at the level of property, like livestock bartered, sold, and passed from one generation of owners to the next. Chattel slavery was an anomaly in human history. Before the Atlantic Slave Trade, slavery was never a lifelong condition and never deprived persons of fundamental respect as human beings. In addition to introducing the disturbing practice of dehumanization, chattel slavery contradicted the principle of God-given inalienable rights asserted in America's Declaration of Independence. Free blacks faired not much better than enslaved blacks. Black persons, both those held as chattel and those able to obtain free status, were regarded as inferior, not just by social class but also by nature.

Theologian and ethicist Riggins Earl claims that the moral and religious crisis of chattel slavery and the racial injustices that followed after it were rooted in a body-soul dualism that depicted blacks as either "soulless bodies" or "bodiless souls."[1] As soulless bodies, black persons are regarded as inferior persons, less than human or not human, whose only value is in the commodification of their bodies. The soulless bodies' highest or only value is in the goods produced by their labor or the uses of their bodies, from which other persons derive the greater benefit. Thus black persons are thought to have no value in their souls but only in whatever can be gained or taken from their bodies. As bodiless souls, black persons are treated humanely but not justly. They are regarded as human in their souls, but the injustices to which their bodies are exposed remain in force.

According to Earl, liberation thought emerges from the desire of the oppressed to be whole. The oppressed do not want to live as fragmented human persons. The wonderful aspects of their souls must be reconciled with the beauty in their bodies. The affirmation expressive of this desire of wholeness is "I am my body." By this affirmation, the oppressed are saying that all of the good and splendor in the human soul are located in the physical body. Both the soul and the body must be valued equally.

African American religion scholars and black and womanist theologians are giving new meaning to the affirmation of liberation in the statement "I am my body." They are increasingly emphasizing the love of the black body. Their emphasis has been influenced by a desire to address the negative depictions of black peoples as well as to utilize the postmodernist method of cultural studies, which threatens these adverse interpretations of the black body and offers a means for studying and critiquing Western culture's social world. The black body was said to be ugly in comparison to the supposed beauty and perfection of white European bodies. The grotesquerie of the black body, as perceived by whites, was exaggerated in the pseudosciences of racism. For example, Dutch anatomist Pieter Camper, asserting that 100 degrees was the ideal facial angle, placed Europeans at an average angle of 97 degrees and Africans at an average angle ranging from 60 to 70 degrees, near that of apes and dogs. In addition to citing the physical differences as evidence of the inferiority of black bodies, white depictions of the sexuality of blacks further reinforced the idea of some fundamental wrong with the black body. Hypersexualized images and stereotypes of African Americans have placed both their humanity and morality in question. "The images of Black women as Jezebels or Mammies and Black men as violent bucks bolster ideas of White male and female superiority by presenting a picture of Black men and women as inferior."[2] African American scholars are now underscoring the close association of social structure with interpretations of the body. Their aim is to recover the humanity of blacks, lost in the racist practice of negatively depicting black bodies. In order to challenge racism and homophobia, their writings on the black body have focused mainly on issues of sexuality as they developed critiques of social and scientific constructions of the human body in general and black (male and female) bodies in particular.

The current focus on the black body may be interpreted as an emphasis on embodiment. Rather than regarding the person as a duality of body and soul, the concept of embodiment regards the person as a unity. Also, the concept of embodiment recognizes that to be (to exist as) a person is to act from a body. Embodiedness is a precondition for perception, moral agency, and life in community. For Anthony Pinn, a confessed atheist who studies religion, the focus on the body may be a form of materialism, where the supernatural or supersensory are neither necessary for nor an ultimate explanation of human behavior. The black body, as an entity with a history and as a product of that history, represents the social world of which it is a part.[3] Cultural study of the human body is a way of tracing events in the social body that impact the persons who comprise that social body. For other persons, who are theologians committed to a well-defined circle of faith, the focus on the body is an affirmation of embodiment that implies God's value of the physical world and expresses concern for humans as creatures with material needs. Stephanie Mitchem says: "Embodiment is a route to considering the material conditions of a particular group of people. The human person, grounded in a given community, becomes the subject of study, integral to the work, rather than the reified object. Embodiment changes the focus of theological reflection because it is centered on the experience of particular people rather than dogma or church polity, both of which are sometimes accepted as universal despite human experience."[4]

BLACKNESS AND THE IMAGE OF GOD

"Black" is a metaphor. "Black," when applied to the identification of persons, is not literal. No one literally has black skin. That the metaphor has become entrenched in American language is due to the fact that a significant number of persons of African descent in the United States and their not-so-distant African ancestors have skin complexion that is relatively darker than European Americans. "Black" symbolizes contrast, not just in terms of physical appearance but also in terms of social, cultural, and ethnic difference.

Martin Luther King Jr., as theologian of the Civil Rights movement, championed the humanity and inclusion of blacks and the other disenfranchised peoples by appeal to their reflection of the image of God. For King, the value on human dignity and worth is attributable to the importance that God gives to it. God creates human beings in God's own image and after God's likeness (Gen. 1:26–27). Black or any other racial or ethnic designation is not the same as the image of God. Rather, it is the image of God that brings dignity and value to each person regardless of their social identification. For King, dignity is innate to each person. This is God-given dignity and cannot be taken away. However, situations of injustice compromise the worth of persons. Our creation in the image of God serves as the foundation for human rights and the struggle for recognition of our worth in social relations. Our law and social policy must value the person, the inherent dignity and worth of human life, in order to fully realize the destiny of human life.[5]

The image of God that we reflect, more so than any other aspect of our existence, is the quality of relationality. Only through a "Thou" does anyone become an "I." We are dependent upon God and upon each other. The "I-Thou" relationship, encountering and interacting with each other as subjects and not objects, allows for mutual personal development. God is the supreme "Thou," whom we encounter and who transforms us into the humanity that we are destined to be.

BLACKNESS AS A "DEEP" SYMBOL

Religion, which provides direction and purpose for human life, is expressed in symbols. Charles Long defines religion as "orientation in the ultimate sense, that is, how one comes to terms with the ultimate

significance of one's place in the world."[6] Religion involves an awareness of self and the relation of the self to other selves and entities
of great significance in the life of the self. When viewed in terms of
human self-understanding, religion is intricately woven into the fabric
of human consciousness. Sense of self is constitutive of external reality
and a basis for certainty of external reality. Consciousness comes to
realization through culture. Religion is the dimension of culture that
focuses on those aspects of experience that are permeated with a quality of sacredness, setting them apart from ordinary cultural objects.
In other words, religion identifies symbols that have the capacity to
pervade and connect various experiences that, if viewed superficially,
may appear to be unrelated. As a historian of religion, Long is looking
for symbols, any symbols, that reveal the matters about which persons
are ultimately concerned and that define who they are and how they fit
into and ought to act in their imagining of the world.

Race is a "deep" symbol. It is one of the symbols that contribute
to the depth of self-understanding sought in religion. Citing Edward
Farley's theory of "deep symbols," Anderson says that race may be
understood as a "deep symbol," a word of power that constrains,
guides, and becomes a focus of human behavior.[7] Farley, however,
does not include race in his listing of deep symbols. He restricts his
theory of deep symbols to the concepts of education, beauty, reality,
rights, nature, freedom, community, and justice. Anderson argues
that, based on Farley's criteria for naming deep symbols, one must
include race and nation as deep symbols. These are words that evoke
passionate response and are descriptive of the loyalties and moral
obligations that persons form.

According to Long, through the prism of race, persons ask questions like these: Who am I? What is my place in the world? What is
the history and experience at which I am the center? These and other
questions probe and possibly challenge the constructions of identity,
community, and historical narrative of which the persons are aware and
seek to reconcile to their experience of life. Race, not to be restricted to
the tensions between white and black, is a social construct that we have
inherited for stating identity. It is a symbol for reflection on culture
and reality.

Symbols reveal and help us reflect upon the "religious dimensions"
of culture. Culture is a feature of human life that clearly sets humans
apart from other living beings on Earth. The ultimate aim of culture is
to enable human survival and fulfillment. The focus that gives culture

a religious quality, deep meaning, and the sense of being something whole is the question: How do we structure, discipline, and deepen subjectively for the survival and fulfillment of the individual and the group to which the individual belongs?

When we use the terms "white" or "black," we must qualify the meanings that we associate with these terms. Though the term "white" is associated with power and privilege in America, there are many white persons in the United States who are neither powerful nor privileged. The largest number of poor people in the United States is white, although blacks are disproportionately represented among the poor class. Of course, not everyone who is black is oppressed in the worst sense of the word. However, each person who is identified (self-identified or identified by others) as black must somehow reconcile their status and experience of life in American society to the past and current injustices of racism in America.

That blackness is a social construct means that it is not merely "skin-deep." Blackness is not a simple matter of skin color, hair texture, and other physical features. It has something to do with these physical properties, but it is not limited to these attributes. Persons use race to create an identity for themselves and in so doing establish some form of community between them. The formation of any community involves the specification of who's in and who's out of that community. Seeking to be a community, persons use race as a perspective from which to tell the story of their past and their shared aspirations for the future. In humans, as with other biological organisms, there has been mutation, random variation, adapting to varied environments, and shuffling of genes through interbreeding over the millennia. The semblance of stability in the physical differences between humans is perpetuated through social and cultural practices with regard to marriage, family, child-rearing, residential location, voluntary association, and so forth, which keep ethnic groups somewhat separate.

Any society has several groups. The United States is made up of many groups. The largest groups in the United States are formed around race. Now, with the migration of large numbers of Spanish-speaking peoples, divisions are being drawn around language. The United States Constitution focuses on the individual but, in reality, life is characterized by interaction within and between groups. As new developments occur that impact social relations, the meaning as well as the configuration of race changes over time. Yet race remains an enduring aspect of American life.

Race is a way to trace the injustices in American society. Although not the cause of injustice, race is correlated with patterns of social injustice. When you cannot identify any persons suffering the injustice, then no one can see where the injustice is. No one sees who is involved in the injustice or who is adversely affected by the injustice. When injustice is nameless, faceless, and colorless, no one sees it and no one assumes responsibility for correcting it. Race is a way of tracing developments and assessing the experiences of persons and the impact of various laws and policies in American society.

Barbara Holmes extends the concept of race, as a symbol, to the largest context possible, which is the cosmos. In *Race and the Cosmos* (2002), Holmes argues that solutions to social problems are linked to the discernment of physical reality through the natural sciences. She uses concepts, which she interprets metaphorically, from quantum physics and cosmology in order to clarify the meaning of justice and the belonging of all persons in a just society. In Holmes's "read" of modern science, diversity and harmony are fundamental features of the universe, and "all of humankind in all of its diversity—gay, straight, female, disabled—[must] match the harmonies of an equally diverse cosmos."[8]

HUMAN BEING AND FREEDOM

In Martin Luther King Jr.'s sermon "Who Are We?," which he preached under different titles, he defines human being and identities the essential attribute that makes humans who they are.[9] King says that the human is an animal with a physical body. He goes on to say that the human is a spiritual being made in the image of God. Lastly, he says that the human is a sinner, that is, an agent with the potential to, and who very often does, misuses freedom.

King defines freedom as (1) "the capacity to deliberate or weigh alternatives," (2) the capacity to make a choice from among two or more alternatives, and (3) assuming responsibility for one's actions, good or bad.[10] Freedom is basic to who and what we are. To be human is to be free. For any human to lack freedom would result in that person's living a life unworthy of humanity. "The essence of [humanity] is found in freedom."[11] Human freedom is not wild, indeterminate, and unrestrained. Freedom ceases to be freedom when there is a lack of order and structure. King says, "Freedom always operates within the limits of an already determined structure."[12] Freedom is the capacity of humanity to do everything that is consistent with its nature as determined by God.

For African Americans, freedom has been defined within the contexts of civil rights, electoral politics, and Christianity. These contexts and the meanings of freedom that emerge from each were discussed in the introduction. According to Cecil Cone, too often the religious meaning of freedom has been neglected in black theology. Cone observes that black religion both is and is not radical, both is and is not otherworldly. Radicalism and otherworldliness wrestle within and are birthed from the womb of black religion.[13] While there are elements in black religious experience that are deeply political, black religion attends to matters pertinent to the health and vitality of the human spirit. African Americans' struggles for freedom and equality in American society and longings for life in the world to come are inspired, to a large part, by their faith in God and encounters with God. African Americans found freedom first and foremost in their encounter with God.

In addition to Cecil Cone, Charles Long gives emphasis to the religious meaning of freedom. According to Long, African Americans' rhetoric on freedom emerges from "soul-stuff."[14] Long contends that freedom was revealed as the ultimate resolution to the deep moral, spiritual, and humanitarian crisis of slavery and its aftermath. This meaning and rhetoric of freedom is markedly different from the rhetoric of freedom that is so pervasive in America and other Western nations. Long says that the Western world "lives under the rhetoric and mark of freedom—a freedom that is supposed to banish [superstition] and reveal a new and a deeper structure of the meaning of human existence."[15] Unfortunately, this rhetoric in Western culture has no sense of sacred time and space. The so-called deeper structure is actually autonomous individualism, framed within constitutional secularism. The African American quest for freedom is aimed at the transformation of the self into an authentic identity relative to the ultimacies of reality and the situation of that transformed self in a just community.

In view of the emphasis on freedom, the major dilemma of human beings has much to do with that which causes human freedom to go awry. The misdirection of freedom and the negative consequences that follow are listed under the category of sin. Unfortunately, the concept of sin is often framed negatively as if the major concern and obsession of God is with punishment of human wrongdoing. The larger concern

around sin is not with wrongdoing as such but with how humans can
get things right. Sin may be defined as the condition resulting from the
misuse or denial of freedom, yours or someone else's, in the context
of the covenant relationship with God. The church's use of the word
"sin" involves a certain conviction about human nature—that rationality, freedom, and responsibility are essential features of human life.
People have the potential (the power) to change the direction of their
lives. Biological urges and selfishness, though strong, are not the only
influence acting upon the human person. A lot of who we are and what
we do results from the exercise of the human will. The church's message on sin and its remedy through salvation implies that humans have
choice in the kind and quality of life they live.

In chapter 9 (below), more will be said about how salvation, in various modes, redresses the problem of sin in human life. For now, something must be said about the association of freedom with salvation. As
a method of setting or making persons free, liberation is a means of
achieving salvation. Here the stress is on liberation as a means to an
end, with that end being salvation. Often persons who are oppressed
must resist oppression, in whatever form it takes, before they can be
full subjects. Efforts to resist oppression are interwoven with efforts
at self-creation, the making of a new self. The ultimate end of all such
striving is universal community, a new reality of justice beyond the
current identities and false sense of superiority and inferiority among
persons in our world.

The conditions of all cultural life depend on political institutions.
The ways in which humans organize their societies for negotiating
their varied and sometimes competing interests has the consequence
of either enhancing or diminishing their culture. The aim of culture
is to facilitate humans' adaptation to their environment and thus their
survival and quality of life. For this aim to be achieved, the subjectivity (the concept and expression of personhood) must be structured,
disciplined, and deepened in ways that make possible the survival and
fulfillment of both the individual and the group. The most efficient
path to this cultural aim is through voluntary action, that is, through
persons acting in freedom and freely.

Power is manifest in a variety of social relations. But more so than
in any other place, power seems to be concentrated in economy, that
is, in how human societies organize for the basics of survival (eating,
clothing, and shelter) and fulfillment (quality of life, convenience, and
enjoyment of goods and services beyond subsistence). Economies are

beset with the problems of scarcity (not having enough for everyone), distribution (determining who will have what and how much each will have), and surplus (having more than enough). Quality of life, and even just surviving, is relative to an individual's or group's position in the economy.

In light of these social and political conditions, the theological meaning of human life may be summarized in four core beliefs. These fundamental beliefs empower and sustain African Americans in the face of life's difficulties, not only in situations of injustice and oppression but also in times of separation, loneliness, sorrow, aging, and sickness. According to Henry Mitchell, the core beliefs at the heart of African Americans, particularly on human beings, are the following: (1) All persons are intrinsically equal and equally valued by God. (2) Each person is unique and worthy of respect. (3) All persons are related as one human family, over which God is the head. (4) Persons "should endure or persevere in their faith and identity" and not "give up in despair" when confronted with the challenge of life.[16]

CONVERSION AND PERSONHOOD

According to Charles Long, revelation of the "sacred," however it is conceived, is a revelation about human existence and how best to live it.[17] If the sacred is represented ultimately in God, human thriving is connected with relationship with God. Freedom, as well as participation in being, if either is to be fully possible, follows the work of God. In addition, "humans learn and practice freedom by imitating God."[18] This learning is complicated and even obstructed by modernity that seeks to "desacralize" the world. As Long intuits, the aim of modernity seems to be a murder of God (or the gods) and a discrediting of the notion and possibility of transcendence.

Though freedom is essential to human being, the assertion of freedom alone is not adequate for the fulfillment of human being. With the emergence of consciousness, humans have become aware of themselves as agents with the capacity to act individually and collaboratively for survival and improvement to their quality of life. Freedom is essential for imagining ourselves in ways other than what we presently are. Maximal freedom and the reimagining of ourselves is possible through encounter with God, the wholly Other, who is supremely perfect and models not just the power of agency but also the moral integrity of an agent seeking to live in community with other beings in the world. This encounter with God and God's example of balancing power and morality are emphasized in the National Committee of Negro Churchmen's historic "Statement on Black Power."[19]

Along with the centrality of freedom, self-transcendence is a recurring theme in African American religion and culture.[20] Through encounter with the supremely perfect Other, the human person is able to transcend limiting or false conceptions of their identity. Self-transcendence is a change in the self that becomes foundational for new constructions of identity, apprehension of one's purpose, and successful engagement with other selves in one's social and cultural environments. In self-transcendence, the person has an awareness of self that goes beyond any of their past and present conceptions of self and immediate circumstances. There is a change in self-identity, the way one images oneself. In the person's attempt to reconcile oneself to a newly perceived identity and potentials, self-transcendence becomes self-actualization.

Conversion and other religious experiences are told as stories of self-transcendence. In African American religion and culture, there are many spiritual narratives; there is no shortage of spiritual autobiographies. One story is described here for the purpose of illustrating how self-transcendence may occur. Elizabeth J. Dabney's narrative is a story of experiencing the glory and power of God through prayer (or the prayer meeting).[21] While persons may and do pray at tarry meeting or service, Dabney's narrative extols the potential of prayer (or the prayer meeting) as a way of experiencing God in ways as profound as the tarry meeting. Dabney tells of how she made a covenant with God, to meet God at the church at nine o'clock every morning, every day, until evening, for three years. This was a physically taxing exercise. She endured extremes of heat and cold, thirst and hunger, not to mention scorn and ridicule from church members and neighbors. During her daily prayer, she communed with and felt God's presence. At the end of the three years, she experienced a flood of God's glory that was overwhelming, the physical sensation of which she describes using the language of a near-death experience. Throughout the narrative, Dabney uses death-language and fears horror and death having come upon her had she violated or failed to keep this covenant. After this three-year covenant and subsequent empowerment, persons sought Dabney out to conduct prayer meetings. Persons attending her prayer meetings testified to miraculous healing. This covenant was, for Dabney, a way of "coming through" or, as she phrased it, "praying through to the glory of God." Dabney's testimony is consistent with other African American religious experiences marked by ecstasy and portraying God as creative-transformative power. Inspired by Dabney's spiritual autobiography, other persons have either imitated or sought experiences similar to Dabney's experience.

Stories of conversion and self-transcendence seem to be culturally conditioned, designed to steer various individual experiences into a predictable pattern. Yet for many persons, conversion and self-transcendence remain meaningful experiences that mark a turning point in their lives. Their testimony is that their lives, from that movement onward, become new. The self is re-created, made anew, becoming more of what God intends for it to be. This profound transformation represents the highest manifestation of human freedom. More will be said about conversion, self-transcendence, and personhood in chapter 7 (below), which is on the topic of religious experience.

Questions for Discussion

1. Must a person be black (or African American) or have some other kind of special experience (social or religious) in order to know God?
2. Must a person actively seek transformation in order to experience dramatic improvements in life?
3. What is the soul, and how might attention to the soul have a positive impact on the body?

Suggested Reading

Copeland, M. Shawn. *Enfleshing Freedom: Body, Race, and Being*. Minneapolis: Fortress Press, 2010.
Hopkins, Dwight N. *Being Human: Race, Culture, and Religion*. Minneapolis: Fortress Press, 2005.
Pinn, Anthony B. *Embodiment and the New Shape of Black Theological Thought*. New York: New York University Press, 2010.

7

Religious Experience

Christians often quote, "In him [God] we live and move and have our being" (Acts 17:28). They interpret this text to mean that there is no part of human life beyond the sight of God or that goes untouched by God. Whatever life or enjoyments we have in life are attributable to God's gift and maintenance of that life. Yet persons, believers included, undergo many important experiences not regarded as religiously significant. The concern of this chapter is with a limited range of experiences that are deemed to be of religious significance.

There are numerous ways of describing religious experience. In most cases, religious experience is thought to be a unique form or category of experience, distinct from all others. The religious experience may be characterized as an event involving encounter with some transcendent reality that gives meaning and direction to a person's life. This transcendent reality is said to be "holy," provoking within human beings a complex of feelings, such as dependence, awe, being overpowered, mystical moods, and longing for union with the transcendent. When the human individual regards this transcendent reality as wholly Other and is brought into contact with it, they achieve self-transcendence, a sense of going beyond social and physical limitations. Some scholars, under the basic assumption that the brain is the seat of consciousness, have argued that religious experience reflects a certain type of activity in the brain. In a great number of African American churches that are influenced by revivalism and Pentecostal-charismatic movements, religious experience is portrayed as the experience of ecstasy, an intense feeling, emotion, or sensation that has profound and lasting consequences.

This chapter examines the meanings and structuring of experience given through human encounter with God. The examination covers the emergence and expressions of African American spirituality, the extension of the concept of conversion to encompass the healing and realization of the self, the meanings of Spirit, and the shout as a response to Spirit.

THE BIRTH OF "SOUL-STUFF"

As discussed in chapter 5, "soul-stuff" is the name that Charles Long gives to the creativity that sprang from enslaved Africans' experience of God as radical otherness.[1] For these enslaved Africans, God was a reality other than and unlike the harsh conditions of life to which they were exposed. They transferred upon the Christian God the attributes and powers that they had ascribed to the Supreme Being and lesser deities of their primal religions. With God now as their source of ultimacy, they took the language of race and altered it to think critically about themselves, their situation, and the culture of the new American nation. This God is gracious, just, all-powerful, all-knowing, and loving. This God loves and values all human lives.

Soul-stuff, and the African American spirituality that it birthed, is a spirituality of freedom—a freedom to create and translate.[2] Carlyle Stewart says:

> If creativity is the power of the spirit to modify or alter material reality through creative soul force according to the presence and power of God, translation is the ability to derive a soul language, lexicon, idiom, or ethos of functional and symbolic meaning and value through the reality that has been created. The capacity to transform material reality into spiritual necessities is essential to black survival in an oppressive society. This means that blacks are able to take the chaos and dross of human experience and to translate them spiritually and culturally into alternative modalities and symbols of black life that promote black identity, sanity and wholeness.[3]

Howard Thurman says that religious experience, which he defines as the "conscious and direct exposure of the individual to God," is a "creative encounter."[4] The religious experience is a process of self-discovery where the person comes into a greater awareness of their true self.[5] The person confronts God bare, and God deals only with persons as they are.[6] The religious experience leads to a truer picture of the self. This religious experience becomes a sound basis for the development of the human person, liberating the person from a static self-conception based on facts alone and the imagined, often nonfactual, notions of self. The religious experience is essential to the individual's achievement of a life in direct proportion to what that person is capable of living.

According to Thurman, this deepening of self-awareness in the encounter with God impacts the whole person and their community in four ways. First, the religious experience leads to a new focal point for the individual's life.[7] This focal point is created from the person's yielding and surrender to God, which may be an immediate turn to God or a gradual closeness to God that happens over time.[8] Second, for the individual, the religious experience becomes a new basis, providing power, energy, and motivation for action.[9] Third, the religious experience becomes, within the person, a desire to be godlike that is expressed in honesty and righteous living.[10] Fourth, the religious experience contributes to the individual's attainment of a set of values for interpreting not only one's own existence but also the existence of other persons and the physical world that they all occupy.[11] The religious person has optimism about life and humanity. The person who feels affirmed and loved fully by God in the religious experience will express their love for others in social responsibility. According to Thurman, in American society the principal areas for the exercise of social responsibility are work (discernment and choice of vocation), voting (citizen participation), and voluntary association (membership in organizations with persons of like minds and faith).[12]

Extending Thurman's analysis of religious experience, Carlyle Stewart points out several sources and functions of African American spirituality. According to Stewart, in addition to the encounter with God, African American spirituality is enriched by other important sources,[13] which include African traditional religions, the Christian Bible, black experience and black culture, and traditions of equality in American democracy. Stewart's intent is to emphasize that, even if God is the principal in religious experience, there are other significant influences that shape such experiences. He says that the basic functions of African American spirituality are formative, unitive, corroborative, transformative, and consecrative.[14] The formative function involves the development of black consciousness, black community, and black culture.

Black consciousness refers to black self-awareness, self-expression, and self-determination. The unitive function involves the relation and integration between the self and community. The corroborative function deals with how spirituality confirms the value and meaning of African American life. The transformative function and consecrative operate together to alter and validate black life as a sacred reality.

CONVERSION, CATHARSIS, AND TRANSFORMATION

In *The Black Church in the African American Experience*, C. Eric Lincoln and Lawrence Mamiya identify conversion as the fundamental concept and means by which African American Christians interpret experience of God.[15] The personal conversion story may be told around the themes of being "born again," receiving "regeneration," or "getting religion." In African American churches, the concept of conversion has taken on several meanings in addition to its normal use in Christianity.

Conversion literally means "a turning." Conversion signifies that a person has experienced a change in attitude, thinking, and behavior. Thus conversion affects a person's outlook on life and how that convert sees oneself.[16] To this radical reorientation, African American Christians have associated conversion, self-transcendence, self-realization, and self-worth.

Conversion, as the experience has been construed in the tradition of American revivalism, is what Jon Alexander calls a "transit of consciousness."[17] The development of the convert's thinking and self-understanding follows a four-stage process.

[In stage 1] the [person's] complacent consciousness is shattered by discovering or encountering something that challenges their customary understanding or paradigm of things, in nearly all cases because it is fundamentally other than they had expected. The most frequently described "trigger" that shatters the complacent consciousness is illness or death. . . .

[Stage 2] is a period of struggle (short or protracted) during which [the person tries] to come to terms with the "otherness" they have encountered. During this period, the [person is] ill at ease, and many experience deracination, alienation, despair, isolation, stagnation, and illness. [They feel] caught between the discredited, complacent world they can no longer accept and a new world they cannot yet fully conceive or affirm. [They spin] around and around, trying to reintegrate things without success, and at this point some [persons] consider or attempt suicide. Sooner or later [they realize] that their discovery or encounter requires a basic change—a difficult transformation and submission to someone or to something or to God—that is beyond their old selves and world. . . .

[In stage 3] the [person describes a] miraculous moment when they find the power to accept and submit. The moment of resolution seems like a miracle because they had come to see their situation as hopeless and because the force that resolves their struggle between two worlds seems to come from outside them—something that happens to them after they have exhausted all their conscious resources. . . .

[In stage 4 the person describes their] new consciousness. Once the old self and its world are transcended, the authors experience the universe as hospitable, the self as hopeful, and they find a new faith, a new generativity, and a new capacity to give of themselves.[18]

Conversion is a healing of sorts. In conversion, the person is delivered from the debilitating sickness of a false identity. Living under a false identity, one that is not true to the self that a person is, can be mentally stressful. Conversion conveys an authentic identity. As a form of reintegration of the self, conversion is a way for persons to attain a true self in relationship with God.

Self-transcendence is a recurrent feature of African American religious narrative. Self-transcendence is a change in the self that becomes foundational for new constructions of identity, apprehension of one's purpose, and successful engagement with other selves in one's social and cultural environments. Instances of self-transcendence can be found in the spiritual autobiographies of Charles H. Mason, Elizabeth J. Dabney, and James O. Patterson Sr.[19] Dabney's story was discussed in chapter 6 (above). Their narratives convey the notion that deeply moving spiritual experience is transformative. Each person rose from obscurity to national and international prominence. Dabney went from homemaker and pastor's wife to national evangelist. Patterson rose from distressed teen to youth leader in the church, eventually working his way to the highest position (presiding bishop) within his denomination. Mason moved from itinerant pastor to found COGIC (Church of God in Christ), the largest Pentecostal denomination in the United States.[20] In the person's attempt to reconcile oneself to the newly perceived identity and potentials revealed in the encounter with God, self-transcendence becomes self-actualization.

In addition to the healing that comes from conversion and self-transcendence, worship represents another means of relieving mental stress. African American worship is characterized by catharsis, to release and relieve the frustrations in life. Gerald Davis says:

> Ecstasy as a form of celebration is not emotional abandonment—it is expression. It is affirmation of sound psychic health. Ecstasy is a manifestation of an insight into one's life and one's humanity. Ecstasy in the African American church is historical. It is not an accommodation to an unrelenting feeling of ill will between peoples of differing races. It is rather a quiet voice made thunderously spontaneous in millions of African American collective minds, reminding folk of an elegant humanism already old in Africa when impudent Europe thought it was the first to discover the power of the celebrating spirit.[21]

Almost never do African American Christians use the words "ecstasy" or "spirit possession" to name their worship experience. They call their expressions in worship "praise." In praise, they find emotional release and comfort. Praise is the thanksgiving and adoration that worshipers offer to God, who in turn allows them into a realm of the Spirit where they experience a foretaste of the glory to come, when the kingdom is fully realized in history.

THE SPIRIT AND THE "SHOUT"

As evidenced by Jonathan Edwards's *Treatise concerning Religious Affections* (1746), the revivals of the Great Awakening and the later camp meetings of the Second Awakening were characterized by expressions of emotion and ecstatic experience. Edwards went to great lengths to disassociate certain emotions and unusual behavior in the revivals from genuine religious conversion, which he interpreted to mean an awakening to Christian living. Yet Edwards's theological work preserved in scholarship the commonly held notion that emotion and subjective experience occupy an acceptable place in Christian life.

In his essay "Of the Faith of the Fathers," W. E. B. Du Bois describes a Southern Negro revival service and asserts that, since the time of slavery, African American worship consists of three basic elements: the preacher, the music, and the frenzy. By frenzy, Du Bois is referring to the shout, the sudden sounds and bodily movements, in response to intensely felt emotion. The music and preaching provoke the frenzy or shout. The shout, more than anything else, defines African American worship. Du Bois says:

> Finally the Frenzy of "Shouting," when the Spirit of the Lord passed by, and, seizing the devotee, made him mad with supernatural joy, was the last essential of Negro religion and the one more devoutly believed in than all the rest. It varied in expression from the silent rapt countenance or the low murmur and moan to the mad abandon of physical fervor, —the stamping, shrieking, and shouting, the rushing to and fro and wild waving of arms, the weeping and laughing, the vision and the trance. All this is nothing new in the world, but old as religion, as Delphi and Endor. And so firm a hold did it have on the Negro, that many generations firmly believed that without this visible manifestation of the God there could be no true communion with the Invisible.[22]

In a manner consistent with Du Bois's intuition that the shout is connected to divine revelation, James Cone describes the emotional expressiveness in African American Christian worship in terms of the participants' awareness of a transcendent reality and revealed truth. According to Cone, the experience not only involves music, preaching, and shouting but also conversion, prayer, and testimony.[23] Ecstatic experience is an indicator of God's comforting and empowering presence among the persons committed to righteous living. The shout is an indication that conversion has taken place and that God is present in the Spirit to enable persons to experience a form of joy that is impossible in their normal experience.[24] In the encounter with God, within the context of worship, they realize as truth that God is liberating them from oppression, not to mention the other distresses in human existence.

EMOTION AND INTELLECT

In African American spirituality, emotion and intellect are interrelated and necessary for apprehension of the truth.[25] Indeed African American worship involves spontaneous, free, and enthusiastic expression, involving hand-clapping, foot-stomping, shouting, dancing, rousing sermons, soul-stirring music, passionate testimony, fervent prayer, call and response, tongue-speaking, prophecy, miracles, conversion, shaking, and even falling out under the power of the Holy Spirit. In response to the Spirit, persons shout (speak spontaneously and sometimes loudly) "Amen," "Glory be to God," "Thank you, Jesus," and "Hallelujah." Sometimes their shouts are in the holy dance that the Spirit moves them to perform. This kind of worship engages persons on the level of emotions but should not be taken to mean mere emotionalism. African American spirituality can be as intense intellectually as it is emotional.

In Barbara Holmes' *Joy Unspeakable: Contemplative Practices of the Black Church*, she challenges the myth that African American worship is essentially emotional and therefore irrational. She argues that thinking, an exercise of the intellect, is at the heart of African American spirituality. The "shout" (ecstatic outburst and spontaneous dance) has a cognitive dimension that involves thoughtful reflection about the encounter with God and its implications for other aspects of believers' lives.[26] According to Holmes, religious experience stimulates emotion, provokes thought, and inspires action. The encounter with God affects all aspects of the believer's personhood.[27]

While humans are capable of and frequently engage in conceptual thinking, most persons live, act, and respond daily on the level of emotion. Worship that touches the emotions reaches persons where they are, in the realm of qualitative distinctions, the place at which they live out their lives from day to day. This realm or place is where persons gage their lives by the barometers of failure and success, sorrow and joy, frustration and happiness, want and satisfaction, pain and comfort. Reflection on these emotions, as measurements of human experience, is essential for our comprehension of reality.

The encounter with God heightens believers' awareness, enabling their intellectual grasp of possibilities yet to be experienced but just as real as life presently known. James Cone describes the encounter with God as a joyous response to an eschatological event where the Spirit breaks into our present moment in order to reveal knowledge, the full truth, of who we are and will become in God's future.[28] It would, however, be a mistake to assume that this joyous response is always expressed audibly or physically in the shout. According to Howard Thurman, emotion may be expressed in silence. In believers' quiet time or quiet place, their silence is a mood that represents an emotional and mental state resulting from the divine encounter and the knowledge disclosed therein.[29]

Questions for Discussion

1. If religious experience is defined as a response to the holy or sacred, where and what is the nature of an otherness (referent to the sacred or holy) that can be a source of meaning and value for black people?
2. What is the entry and best way to access this source? Is the entry God? Is the entry through conversion, Spirit, or worship?
3. If there is more than one entry or point of access to the "sacred," how might these different approaches be correlated and harmonized into a single perspective?

Suggested Reading

Bostic, Joy R. *African American Female Mysticism: Nineteenth-Century Religious Activism.* New York: Palgrave Macmillan, 2013.

Holmes, Barbara A. *Joy Unspeakable: Contemplative Practices of the Black Church.* Minneapolis: Augsburg Fortress Press, 2004.

Stewart, Carlyle Fielding. *Black Spirituality and Black Consciousness: Soul Force, Culture, and Freedom in the African-American Experience.* Trenton, NJ: Africa World Press, 1999.

Thurman, Howard. *Creative Encounter: An Interpretation of Religion and the Social Witness.* Richmond, IN: Friends United Press, 1972.

Whelchel, Love Henry, Jr. *Hell without Fire: Conversion in Slave Religion.* Nashville: Abingdon Press, 2002.

8
Suffering

Though suffering is not a problem unique to any particular racial or ethnic group, the focus of this chapter is on the interpretations that African Americans have given to the suffering that they have endured from racism manifested in the history of the United States. Common to all forms of human suffering is the pain caused and diminishment to the quality of life, and even the termination of life in physical death. In American society—so stratified by gender, race and ethnicity, income and wealth—a person's quality and length of life is affected, for better or for worse, by their social status.[1] Injury, sickness, hunger, conflict, loneliness, loss, and other ails of human finitude are experienced disproportionately on account of the inequality and injustice in human societies.

African American theologians have addressed suffering both generally as a predicament of human existence and, in particular, as the distresses stemming from or intensified by racism. Sufferings of both kinds have raised questions about God's solidarity with the oppressed, God's intentions for human life, and even God's existence. For the most part, in African American churches and communities, the various forms of suffering have been interpreted in light of God's righteous purposes and therefore deemed as redemptive. This chapter examines the critique and defense of redemptive suffering and the conception of God as a liberator for persons oppressed by suffering.

CRITIQUE AND DEFENSE
OF REDEMPTIVE SUFFERING

Whether resulting from the experience of finitude, social injustice, or natural disaster, African American Christians have overwhelmingly regarded suffering as redemptive. This idea of redemptive suffering has meant for them that unmerited agony, though intrinsically evil, can lead to a positive outcome. The reward for enduring suffering may have a soul-building effect: a person may become stronger in faith, more virtuous in character, or more knowledgeable. Perhaps the person will experience a blessing of some kind in this life, when the season of suffering ends. If it does not end here, then the person can expect the reward of eternal life in the world to come. Evil and suffering in this life would have served a divine purpose.

To the question of why God would allow something as terrible as chattel slavery, Alexander Crummell answered that slavery was a "chastisement" that God used in order to make the Negro superior (an exemplar) in morality and religion.[2] Not all African American Christians have adopted Crummell's view; yet they have, in their own way, maintained an emphasis on redemptive suffering, the idea that any suffering experienced is due to God's will and purpose and desire to reward those who endure it. African American theologians espousing some form of redemptive suffering, less extreme than Crummell, include the following: Karen Baker-Fletcher, James Cone, M. Shawn Copeland, Martin Luther King Jr., JoAnne Marie Terrell, and Howard Thurman. Notwithstanding their explanations of redemptive suffering, questions persist regarding commonly held assumptions about the purposefulness of suffering, God's solidarity with the oppressed, and God's will to liberate them.

The Criticisms

Delores Williams and Anthony Pinn are two formidable opponents to the idea of redemptive suffering. Williams questions the use of Christ's atonement as a justification for redemptive suffering. Pinn argues that the concept of redemptive suffering is incoherent, leading to oppressed persons' quietism and complicity with systems of injustice. Thus its use in liberation theology is counterproductive.

Williams argues that the oppressed are not sufficiently motivated to resist oppression when, in the Christian doctrine of atonement, Jesus' suffering is glorified to the degree of becoming a pretext for the inherent virtue of suffering. Nothing so influences persons' acceptance of their sufferings, even when wrongly imposed, than the idea that Jesus, their Savior, suffered as a surrogate for someone else's benefit. According to Williams, the traditional interpretation of atonement has led to a misunderstanding of how God accomplishes the salvation of humanity. The root of the misunderstanding is the inordinate focus on suffering. Williams insists that the main focus of Christians should be on Jesus' ministerial and eschatological vision.[3] Jesus suffered and died in pursuit of this vision. So, rather than Jesus' suffering functioning as the principal means of salvation, it is the power of Jesus' vision that saves. The traditional doctrine of atonement does not inspire persons to suffer in pursuit of a vision of new possibility. The traditional doctrine misleads them to believe that their sufferings, wrongfully and unjustly imposed by their oppressors, must be endured in patience. Any relief of their sufferings comes, if at all, through divine intervention. Instead of altogether rejecting the idea of redemptive suffering, Williams is actually questioning the sufferings that are incorrectly labeled as redemptive.[4] Jesus' suffering was not redemptive but illustrative of the gross sin and evil that resisted his transformative vision and ministry.

As a committed Christian theist, Williams maintains belief in God but points out, using the story of Hagar, that God does not always liberate. Hagar, the slave of Abraham's wife Sarah, was forced into surrogate motherhood and then despised by Sarah when she perceived that Hagar's son, Ishmael, may become a rival to Sarah's son, Isaac. After Hagar and Ishmael were banished to the wilderness and there about to perish for want of food and water; God heard Hagar's prayer and provided sustenance and promised greatness to her son. God did not correct the injustice, in the sense that Ishmael would grow up in Abraham's house and be the heir of Abraham. Williams points out that sometimes, as illustrated in Hagar's story, God enables survival, which can be just as important as liberation is for those who are oppressed. Always, God offers the vision of new and better possibilities. According to Williams, Jesus' life was devoted to a God-given vision of possibility. Williams acknowledges that, in the Bible, God is revealed in the stories of Hagar and Jesus. Her aim, however, is to reinterpret these biblical stories in order to emphasize survival and ministerial vision.

Anthony Pinn raises the problem of evil and suffering both as a logical problem and an evidential problem.[5] As a logical problem, the statements "God exists" and "Evil exists" cannot both be true. The assertion that God exists cannot be squared with the unquestionable existence of evil and the suffering that occurs on account of it. As an evidential problem, the persistence of evil raises doubt as to whether any type of definitive event such as Jesus' crucifixion and resurrection has ended evil. If God defeated evil, then why does it continue? If it continues, then God, if God exists, is unable or unwilling to stop it. According to Pinn, however the problem is raised, the commitment to the notion of redemptive suffering may inhibit liberation because oppressed people are tempted to justify and tolerate suffering out of their deference to some mysterious or supposedly known plan that God has for the betterment of human life. As an atheist, Pinn does not deal with the topic of God's existence, attributes, and actions. Instead, he argues that the concept of redemptive suffering is logically incoherent and antithetical to black people's desire for ultimate freedom. There is no special need for belief in God or any other religious belief in order to sanction a people's aspirations for freedom.

Karen Baker-Fletcher, in *Dancing with God*, discusses Anthony Pinn's criticism and rejection of redemptive suffering, which for Pinn means the justification of continued suffering after Jesus Christ's triumph over evil in his resurrection from death.[6] According to Pinn, if Christ truly overcame evil, then evil would no longer exist in the world. Baker-Fletcher's best response seems to be a reiteration of instances where the Holy Spirit miraculously enables persons to endure and overcome sufferings in this world, although the final deliverance from evil is in the remote future.[7] She seems to not recognize that Pinn's critique rests upon a misunderstanding of historical and social change.

Pinn disregards the fact that certain events are decisive and forever change the course of history. There are singular events that can be cumulative in effect. For example, the discovery of fire (though cold and darkness still exist) changed human society. The American Revolution (though the United States' sovereignty and security is still being challenged) propelled and continues to drive forward the American Republic. The Civil War (though divisions rooted in injustices surrounding race and ethnicity continue to plague America) resulted in an American nation composed now of only free states. In the New Testament, Jesus' and Paul's eschatology attest to the idea that the process of change (i.e., God's transformation of the world) has started and is irreversible. The above cases illustrate that change is incremental.

The Defense

Depicting Pinn's and Williams's critiques as modernist perspectives that are out of sync with the faith expressed in the majority of African American churches, Victor Anderson proposes an alternative conception of redemptive suffering.[8] Anderson takes objection to Pinn's and Williams's suggestion that faith is a derivative or benefit of suffering. Anderson says: "We do not suffer in order to obtain faith. Such virtues as faith, courage, endurance, temperance, friendship, and magnanimity are not excellences peculiar to Christians, whether black or other. These human excellences, these human capacities and possibilities, are already present in human miseries, struggles, and sufferings."[9] Faith is a human capacity that may or may not be interpreted by using Christian theology.[10] Faith emerges from creative exchange.

According to Anderson, creative exchange is the process by which something, as well as the world itself, comes to fulfillment by drawing upon an available network of relations and/or meanings. Anderson takes Henry Nelson Wieman's term "creative interchange"[11] to label what Wieman says is the satisfaction of the demands of each individual participating in their community's goal-seeking activities. Based upon Wieman's theory, creative exchange "expands the valuing consciousness of each [participant]," "widens and deepens mutual support between individuals and [groups]," and develops the unique individuality of each person."[12] The network of relations and means, as they are initially experienced before interpretation, is ambiguous.[13] In experience, there are realities that exhibit no apparent coherence. Yet they are present in the same environment. In the same world of possibilities, misery, suffering, and wickedness exist, as do faith, hope, and love. In creative exchange, faith emerges as a possibility that some persons will choose in order to live meaningfully, in spite of the presence of evil and suffering.[14] For Anderson, redemptive suffering is a symbol of creative exchange, that is, the transcendence that we achieve in spite of the ambiguities and contradictions in our experience.

Pinn and Williams's suspicion that the acquiescence of the oppressed to suffering follows from their belief in redemptive suffering is clearly not the case in the theology and activism of Martin Luther King Jr. His concept of redemptive suffering is associated with nonviolence, a form of social action signifying that the oppressed are not passive but are asserting themselves, albeit peacefully, to achieve social change. King believed that suffering is altered and overcome by higher divine purposes, especially when persons channel their energies into constructive action to resist injustice. For King, suffering is redemptive because it is demonstrated in the cross as well as in his personal experiences of fulfillment found in enabling others to attain healing, a sense of wholeness, in spite of the injustices of racism.[15] King regarded the cross as "the power of God unto social and individual salvation."[16] At the heart of the gospel is the triumph of Jesus Christ: his crucifixion, followed by resurrection, is a message of redemptive suffering, showing that the struggle for good, right, and justice is not in vain. The cross is a symbol of hope and divine love. Yet the cross is part of the gospel, not the only event in the gospel message. In the gospel of Jesus Christ, the cross (his suffering and death) is followed by resurrection (being raised from the dead and receiving vindication of his ministry). As a symbol of God's love, the cross illustrates the extent to which God will go to save humanity. According to King, as surely as Jesus achieved our salvation through suffering, we must be willing also to suffer in our struggle to be free and transform our society. King is a significant figure for explaining as well as demonstrating that nonviolence, which requires of its practitioners the endurance of suffering, does work. Suffering is often necessary for a righteous cause.[17]

THEODICY AND BLACK SUFFERING

In addition to redemptive suffering, theodicy—the task of reconciling the empirical reality of black people suffering to belief in a benevolent and powerful God—is a concern of black and womanist theologians. William Jones contends that theodicy is the central category of black theology. In Jones's opinion, black theology can be nothing more than an expanded discourse on theodicy. He critiques the prevailing model of God (black liberation theism) in black theology and offers humanocentric theism as its alternative. Black liberation theism is the belief that God is in solidarity with oppressed African Americans and will liberate them. Humanocentric theism is the belief that liberation or any other action necessary for transforming society is mostly the work of human beings. Jones argues that black liberation theism is grounded in traditional Western biblical theism, which posits belief in a perfectly good God, who is beyond questioning and not subject to empirical investigation.

Jones's critique of black liberation theism was discussed in chapter 5 (above). The gist of his argument is that, given the magnitude of black suffering and the absence of compelling empirical evidence in support of divine liberating activity, an alternative form of theism, which he calls "humanocentric theism," is necessary. Humanocentric theism, the last point on the theistic spectrum before adopting a position of complete humanism, emphasizes human agency and responsibility for improving social conditions. Liberation is principally the work of human beings and not God's work. God may provide the vision and inspiration, but humans must do the work. Jones says that secular humanism is the best framework for liberation.

In an attempt to justify black liberation theism against Jones's argument, James Cone developed a response to Jones's evidential objection to black liberation theism.[18] Jones argues that there must be some evidence to support black Christian theism: the belief that God is in solidarity with black people and is liberating (or will liberate) them. Jones says there must be a decisive event of liberation in the history of black people. James Cone says that this decisive event of liberation is the resurrection of Jesus Christ. In the resurrection of Jesus Christ, God has shown definitively God's triumph over evil and initiated the ending of history, which is to be finalized in the second coming (return) of the resurrected Jesus Christ.

In Jones's opinion, citing biblical motifs of God's supposed acts of liberation and the verification of black liberation theism in the postulation of a distant future does not constitute sufficient evidence. On the one hand, Jones argues that biblical motifs are not direct acts of divine liberation in the history of African Americans. A legitimately held belief in black liberation theism requires (what Jones calls) a "liberation-exaltation event." That is to say, belief in black liberation theism would be justified if there was a definitive event in African American history clearly demonstrating that God favors African Americans and is working to liberate them. Jones argues that eschatological verification does not add to our certainty but instead begs the question of why God is delaying liberation. Is God able but not willing to liberate black people? Or is God willing but not able to do so?

Cone espouses a kind of fideism, contending that theologians operate under a system of logic that differs from other forms of rational discourse. Yet his response begs the question of the relation and relevance of salvation (or biblical) history to African American history. How are the two distinct and yet the same or overlapping? From Cone's perspective as a black Christian theologian, suffering and philosophical critique do indeed challenge black Christian faith, but neither negates it. According to Cone, although racism might be eliminated from human society, suffering in general is unlikely to disappear from human existence.

FAITH THAT EMERGES ALONGSIDE SUFFERING

The concept of God at the center of African American Christian faith is God as "Waymaker." As Waymaker, God creates (out of nothing) or makes (from existing things) ways, that is, opportunities for persons to survive and thrive. Faith in God, who is conceived as such, seems crucial for African American believers' effort to make sense of suffering as well as to endure and overcome suffering. Their faith fortifies them against being demoralized by suffering resulting from events in nature as well as from actions of other humans. Even amid suffering, their faith asserts that God is in charge. God's power is ultimate. God has made a world that is fundamentally good, and the life in it is worth living. God makes a way for life to continue, against all the threats to being. Their faith is expressed in testimony and song in statements like the following:

> I say to my soul don't worry; the Lord will make a way somehow.
> In all of my appointed time, I will wait until my change comes.
> Lord, help me to hold out until my change comes.

This is the faith expressed in the majority of African American churches; such faith has enabled African Americans to survive and thrive.

Questions for Discussion

1. For Christians, what does Jesus' suffering reveal about the nature of human suffering and the association of suffering and its endurance with social change?
2. How does a person determine when suffering is or is not redemptive?
3. Can the belief that suffering is redemptive (the conviction that there is a divine purpose and reward for those who endure suffering) be empirically verified or falsified? If there is no indisputable evidence that can be presented in support or rejection of this belief, is the belief irrational?

4. If a life without suffering is impossible, what validity is there to arguments like Pinn's that reject the endurance of suffering for the purpose of achieving commendable moral and spiritual purposes?

Suggested Reading

Pinn, Anthony B., ed. *Moral Evil and Redemptive Suffering: A History of Theodicy in African American Religious Thought*. Gainesville: University Press of Florida, 2002.

Terrell, JoAnne Marie. *Power in the Blood? The Cross in the African American Experience*. Maryknoll, NY: Orbis Books, 1998. Reprint, Eugene, OR: Wipf & Stock, 2005.

9

Salvation

In African American theology, as in Christianity in general, the life, death, and resurrection of Jesus Christ are central to the occurrence of salvation. If humans are transformed, it is accomplished by what Jesus does. In chapter 6 (above), sin was defined in terms of how human freedom, an essential feature of our humanness, is misused. More will be said about sin in this chapter as well as how salvation represents the ultimate remedy for sin. This chapter will offer definitions of both sin and salvation, an explanation of how sin and salvation are manifested personally and socially, descriptions of the person and work of Jesus Christ, and a survey of the metaphors and models of salvation in African American experience and theology.

PERSONAL AND SOCIAL MANIFESTATIONS OF SIN

Black theology understands sin as something that is social and not personal only. Hence, black theology exposes racism as a sin. Racism is an oppression with which persons ought not to be complicit. Black theologians have expanded the notion of oppression to include classism, sexism, heterosexism, and ecological destruction as evils to be combated.

James Cone states that one of the strengths of the contemporary black theological movement is its attack on racism and labeling racism a sin.[1] Whenever an act is identified as sin, we have to cease doing it and start resisting it. Evangelical Protestant Christianity, which exerts a strong influence in African American churches, tends to regard sin as something personal, namely, any act that supposedly transgresses God's commandments and, as well, implies a moral failure on the part of the individual committing the act. The inordinate focus on individual acts leads to an oversight of the social practices, maintained by a complex web of individual actions that are oppressive to certain groups of persons in society. African American theologians contend that the matter of sin cannot be limited to a discussion or corrective of personal conduct. Sin must be dealt with in its social manifestation. Since sin is manifested socially, it needs to be addressed in a social manner. Similarly, salvation, as the remedy for sin, must be discussed and pursued with regard to how it too may be manifested socially. Salvation is personal but not individualistic; it is a possibility for the entire human society.[2]

In the context of racism, sin is blacks' condition of nonbeing and whites' condition of privilege at the expense of blacks' and others' oppression.[3] Racism is a splintering not just in American society but also in humanity. Thus racism is an estrangement from God and from each other that has resulted in both physical and spiritual death. Persons oppressed by racism have thereby endured a denial or loss in their quality of life and even suffered physical death. Those who contribute to their suffering and death are often incapable of discerning the sins committed.

Though racism and the other myriad of moral evils identified by black and womanist theologians are serious problems, they are not the only forms of social action that are sinful. Martin Luther King Jr. claimed that along with racism, militarism and poverty comprise the three great evils in the modern world. Greed, the suspected motive of corporate executives, is often cited as the human failing that contributed to the Great Recession in the United States and weakening of financial markets in Western Europe. The idolatries of capitalism and its dehumanization of persons through alienation and exploitation is also sinful.[4] Rather than trying to defend one action or practice as far worse than others, attention should be placed generally on sin as any activity, personal or social, that diminishes the quality of life or results in the destruction of life.

Sin is best defined in terms of the larger context of persons in community. It is denial of community, not just any community, but especially the human community intended by God.[5] In the Hebrew Bible and the Christian Testament, the idea of covenant is central to understanding human life in relation to God. A covenant is an agreement, a contract, between two or more parties where each promises to perform certain actions. God agreed to be Israel's God. Israel promised to accept God as their God, their only God. In return for Israel's pledge, God promised to make them a great nation and to bless all nations of the world through Israel. The first thing that God did in order to establish the covenant was to save Israel, that is, to deliver Israel from bondage in Egypt with a mighty hand and give Israel victory over the peoples of Canaan. God never wavered in keeping God's promises, although Israel violated the terms of the covenant. Still God acted with mercy and grace in order to keep the covenant in force. The covenant with God not only specifies God's actions toward humans. It also specifies how humans must act toward each other. In the covenant, God gave Israel the law, which defined just relations between persons in the nation.

Sin is the condition resulting from the misuse or denial of freedom, yours or someone else's, in the context of the covenant relationship with God. The church's use of the word "sin" involves a certain conviction about human nature—that rationality, freedom, and responsibility are essential features of human life. People have the potential (the power) to change the direction of their lives. Biological urges and habits formed in socialization, though strong, are not the only influences acting upon the human person. The church's message on sin and salvation implies that humans have choice in resisting injustice as well as in determining the quality of life they will have. As the church models and promotes the beloved community, persons are restored to their essential humanity, to their status as free beings capable of relating to God and each other in meaningful and healthy relationships.

The proliferation of oppressions—or expanding the concept of oppression to include some terrible acts without a clear sense of how these oppressions are related—is resolved by this definition of sin as human agency gone awry. The misdirection of freedom and the negative consequences that follow are listed under the category of sin. Also, the vagueness of oppression is eliminated by this definition. Naming remains important for the purpose of calling person's attention to what they are doing. If there is any oppression, it is due to the misuse of freedom by persons who commit acts that contribute to the situation of oppression, or by persons who are complicit or cooperate with their oppressors.

JESUS CHRIST AND SALVATION

Salvation from sin comes from Jesus Christ, whom African Americans have imagined in various ways. According to James Cone, these imaginings have emerged from the interplay between social context, Scripture, and tradition.[6] Cone presupposes a dual-source theory of Scripture and tradition, with each being distinct sources of revelation that are unequal in authority. For Cone, Scripture carries greater authority than tradition. According to Cone, we experience Jesus Christ in the context of our struggle for freedom. However, the Jesus encountered in our social context is wholly other, someone who is different from us although he identifies with us. This otherness of Jesus requires that we turn to the Scripture in order to better understand who he is. In addition to Scripture, tradition (which represents the church's affirmation of faith in Jesus Christ at different periods in history) opens us to the meaning of Jesus beyond the subjectivity of our present social context.

African American Christians affirm images of Jesus Christ that are valued similarly by other Christians. James Cone and Jacquelyn Grant identify these traditional images, which have been appropriated in African American experience. According to Cone, African Americans have confessed that Jesus is human, risen Lord, and hope.[7] According to Cone, Jesus' humanity is underscored by his Jewish ethnicity. Jesus was a historical person who lived at a certain time in history and who belonged to a particular group of people. Jesus is divine. He is God incarnate, God in the flesh. Jesus was resurrected from the dead, is forever alive, and forever is God with us. Jesus is Lord of the future. He is our soon-coming Lord. To Cones's affirmations about Jesus Christ, Grant adds that Jesus is "Divine Co-sufferer" and "the One who empowers the weak."[8]

According to Jamie Phelps, very distinct kinds of images of Jesus emerge from the types of oppression that African Americans experience. If the oppression is institutional, such as racial inequality and racism, African Americans imagine Jesus as "Liberator, Social Prophet, and Social Equalizer."[9] If the oppression is psychological and leads to emotional distress or mental anguish, Jesus is imagined as "Friend, Heart Fixer, and Mind Regulator."[10] Jesus is the "friend who sticks closer than a brother" (Prov. 18:24 NIV).[11] For African Americans faced with spiritual oppression, Jesus is imagined as "Homeboy who is always covering their backs and who risked and embraced death that they might live."[12]

Several black and womanist theologians contend that Jesus Christ is black. According to James Cone, Jacquelyn Grant, and Kelly Brown Douglas, Jesus' blackness is ontological. James Deotis Roberts declares that Jesus' blackness is mythological. According to Dwight Hopkins, Jesus' blackness is pneumatological. Albert Cleage claims that Jesus was, as a matter of historical fact, black; he was a revolutionary leader of a black nation seeking liberation. For Cleage, Jesus' blackness is physical. That Jesus is ontologically or symbolically black means that he identifies with the suffering poor. He is revealed in the sufferings, struggles, and joys of black people. For Cone, Jesus' blackness is an ontological symbol that describes what oppression means as well as shows those with whom God is in solidarity.

Grant claims that the black woman, as the most oppressed in America, is a genuine liberating symbol of Christ for the oppressed. African American women are disproportionately represented among the poor and suffer from the interconnecting oppressions of racism, sexism, and classism. Douglas shares Grant's conviction about the symbolic power of the black woman; however, she believes other symbols can be just as powerful and ought not to be disregarded. According to Douglas, Christ can be in any image that provides an analysis of oppression. Roberts argues that Christ's representation as black or any other feature of ethnic and social groups can only be mythical. Mythical representation is a way to relate the gospel directly to a group of people and instill within them a sense of worth by closely associating their physical characteristics with the divine. However, Roberts insists that the biblical Jesus Christ must stand as the measure for all mythological images of Christ. Hopkins, seeking to avoid gender and race-specific terminology, claims that Jesus' blackness is metaphysical. In Jesus, God is revealed as the "spirit of liberation" operating in the world.

Recently J. Kameron Carter and Willie J. Jennings, African American theologians at Duke Divinity School, have emphasized the significance of Jesus' Jewish ethnicity for Christology and salvation.[13] The story of Israel (ancient and modern) is the struggle of a people to assert their identity, to survive, and to be fulfilled. God's covenant with Israel, through which the quest of the Jewish people is satisfied, is expanded to include all nations in the world. Jew and non-Jew (Gentile) alike are baptized into Jesus' body. The incarnation, God's entry into human flesh, is in a Jewish body, and this Jewish body, Jesus, welcomes the diverse peoples that make up the human race. The challenge then and now, for Israel and all nations, is for peoples of all kinds to coexist peacefully. To be authentically church, Christians must embrace the hospitality of Jesus Christ toward other peoples.

METAPHORS AND MODELS OF SALVATION

If God saves through Jesus Christ, how does salvation happen? Numerous meanings have been proposed for salvation. Based on the notion that freedom is essential to human nature, salvation may be defined in terms of that which makes possible the full and proper exercise of freedom. In that regard, *salvation is deliverance (relief or release) from situations that the individual (or group of persons) alone cannot escape and the subsequent achievement of an improved life.* The Hebrew Bible and the Christian Testament teach that in order to live in covenant relationship with God, we often need to be delivered from that which impairs our ability to fulfill our terms of the covenant (Exod. 20:1–3; Lev. 26:12–13; Deut. 7:8; Rom. 6:18, 22). We must trust God for salvation because there are moments in our lives when we cannot handle the situation all by ourselves. We need help, and God, through Jesus Christ, supplies that help. God offers this help freely. God acts with integrity in the covenant relationship, always fulfilling God's part with mercy and grace, forgiving us and even providing assistance that enables us to fulfill our obligations in the covenant.

Salvation is a valid concept for personal and social transformation. Humans are contingent beings, dependent on something else for their existence, and creatures of finitude, beings with limitations. In the environment that forms our world, we are not the only agents with freedom. There are many entities and forces over which we have little or no control. To seek salvation is to acknowledge the conditions of human existence yet to strive for connection with God, the ground of our being, and in so doing, transcend what appears before us as an obstruction to our enjoyment of life. If rightly interpreted by Christianity and other religions, the identification of sin (i.e., the major predicament in human life) represents a significant insight about human nature and reinforces the notion that, for human beings, profound change occurs through self-transcendence.[14] The discourse on sin and salvation is a language of identifying major predicaments in human existence and finding ultimate remedies that will lead to outcomes for human flourishing.

In Christianity, several sets of metaphors are used to explain what salvation is and how it is achieved. The predominant metaphor and model of salvation is atonement. Womanist theologian Delores Williams questioned the adequacy of the atonement model for the liberation of the oppressed, objecting to its glorification of suffering. Rather than liberation, she emphasizes survival and quality of life as a form of salvation. Yet most black and womanist theologians interpret salvation in terms of liberation. Rivaling both Williams and her colleagues are African American megachurch pastors and televangelists who interpret salvation in terms of blessings that follow from divine forgiveness and favor.

The various biblical metaphors for salvation are capable of coordination by using the root metaphors of "problems are puzzles" or "problems are difficulties."[15] The puzzle begs for a correct solution. Once solved, the puzzle is solved forever. Sin is regarded as a problem. Salvation solves the problem. The difficulty, the state or condition, is treated as a container that holds the person. Sin is a difficulty into which persons are confined. Salvation releases them from the state or condition that binds them. Like the movement from puzzle to solution as well as from the constraints of difficulty to an independence from those constraints, the movement from sin to salvation represents better and lasting change.

The following chart shows how the basic principle of the above root metaphors brings structure to the language of sin and salvation:

Problem	Solution	Outcome	Biblical Reference
absence (lost)	recovery	presence (found)	Luke 15; Matt. 10:5–8; 18:11; Luke 19:10
bondage (oppression)	emancipation (liberation)	freedom	John 8:32, 36; 6:18, 22; 8:2; Gal. 4, 5:1, 13–15
death	resurrection	life	John 3:14–16; 10:9–10; Rom. 5:12–21; 6:22–23; 8:11
difference	deification	likeness	Luke 20:36; John 17:22–23; 1 Cor. 15:42–49; 2 Cor. 3:17–18; Gal. 2:20; 2 Pet. 1:4; 1 John 3:2
disorder	re-creation	harmony	Rom. 8:19–22; 2 Cor. 5:17; Rev. 3:12; 21:1–2

(continued)

Problem	Solution	Outcome	Biblical Reference
estrangement	atonement*	reconciliation	Lev. 16; John 1:29; Rom. 5:8–11; Heb. 10:1–18; 1 John 2:1–3
exclusion	adoption	inclusion	John 1:2; Luke 20:36; Rom. 8:14–17, 23, 29; Gal. 3:26; 4:4–7; Eph. 1:5; 1 John 3:1; Rev. 21:7
lack (poverty)	blessing	abundance (prosperity)	Deut. 7:12–16, 8:18; Ps. 34:9–10; Prov. 3:9–10; Joel 2:25; Mal. 3:10; 2 Cor. 8:9; 3 John 1:2
loss	redemption	victory	Lev. 25; 1 Cor. 9:24–27; 2 Tim. 2:10
offense	acquittal (or pardon)	forgiveness	Matt. 9:1–7; Rom. 3:23–28; 4:22–25; 10:8–10
sickness	healing	wholeness	Matt. 15:29–31; Luke 4:17–21; 6:18–19; Jas. 5:14–16; 1 Pet. 2: 24
wickedness	justification**	righteousness	Rom. 1:18–3:20; 3:21–26; 4:20–25; 5:1.

* Another outcome of atonement, in addition to reconciliation, is justification.
** Justification is also treated as a remedy for wickedness.

Most (but not all) of the above metaphor sequences can be found in African American evangelical Protestant and Catholic churches. The sequence of difference-deification-likeness is a coordination of metaphors for salvation that one will find emphasized primarily in Orthodox churches. In the Orthodox tradition, humanity's predicament is attributable to our dissimilarity to God. By the process of deification (*theōsis*), we are united with Christ both in his humanity and divinity and thus become like God in character and person, participating fully in the divine nature of God. The biblical references for this and other metaphor sequences are by no means definitive; the selected biblical references in the chart (above) are given merely for illustration of how Scripture may be correlated with the metaphors.

Contemporary black and womanist theology offers both direct and indirect comments on certain metaphor sequences more than on others. Rarely in their discussions of salvation is there an awareness or acknowledgment of the linguistic structure underlying the terms they have selected for emphasis. The terms affirmed or critiqued include atonement, liberation, reconciliation, freedom, re-creation, healing, inclusion, and prosperity.

Atonement

Atonement is the dominate concept for interpreting Jesus Christ's work of salvation. This is the concept used by the New Testament writers to explain Jesus' suffering and death. They use the ritual of atonement (the killing of an animal) to depict Jesus' suffering and death as an appeasement of God's anger that restores the broken covenant (Rom. 3:24–26; 5:9; Heb. 10:1–18). Like the majority of Christians throughout the history of Christianity, African American believers have utilized the concept of atonement to talk about God's saving work.

In James Cone's *God of the Oppressed* and *The Cross and the Lynching Tree,* he says that Jesus' death was a sacrifice for the liberation of the oppressed, whose condition is one of physical and figurative death. Cone utilizes the death-resurrection-life metaphor sequence in order to emphasize that the oppressed are not only being liberated for freedom but also being restored to life. The cross of Christ reveals the extent of God's involvement in the suffering and pain of the oppressed. The resurrection of Christ is a sign of God's once-and-for-all victory over suffering, death, and the powers of evil represented in the cross. Resurrection is the power of God to bring new life in the here and now and in the hereafter. The resurrection is God's breaking into history in order to open for humanity a divine realization of life beyond those options given by any oppressive social system. The cross is understood best by its correlation to the lynching tree. Lynching is literal and figurative of the horrible death and ruination of life that black people have experienced in America. The cross needs the lynching tree in order to remind American Christians of the suffering and barbarity that is very real in our world. The lynching tree needs the cross, which points to resurrection and the hope of there being a dimension of life beyond the control of the oppressor.

As discussed earlier (in chap. 8), Delores Williams questions the preoccupation of African American Christians with the concept of atonement, especially its use in liberation theology. In addition to Williams's critique of atonement for the misunderstanding it promotes about Jesus' life and vision, the concept of atonement is problematic for three reasons: (1) Its glorification of suffering is likely to make oppressed persons complicit and docile. (2) Atonement is, as the chart shows, within a set of metaphors and models different from those of which liberation is actually part. (3) No one set of metaphors and models alone can exhaust the meaning of salvation. In the broadest possible sense, all metaphors and models, as symbols, point to our ultimate concern about survival and quality of life.

Liberation and Reconciliation

Very early in the black theology movement, James Cone and James Deotis Roberts began a debate about liberation and reconciliation. Cone took the position that liberation precedes reconciliation, insisting that reconciliation between the races commences after blacks have achieved power and equal status with whites. From Cone's point of view, reconciliation between unequal racial groups is impossible and irrational. Roberts took the position that reconciliation precedes liberation.

According to Roberts, the human condition is basically the predicament of estrangement, alienation from God and from each other. Using atonement (the ritual of animal sacrifice) to explain Jesus' crucifixion, salvation is interpreted as forgiveness of sin. The sacrifice (of Jesus' life) appeases God's wrath and brokers reconciliation between human beings and God (Rom. 5:8–11; Col. 1:21–22). Through Jesus' exemplary moral behavior, expressed ultimately in his agape love and martyrdom (death on the cross) for a higher cause (our salvation), we are restored to right relationship with God and each other. When reconciliation is understood eschatologically, reconciliation between the races commences before white racism ceases to exist because of Christ's love operating presently in the hearts of individual black and white Christians.

The debate between Cone and Roberts occurs across two sets of metaphors. Within the internal logic of each metaphor sequence, they are both right. Given that Christianity has historically privileged atonement and that the estrangement-atonement-reconciliation metaphor sequence identifies reconciliation as the outcome leading to human flourishing, it stands to reason that reconciliation is privileged in Christian theology. Cone's claim that liberation precedes reconciliation is correct when the basic structure of the metaphor sequence is taken into consideration. Liberation is a method for salvation, whereas reconciliation is an outcome that defines salvation. The debate between Cone and Roberts may be interpreted as a clash between two systems of rhetoric, with each having its own unique grounding in metaphor and preference for modeling salvation.

Freedom

The Christian interest in sin is attributable, in large part, to the human concern about the barriers to and misuses of freedom (human agency) and the human quest for fulfillment, which is impossible apart from the proper exercise of freedom (human agency). A large part of humanity's existential crisis has to do with the challenge of discerning how to use its freedom, individually and collectively. Thus the major dilemma of human existence revolves around the question of agency: What must persons do with their freedom?

As an outcome that names salvation, freedom is wedded to the concepts of self-actualization and self-realization. Freedom is distinguishable from liberation, that is, the means utilized for emancipating persons from bondage. Cone defines freedom as the liberty for self-actualization, where the self is defined by the image of God (*imago Dei*).[16] To be free is to be black in the manner in which God seeks to use one's blackness in the fulfillment of that person's existence in the world. Anthony Pinn names this freedom "complex subjectivity," that is, black existence in a variety of modes.[17] Pinn says, "Sin . . . has to do with the objectification of the body or body collective in such a way as to render its significance relegated to its one dimensionality as an instrument of others' enjoyment or abuse."[18] Freedom is African Americans' privilege to live as they wish, without restriction to a singular identity imposed on each of them or to one feature of any individual's personhood. As African Americans truly exist and seek to thrive in the various social spaces where they live, they are different in gender, sexual orientation, educational attainment, income status, religious beliefs, cultural traditions, and numerous other areas of life.

Re-creation

According to Karen Baker-Fletcher, salvation is transformation of the world. She describes the predicament of human existence as our plight in a world with horrible and disorienting evil. God is re-creating, better still, bringing the creation of the world into its completion. God is involved in a dance with the universe. The divine dance is the creative, liberating, and healing activity that overcomes evil.[19] The good that God seeks to bring from the dance is inevitable.[20]

Healing

Monica Coleman defines salvation as the wholeness that happens in and through community.[21] The activities in community that bring salvation include the healing of mental and physical illness, teaching by personal testimony of God's healing, remembering the past and honoring the ancestors, and possession by the Spirit. Salvation is not an individual attainment. One can witness to being saved because one is a participant in a community that acts upon the vision and possibilities that God offers, time and time again.

Inclusion

Inclusion is a catchword in current liberation-oriented discourses in theology. This catchword, when incorporated into the framework of salvation, is key to interpreting the enormity and agony of marginalization in our society. In the exclusion-adoption-inclusion sequence, the concept of exclusion refers to the predicament of being disconnected, unrelated, and distant. Adoption is a voluntary act, a legal action to make someone your child. Beyond its literal meaning, adoption refers to any act or actions whereby relationship is established and thus brings persons from or outside the margins into the inner circle of community. Inclusion refers to kinship, belonging, inheritance. The person who is included enjoys not only being in community but also all that the community has to offer to those who are its members.

Prosperity

Despite black and womanist theologians' criticisms of Pentecostal, charismatic, and Word of Faith preachers who define salvation by the outcome of abundance, the so-called prosperity gospel has tremendous appeal in African American churches. The black televangelists and megachurch pastors, whom black and womanist theologians' criticize, are not representative of the many African American preachers espousing modest interpretations of the prosperity theme. The prosperity gospel message is simple: if you accept Jesus Christ as your Lord and Savior and follow God's word, as in the Bible, God will bless you with success, wealth, health, and abundance. The message has appeal for several reasons. First, the message affirms a basic truth about God. In the covenant relationship, God makes promises. God promises to show mercy, offer grace, and bless. Second, the message affirms the essential nature of humans as creatures with freedom. The message affirms persons as agents who can do something about their conditions. This is particularly important, given the fact that civil rights legislation does not automatically result in all persons having equal enjoyment of the goods and services produced in America. Persons like the notion that their enjoyment of life does not depend upon someone else's recognition of their rights. When the law lacks enforcement, they can still thrive. Third, the message is a declaration that faith and spiritual discipline work. The message is pragmatic and hopeful. This proclamation is appealing especially when persons' use of or restriction from the normal social channels for fulfillment has led to their condition of unmet needs and desires. This message is an announcement of empowerment. However, the message is not a communiqué on salvation by works alone. Abundance, as the metaphor sequence shows, is the outcome that follows from blessing, that is, from God's blessings. The believer is blessed for obedience (to God and God's word) and for worship, praise, and sacrifice offered to God. Last, the message appeals to the "spirituality of longing" in African American communities.[22] Racial injustice and economic inequality have combined to frustrate African Americans' attainment of the American dream, as defined by a certain quality of material and financial well-being. They experience poverty, abject and relative, in the midst of an affluent society. Even middle-class African Americans lag behind their white middle-class counterparts. The prosperity message appeals to the desire of African Americans wanting to have and wanting to survive and thrive in America.

Common Affirmations about Salvation

In spite of the fluidity (multiple meanings) of salvation, there are three commonly held notions. First, theories of salvation consistently maintain the theme that *Christ saves*. There may be different ideas about how Christ saves, but the affirmation that Christ does save is upheld. Second, theories of salvation consistently maintain the theme that *divine action cannot be substituted or superseded by human action*. To whatever degree the divine act is defined or complemented by human effort, salvation is never thought of as being possible without God's act.

Salvation does not happen without God's activity. Third, theories of salvation consistently maintain the theme that *transformation happens*. After the divine act, change follows. This change is always regarded as a positive result and improvement over the previous state of affairs. Concerns about agency in salvation are expressed in questions about what God does and what human beings do. God's actions are described as or under the topic of grace. Questions about human agency are raised about the meaning and relation between faith and works.

The concepts of sin and salvation are grounded in the recognition of human imperfection and finitude. To repeat: humans are contingent beings, dependent on something else for their existence, and creatures of finitude, beings with limitations. In the environment that forms our world, we are not the only agents with freedom. There are many entities and forces over which we have little or no control. To seek salvation is to acknowledge the conditions of human existence yet to strive for connection with the ground of our being and, in so doing, transcend what appears before us as a barrier to our existence and quality of life.

SALVATION AND COMMUNITY

Olin Moyd claims that salvation is "the root and core motif in Black theology."[23] According to Moyd, salvation means liberation and community.[24] Having defined salvation in this way, sin is estrangement from God that is manifest in human pride (our standing in the place of God), the denial of other persons' humanity, cooperation with systems of oppression that diminish the quality of or destroy human life, and the refusal to participate in God's work of redemption in the world.[25] God is liberating, freeing persons, with the ultimate aim of creating just community, local and global, for the survival and fulfillment of all persons. The liberated person is free from control by others and is a self-determining agent in community. The meanings of community and the moral conduct that characterizes life in just community are discussed in the next chapter.

Questions for Discussion

1. In what way is personal sin distinct from but yet related to social sin? Can a person be guilty of personal sin but innocent of social sin, and vice versa? Is one ever worse than the other?

2. Given the centrality of the concept of atonement in New Testament interpretations of the cross, not to mention the almost exclusive focus on atonement in the history of Christian thought about salvation, which alternative concept or metaphor has the highest probability of gaining acceptance in African American churches?
3. How well or poorly does the correlation of the cross of Christ and the sufferings of black people make the gospel meaningful, relevant, and of consequence to contemporary American society, which is now more multiethnic, plural, and inclusive than at any other time in its history?

Suggested Reading

Coleman, Monica A. *Making a Way out of No Way: A Womanist Theology*. Minneapolis: Fortress Press, 2008.

Cone, James H. *The Cross and the Lynching Tree*. Maryknoll, NY: Orbis Books, 2011.

Moyd, Olin P. *Redemption in Black Theology*. Valley Forge, PA: Judson Press, 1979.

10
Moral Life and Community

This chapter turns to the topic of morality, in particular how faith in Jesus Christ and how the church as a sign of the community that God is creating inform ethical actions on various social and political issues. Morality is not, however, a matter of concern only to Christians. All persons, Christian and others, have a vested interest in morality, if defined as conduct influenced by that which is regarded as a value. Whatever is deemed to be of great importance has value. Persons value life, freedom, justice, community, knowledge, truth, family, work, friendship, and democracy. The list can go on. There are many things that persons value and that are of consequence for how they live and relate to one another. In black and womanist theology, liberation and freedom seem to hold priority over, or suggest a pattern of, organization of additional and related values.

This chapter makes a limited examination of morality and moral values. The coverage of the chapter includes the relation of black solidarity to the concept of community; images of the church, in particular those of the church as community and moral conscience of society; the meaning of freedom and its expression in morality and ethics; and opinions on the use of violence in the struggle for liberation.

BLACK SOLIDARITY AND COMMUNITY

The black population of the United States has never been a monolithic, undifferentiated group. Class division between slaves and free blacks, though some free blacks experienced unemployment and poverty, emerged early and slowly increased during the period of slavery. Today, especially since the civil rights movement flourished, the black middle class is larger than it has ever been yet equals the underclass in number. Class division is evident in and contributes to the widening disparities in education, income, wealth, and housing. After the Emancipation Proclamation on January 1, 1863, and then actual emancipation, many African Americans migrated from the South to the North and to the West. In recent decades, migration has reversed direction and is occurring from the North and the West to the South. The economic and social realities vary from one geographical region to the next. There exist divisions by class, gender, region, ethnicity, and cultural sensibility. Since the 1960s, increasing numbers of Africans and African diasporic peoples have migrated to the United States. The rate of African immigration has doubled each decade since that time.[1]

Since the Immigration and Nationality Act of 1965, a substantial and rising number of Africans, with the largest contingency from Kenya, Nigeria, Ethiopia, and Ghana, have settled in the United States. Another significant wave of immigration has come from blacks in the Caribbean, mainly from Jamaica, Haiti, Trinidad and Tobago, Dominican Republic, and Barbados. They are preserving and perpetuating their language, religion, and culture. Recent African and Afro-Caribbean immigrants have not assimilated into the native-born African American population (as they did when their numbers were smaller) but instead have formed communities to continue their unique religious and cultural traditions, which may or may not be Christian. About 40 percent of these immigrants are college-educated persons and in the professional class. They are sending money (U.S. dollars) back home. This flow of money is indicative of their affinities, attachments, commitments, and political concerns.

In Eugene Robinson's *Disintegration: The Splintering of Black America*, he identifies four divisions among African Americans.[2] They are the transcendent elite, the mainstream middle, the emergent groups, and the abandoned minority. The transcendent elite are the upper-class blacks—mostly athletes, entertainers, media personalities, corporate executives, and high-ranking politicians—who are financially secure, insulated from the fluctuations in the American economy. The mainstream is comprised of the black middle and working classes, with incomes comparable to their white counterparts but lacking in the same level of material wealth and assets. The two emergent groups are the biracial persons and recent black immigrants who are varied by class. The abandoned minority are those blacks, mostly in the inner cities, who are at or below the poverty line and have not benefited as much as other blacks from the changes resulting from the civil rights movement of the 1960s. In view of these class differences, African Americans are increasingly reluctant to consider themselves as belonging to a single race or ethnic group.

Though the black population is diverse, the narrative of slavery is central to defining black identity in the United States. This central narrative is the story of the enslavement of Africans and their descendants, who by law were declared to be chattel (property) and who struggled to be recognized as both fully human and fully citizen. The narrative preserves the memory of how and under what conditions Africans en masse were introduced to America. This account has a moral dimension in that it demonstrates the injustices of chattel slavery and the racism in the American experiment in democracy. Slavery violated the fundamental principle of the American Revolution, that all persons are created equal and entitled to freedom. The American nation's struggle to resolve the contradiction of slavery and later struggles to follow the dictates of democracy is a theme that invites reflection on the purposes or ends of life in America.

Among African Americans, community has meant black solidarity, a kind of racial solidarity or black unity. For example, the sense of bond across class and other differences was declared by the delegates to the Colored National Convention of 1848: "We are one people, chained together. We are one people—one in general complexion, one in common degradation, one in popular estimation. As one rises, all must rise. . . . Every one of us should be ashamed to consider himself free, while his brother is a slave."[3] Frederick Douglass also expressed this communal feeling and shared suffering with the black masses. In Douglass's newspaper, *The North Star*, he wrote: "We are one, . . . our cause is one, and . . . we must help each other, if we should succeed."[4]

Community has been influenced and shaped by authoritarianism and individualism. African American leaders have advocated the notion of authoritarian collectivism in African American social and cultural life.[5] The black masses are to be led by a black elite. Racial unity and loyalty are valued over individualism. According to W. E. B. Du Bois, "The history of the world is the history, not of individuals, but of groups, not of nations, but of races."[6] Individuals are representative of the groups to which each belongs. Individuals are expected to subordinate their personal interests to the larger goals of the group. Under the ideal of individualism, the African American community is perceived as an aggregate of individuals.[7] Such a community is structured around personal initiative, self-assertion, self-determination, and self-reliance. In either case, whether under authoritarianism or individualism, emphasis is placed on strong leadership from an elite class. Alexander Crummell, W. E. B. Du Bois, and certain other black thinkers argued that this leadership should consist of scholars, philosophers, cultural historians, and statisticians. But Frederick Douglass, Booker T. Washington, and other practical black leaders argued that this leadership should consist of agronomists, economists, engineers, technicians, and bureaucrats.[8]

The concept of beloved community has been employed in African American religious thought in order to shape the meaning of black solidarity and connect with a larger project of unity among humans. Recently Victor Anderson has argued that, in African American religious experience, persons are not indiscriminately seeking a new or alternative community; they are seeking beloved community. Anderson uses the concept of creative exchange, which was discussed in chapter 5, in order to define beloved community. By creative exchange, Anderson means the orientation by and toward community represented in God's capacity to bring harmony, wholeness, and integration. He argues that, in human society, this vision of relationship is best described as beloved community.

The term "beloved community" was popularized by Martin Luther King Jr. but first coined by Josiah Royce. By use of the adjective "beloved," Royce is emphasizing individuals' loyalty (devotion) to community, love of community, and search for community. Beloved community is "universal" community in the sense of (1) the inclusion and affirmation of all persons and (2) an ideal and objective that is relevant to all human societies. Human groups become community with shared memory, shared hope (a vision of the future), the involvement of persons in the process of interpretation aimed at seeking truth, and the demonstration of loyalty, which is a love of and sacrifice for community once it is formed. Individuals then become a "community of

memory," "community of hope," and "community of interpretation."
Humans are not content to merely exist in a group but want life in
that group to be characterized by a certain quality in relationships.
For both Royce and King, beloved community is the ultimate goal of
human life (all human striving), the creation of an inclusive community where all persons are able to develop and realize their potential.[9]
For King, "beloved community" is the norm (model, pattern, or measure) and goal (ultimate stage of development) for human society. The
American dream, though not exactly the same as beloved community,
is in several respects compatible with the idea of beloved community
and has the potential for moving human civilization toward a greater
quality of life and/or the beloved community itself. Long before King
would make this application of the concept to life in America, Royce
claimed that beloved community has the capacity to breed patterns
and networks of organization in society well beyond the church from
where it begins.[10]

Though the term "beloved community" has appeal in African American religious thought, the meaning of community for most African
Americans still revolves around the concept of black solidarity, a term
that is difficult to define. The African American philosopher Tommie
Shelby offers a solution to the dilemma of African Americans' wanting
to hold on to the idea of black solidarity but experiencing difficulty
and controversy with the commonplace notions of black solidarity that
circulate among the African American population.

In Tommie Shelby's *We Who Are Dark*, he states that there are
two principal views of black solidarity: (1) the view that black people
are a distinct, politically autonomous subnation or subculture in the
United States; and (2) the view that black people are a community
bordered by race, seeking pragmatic ways to eradicate the stigma of
race from the United States.[11] In view 2, solidarity is possible without a common black ethnocultural identity. Shelby warns against the
dangers of a "groupthink" mentality in view 1.[12] For view 2, Shelby
recommends a form of "pragmatic nationalism," which he calls "transinstitutional black solidarity."[13] Instead of trying to build solidarity on
the basis of physical characteristics, religion, culture, language, and so
forth, this transinstitutional black solidarity is focused on mobilizing
persons (who are African American and of other ethnicities) for action
on "black interests," especially on addressing the ideology and structures of injustice detrimental to black peoples.[14]

THE CHURCH AS COMMUNITY
AND MORAL CONSCIENCE

W. E. B. Du Bois stated that, for African Americans, their churches constitute an all-encompassing institution.[15] The church remains the central institution in African American communities. However, it is unlikely to have this centrality in the realm of politics and culture. The church faces competition from other institutions, not to mention the internal problems that distract from its mission and rob its potential for impact.

According to Dwight Hopkins, economic globalization today functions like a religion.[16] Hopkins defines religion as a system of beliefs and practices centered on a god, recognized leadership, and institutional organization.[17] Within a religion, there are specified values, justifications of its beliefs and practices, and commended ways of attaining knowledge of its god's nature and purpose.[18] He says that the god of globalization is monopoly finance capitalism, which concentrates wealth in the hands of the few and beyond the reach of government control. The religious leadership of globalization is this small group of persons who own and control the world's wealth as well as the means by which this wealth is produced. The institutions of globalization are the World Trade Organization, the International Monetary Fund, the World Bank, and multinational corporations. The religion of globalization leads to the creation of a world culture where the humanity (value and worth) of the person is based on their participation in the economy and their accumulation of commodities sold by major corporations and businesses.

Capitalism and consumerism have the effect of bending all cultural institutions, including Christian churches, toward materialism. This materialism is seen in those congregations that embrace the prosperity gospel as well as in the youth culture obsessed with "bling-bling," the sound of a cash register when a purchase, usually an expensive one, is made for an item that can signify status and importance. Prosperity gospel has flourished because of its use of a basic metaphor for salvation (discussed in chap. 9) and the tradition of venerating leadership in African American churches. African Americans have often well rewarded their religious leaders and lived vicariously through their leaders' material success. As Du Bois noted in *The Souls of Black Folk*, the preacher is a key figure in shaping African American religious experience. Many young people are attracted to a commercially driven global hip-hop culture that often is at odds with the morality and social responsibility taught in Christian churches. At its worst, hip-hop "exudes a hedonistic spirit and oppositional outlook which challenges conventional Christian morality. Uninhibited expressions of sexuality, confrontational human behavior, and outlaw identities are dominant aspects of global Hip Hop culture."[19] Cornel West says that the political engagement of American youth is unlikely until they first overcome disillusionment, addictions (to drugs, alcohol, and sex), and the market-driven media, which bombards youth with amusements, sensual and overly sexualized imagery, and glorification of individualism, materialism, and violence.[20]

Another force that competes with the church is social media, although some congregations make effective use of social media to reach people. The youth are increasingly organizing in social media (i.e., Facebook, Twitter, etc.) instead of the church. People are connected electronically through communication technology but are more isolated and alienated socially and empathically than at any other time in history. Some churches have utilized TV, Internet, and radio to form "virtual communities." The downside of the churches' use of social media is the absence of exemplars in prophetic ministry and social justice. The churches, mostly megachurches, that are on the cutting edge of Internet communication and television production are nondenominational (or loosely connected to a denomination) and lack the long history and role models (heroic figures) for ministry in social justice. Martin Luther King Jr. lamented that science and technology are outpacing human moral development.[21]

For King, as with other African American theologians, the church is the moral conscience of society but, without reform, does not fully realize this potential. As early as 1904, four decades after the close of the Civil War and the period to which most historical black institutions trace their origins, African American intellectuals were dismayed by the ethos of the Negro (later the black) church. At the 1904 meeting of the American Negro Academy, Orishatukeh Faduma (christened William J. Davis) presented a paper titled "The Defects of the Negro Church."[22] The defects that Faduma identified and described were the following: superficial, external display of religion rather than contemplation and piety, neglect of the rural churches as the United States was undergoing urbanization, a lack of seminary-trained ministers, poorly discipled and passive laity, and excessive emotionalism. Faduma recommended the opposites of each defect and called for curbing the excesses in the church. Today, King would likely recommend that churches

(1) find new ways of interpreting and practicing its worship traditions; (2) cooperate with government, at various levels, but maintain its independence so that it can carry out its mission on its own terms; (3) utilize its resources (including money and assets) and influence for the common good; and (4) ground its ministry in the prophetic (justice) tradition as exemplified by the Hebrew prophets and Jesus' own vision and proclamation of the kingdom of God.[23]

In order for African American churches to truly function as the base for liberation, freedom, and justice, black and womanist theologians have suggested several reforms in the belief, worship practices, organizational structures, and worship of African American churches. In Victor Anderson's words, he would say that the church is grotesque: it is ambiguous, a place from where great good as well as great harm comes. Confident of the good that can emerge from the church, he and other African American theologians further recommend a number of improvements.

Given the centrality of African American churches, several reforms and initiatives are required in order for these institutions to truly function as a base for personal and social transformation in African American communities. Cornel West contends that the churches alone cannot achieve liberation. They must partner with other institutions such as families, schools, businesses, and communication organizations in order to achieve wide-scale social change.[24] James Cone argues that reforms within the churches and the achievement of black solidarity must precede coalition building. He has in mind a number of specific reforms in the belief, worship, practices, organizational structures, and ministry of African American churches.[25] Among these reforms are: reallocation of time and resources for greater investments in transformational ministry, self-criticism of the church's own beliefs and practices, improvements in the seminary education and training of ministers, improvement in denominational/ecumenical relations, and eradication of sexism and other forms of discrimination within the churches' domain. All womanists have stressed the need for African American churches to address the problem of sexism and the exclusion of women from ordained ministry and key leadership positions in the churches. When African American churches truly function as the church, they are the people of God, proclaiming the gospel, working for the liberation of the oppressed, and being a model and manifestation of the new humanity in Jesus Christ.[26] The mission and ministry of the black church is variously conceived but mainly focused on enabling African

Americans to enjoy full participation in American society and more importantly to be fulfilled in their humanity.

THE ETHICS OF FREEDOM IN CHURCH AND SOCIETY

According to Carlyle Stewart, African American spirituality is a practice of freedom. He says that it is "a process, a style of existence, a mode of consciousness and being which [enables] black Americans to survive."[27] It gives rise to a way of being in the world. African American theologians and ethicists have delineated the moral and ethical expression of this spirituality of freedom in a distinct set of virtues, themes, values, and principles.

Virtues

According to Peter Paris, African and African American ethics is a "virtue ethics" and is concerned primarily with the development of moral character. Paris identifies six moral virtues of African and African American peoples. These moral virtues are (1) beneficence: facilitating the well-being of others and the community; (2) forbearance: patience and tolerance, perseverance in the struggle for good; (3) practical wisdom: the best thought that guides good action; (4) improvisation: creativity, ingenuity, adaptability/flexibility to new or changing situations; (5) forgiveness: refusal to hate or harbor long-term resentments; and (6) justice: fulfilling obligations to others in community and the community's obligations to its members and to itself.[28] To Paris's six virtues, Henry Mitchell would add (7) perseverance: enduring even when confronted with challenges and the ensuing feelings of despair.[29]

Themes

In African American religious thought, several recurring themes influence moral life and the meaning of community. These themes were discussed earlier (in chap. 3). When stated propositionally, these themes are that (1) African American Christianity is an authentic expression of Christianity; (2) African American people are special (distinct, having qualities not found in other peoples); (3) community (black solidarity) is vital for liberation, survival, and quality of life; and (4) education (literacy and knowledge) is a path to freedom.

Values

Martin Luther King Jr. foresaw the need of morality and suggested a set of moral values to resist the great evils in the world. His ideals are vital for forming a critique of the troubling trends in globalization, as described by Hopkins. Based on a reading of King's speeches and writings, a global ethic that affirms human dignity would entail (1) learning how to sustain diversity in positive and meaningful ways, (2) overcoming materialism and greed, and (3) nurturing an adherence to the idea that the resolution of conflict by the use of nonviolence is far better than resorting to war.

Aware of the conflicting tendencies of values in American society, King called for a "revolution in values."[30] According to King, a revolution of values means bringing the democratic ideals from the bottom (or periphery) to the top (or center) and giving priority to these values as a way of preserving our other moral values and thereby better facilitating our survival and fulfillment. The revolution of values is about establishing priorities within our system of moral values.

The values recommended by King and the values to which we ought to give priority are the following: (1) life: the dignity and worth of human life, (2) freedom, (3) justice, (4) equality, and (5) community. "We must "shift from a 'thing'-oriented society to a 'person'-oriented society."[31] The infinite and uncompromised dignity of human life and the sacredness of all life must be at the center of our social activity. For King, the very essence of being human is freedom.[32] He defines freedom as the capacity to deliberate alternatives, the capacity to choose or decide, and the capacity to take responsibility for those choices, for bad or good.[33] The rules of our social institutions must change. Power and resources must be reallocated. For King, justice is more than a balance of competing interests: justice is also a continual questioning of the fairness of past and present policies.[34] The value of equality is realized in a world without poverty, a world where every family is guaranteed of having an annual "livable" income.[35] King came to realize that state and federal minimum-wage standards were too low to ensure that the average worker can afford education, healthcare, food, transportation, and decent housing. For King, community is characterized by open-mindedness, acceptance of diversity, a vision of the common good, being moral and respectful toward one another, and demonstrating loyalty to humankind that supersedes loyalty to one's own tribe, nation, ethnic group, or part of the world.[36] For King, life, freedom, justice, equality, and community are not to be our only values; they are, however, to be the values that take precedence over the rest of our moral values.

Like King, Robert Franklin suggests that priority be given to certain values in order for African American communities to thrive. In the context of Franklin's work, a value is something highly important, so much so that it influences our behavior. A value is something (1) that we seek to obtain or preserve, (2) that we admire and respect, (3) for which we long, (4) that is indivisible, and (5) that cannot be compromised. Since the priorities recommended by Franklin may advise or influence the way we relate to each other, they are called "moral values." In Franklin's *Crisis in the Village: Restoring Hope in African American Communities*, he centers moral value in family (love and commitment), church (spirituality and mission), and college (moral purpose). In Franklin's strategies, renewal will involve the steps of dialogue, collaboration, vision and planning, accountability and action, allocation of resources for new initiatives and policy changes, and documentation and celebration of success.[37]

Principles

One principle asserted is that of loving the body. As mentioned in chapter 6, African American religion scholars, including black and womanist theologians, are giving new meaning to the affirmation of liberation in the statement "I am my body." They are increasingly emphasizing the principle that the black body should be loved and appreciated instead of being ignored and scorned. Inspired by Alice Walker's definition of womanism—which includes a black woman's love of other women, the community, the spirit, and herself—African American women theologians have likewise emphasized this love of the black body, female yet also male. In African American theology, love of the black body is expressed in scholarship that values human embodiment (the way humans actually exist in their bodies in time and space) as a way of studying social and political bodies.

Stephen Ray proposes rules for ethical conduct based on his study of the harm, potential and actual, in the language about sin. Patterns of oppression may be intensified when the so-called sinner is viewed as a corrupting influence, one who is thought to be irresponsible and defiled.[38] The problem with sin-talk is that it situates persons in a socially marginalized condition not of their making. Sin-talk imputes guilt. Persons with little or no control of the formation of public discourse may be blamed for problems in society that they did not create. Some of the worst of sin-talk has been targeted at homosexuals and the poor. In order to redeem sin-talk from its misuse in American society, Ray recommends that theologians follow four rules: (1) Do not seek only your own privilege: examine and confess how sin-talk serves your own interests. (2) Follow the money: examine how sin-talk benefits other persons' interests. (3) Heal thyself: examine and confess how one's own contexts and actions might be reinforcing the marginalization of persons labeled as sinners. (4) Listen to the sinner: as a corrective to your own sin-talk, incorporate the perspectives of marginalized persons into your perspective.[39]

In African American churches and communities, there is a practice of identifying certain persons as exemplars of the moral virtues, themes, values, and principles mentioned above. These persons form what Victor Anderson calls "the cult of black heroic genius."[40] The meanings of moral and ethical action are inseparable from the admiration accorded to the persons who demonstrate the moral agency that the churches and communities commend for their members. For example, the circle of African Americans admired by black and womanist theologians includes Martin Luther King Jr., Malcolm X, W. E. B. DuBois, Fannie Lou Hamer, Jarena Lee, Zora Neale Hurston, and Sojourner Truth. In addition to actual historical persons, Dwight Hopkins claims that characters in black folklore are models of moral and ethical action.[41] These fictional characters include Brer Rabbit, the Conjurer, and Outlaw figures such as Shine and Stagolee. Another hero in African American folklore is John, sometimes called John the Conqueror, High John the Conqueror, or High John, who evades his master, outsmarts the Devil, or devises clever ways to beat the system.[42]

VIOLENCE IN THE STRUGGLE FOR LIBERATION

According to Carlyle Stewart, African American spirituality expresses itself in mercy and nonviolence.[43] Blacks have not resorted to whole-scale violence against whites. There have been incidences of violence but never extending for a long period of time or amounting to success.

Other African American theologians have taken positions as well on the use of violence.[44] James Cone argues that violence, in the form of self-defense, is permissible. James Deotis Roberts and Major Jones maintain that under no conditions is violence ever moral or ethical for Christians. Thus Roberts and Major Jones take a position that resonates with Martin Luther King Jr.'s absolute commitment to nonviolence and total rejection of violence. For Major Jones, the sanctity of human life is absolute; under no conditions is killing permissible. William R. Jones takes the position that violence, as a strategy for liberation, cannot be dismissed if it can be shown that the use of violence will emancipate an oppressed people.

Moral and ethical action not only emerges from the sense or intuition of what is right but is also called forth and pursued in hope for the change sought. Persons hope for change to come soon. They hope as well for the change to come in the distant future. This hope has been given many names: the American dream, beloved community, the second coming, and heaven. In the next chapter, we turn to an examination of hope, variously named and intensely desired.

Questions for Discussion

1. How, in African American spirituality, do believers grow in grace and holiness?
2. Could personal transformation and meaningful religious experience occur in the lives of believers without the reforms of the black church suggested by African American theologians?
3. In which ways does the church best model community?
4. What is the relation of black solidarity to broadly cast global visions of human unity? Is anything lost in the shift of focus from black solidarity to global community?
5. How might the various stipulated moral virtues, values, themes, and principles be integrated into a single ethical perspective?

Suggested Reading

Fluker, Walter E. *Ethical Leadership: The Quest for Character, Civility, and Community*. Minneapolis: Fortress Press, 2009.

King, Martin Luther, Jr. *In a Single Garment of Destiny: A Global Vision of Justice*. Edited by Lewis V. Baldwin. Boston: Beacon Press, 2014.

Sanders, Cheryl J. *Empowerment Ethics for a Liberated People*. Minneapolis: Fortress Press, 1995.

Warnock, Raphael G. *The Divided Mind of the Black Church: Theology, Piety, and Public Witness*. New York: New York University Press, 2014.

11
Hope

Whereas William R. Jones contends that theodicy is the central category of black theology, Olin Moyd argues that eschatology is the basic category. Eschatology is vision not only of a certain end but also of a people's true humanity. This vision inspires people to moral and ethical action in pursuit of the object of their longing. Their efforts, no matter how small or frustrated, are not futile. Whatever they fail to achieve at any particular moment does not diminish the certitude that they have about the eventual outcome of history. Eschatology represents a perspective not only on what God does in the past or present but also on what God does in the future. This perspective is encased in a grand narrative of divine action, viewing the entire course of the universe's history. It is a story of hope: longing for and dreaming of a place in the future being fashioned by God.

In addition to Moyd, other theologians and religion scholars have emphasized the importance and implications of eschatology in African American churches. This chapter examines some of their interpretations of eschatology. Covered in this chapter are topics of the meanings of hope, the casting of vision or imaginings of alternatives to the existing social order, traditions of millennialist thought, belief about heaven and the afterlife, and the use of eschatology for verification of religious beliefs.

HOPE AS OBJECT AND LONGING

Hope is both the *object* for which persons long as well as the *longing* they have for the object. There are, therefore, two things that are crucial to defining hope. First is the task of identifying the object. This task can be expressed as a question: *For what do persons hope?* Second is the task of articulating the longing for the object. This second task can also be expressed as a question: *What affections and actions are aroused in response to and in quest of the object of hope?*

African American theologians employ Christian eschatology for articulation and critique of ideas about human destiny, particularly those visions of and aspirations for an improved future. Black theologians, as well as other African American thinkers, have developed conceptions of an ideal form of society and/or culture—which might be located in the past, present, or future—for use as a norm for judgment, model for reform, and/or goal of human life. Some of these conceptions are the "glorious black past," the "American dream," "beloved community," the "millennium," the "second coming of Christ," and the "day of judgment." These concepts not only function for the imagination of an improved human condition but also for inspiring, sustaining, and justifying efforts and thinking toward achieving that ideal human condition.

From a womanist perspective, A. Elaine Brown Crawford defines hope as a bridge.[1] Hope is that which enables black women to journey from oppression to liberation. Hope also enables black women to connect with each other in time and space, linking them to a shared quest for survival and quality of life. According to Crawford, this hope is anchored in Jesus Christ.[2] This hope, a power from God, is a definitive response to the holler of black women. Brown says that the holler of black women is a cry of pain, deep agonizing pain, that refuses to be silenced and can only be calmed by the full recognition and appreciation of black women's humanity.[3] Hope is healing and builds anticipation of new possibilities that God has prepared for the oppressed.

UTOPIAN AND ESCHATOLOGICAL VISION

Presupposing and fundamental to liberation and other inclinations of African American spirituality is the propensity toward utopian and eschatological vision, what I call the mythic dimension of racial consciousness. Here is where the turn to another reality takes place and where belief and hope are born. In turn, the sacred is located. The sacred may provoke, in those who encounter it, a nostalgic longing for recovery of a lost past or dream of a promising future.

According to Charles Long, parallel to the rise of modern Western culture, a mythic world was formed in the imagination of oppressed Africans.[4] The New World had no single hegemonic identity shared by all Europeans. The identity by which Europeans proscribed Africans did not fully affirm their humanity. Brought forcefully and violently into a new and emerging global system, oppressed Africans formed different ideas about American identity. In the Western Hemisphere are several meanings of the term "American" (not just one sense) and differing ideas about the role of America and its future in the world.[5] In the background of the mythic consciousness of these Africans is their sense of (aspirations for) dignity and worth, originating before cultural contact with Europeans. In the foreground is their conception of human community that is not based on racial caste and inequality. Several questions likely guide their reflection: To what extent should those who have endured a history of systemic and legitimized oppression wish to become a part of and continue such a system? Do the oppressed imagine a world of possibility for what America can be? Do they imagine and strive for a place of destiny beyond or after America?

More than a mere basis for critique of social structures and cultural ideas that adversely affect the lives of people of African descent, black mythic consciousness is a locus for the sacred. With the gaze into another world, God is found and encountered. God substantiates the reality of something, somewhere, or someone other than what is. Yet God is an altogether different reality. Mythic consciousness not only imagines God but also produces new conceptions of humanity and community consistent with its understanding of God. This new humanity, partially realized in gatherings of the oppressed, is thought to come into fruition sometime in the future.

Black mythic consciousness is expressed by using Christian symbolism. Africans' first exposure to Christian symbolism was in the religious meanings that Europeans gave to their journey and settlement of the Americas. In the United States, British millennialism and apocalypticism construed the settlement of the Americas as a divinely inspired and guided mission, favoring the expansion of a new people and new country entitled to opportunity and wealth. Excluded from this entitlement were African slaves as well as Native Americans. Oppressed

Africans dreamed of another world. For example, in slave spirituals and David Walker's *Appeal*, there are different correlations of Christian eschatology to racial consciousness.[6] Many Spirituals depict Jesus as king and warrior, for example, in statements such as "Ride on, King Jesus. No man can hinder thee" and "He's a battle axe in the time of war." Walker describes Jesus as the King of heaven and earth and God of justice who will soon punish racial injustice. The kingdom of God, lying in the future, is peopled with ancestors and friends and described by using imagery that depicts it as home, a place where freedom is abundant, inequality is nonexistent, and all needs and desires are fulfilled.[7] In Christian churches, during worship, Jesus Christ comes to the black community in the ecstasy of worship.[8] The joys of life in Christ, experienced in the here and now, are regarded as but a foreshadowing of God's eventual transformation of the world, a time when the wicked are punished and the righteous are rewarded.[9] During the worship event, the worshiper experiences ecstasy that, in turn, reveals how human life is or should be characterized by joy, pleasure, and fulfillment. The worship experience confirms God's existence and accentuates the dignity and worth that God places upon the lives of the worshipers. The aim or permanent condition of human life is not misery and unhappiness, though conditions may appear that way for persons beset with suffering and hardship. Besides revealing the aim and divine will for human life, celebrative worship gives persons a "taste" of the ultimate joy, deliverance, or prosperity that is to come.

TRADITIONS OF BLACK MILLENNIALISM

Christian eschatology is defined and refined through Christian millennialism (or chiliasm) that interprets the eschaton (the second coming of Christ) in terms of the millennium, a "golden age" or "paradise" on Earth, mentioned in the book of Revelation, chapter 20. Based on convictions about when Christ will return (before the millennium, after it, or not at all in connection with it), Christian millennialism divides into three perspectives: (1) premillennialism, in two forms, (a) classical or nondispensational and (b) dispensational; (2) postmillennialism; and (3) amillennialism.

The three conceptions of Christian millennialism emerged at different times in the history of Christianity. The very idea of a millennium took hold in the second century. In the first century, the early

Christians believed that their life between the "already" and the "not yet" was the only era linking the resurrection of Jesus Christ to his second coming. They therefore thought that in their lifetime they would witness the return of Jesus Christ. As the decades passed and Christianity entered the second century, Christians believed that Jesus Christ would return in their era but thought that their present era would extend for a millennium (a thousand-year period) before the end of the world. In the fourth century, Augustine of Hippo argued that the millennium is a symbolic number and represents the current church age. For Augustine, Jesus Christ reigns spiritually on the earth through the church, until his physical return. Augustine's view, called *amillennialism*, has been adopted by most Christian denominations and has been the dominant eschatological perspective in Christianity from the fourth century unto the present.

In the eighteenth century, in colonial America, the New England Puritans developed a new perspective on the end times. From their point of view, called *postmillennialism*, Jesus will return after a literal thousand-year period of peace and prosperity, a golden age in human civilization. Distinctly American, this eschatological view emphasizes progress (social, economic, and cultural) as the sign of the end and even a way to hasten its coming. The optimism of American postmillennialism was laid to waste in the devastating aftermath of the Civil War, the complications of America's urbanization and industrialization, and the carnage of the First and Second World Wars.

Starting in the nineteenth century, radical Holiness leaders (and later Pentecostals, fundamentalists, and evangelicals) introduced *premillennialism* as an alternative interpretation of the condition of the world and how it will end. Whereas postmillennialists viewed improvement as a sign of the end, premillennialists view deterioration as a sign of the end. In premillennialism, it is believed that Christ will return visibly and bodily before his thousand-year reign on the earth, as stated in Revelation 20. Classical premillennialism is based merely on a literal reading of Revelation 20, which indicates that Christ returns before the millennium. Dispensational millennialism embraces the same idea of Christ's return before the millennium but presupposes that all events in the Bible can be arranged in a schema of dispensations (periods that denote God's chief means of accomplishing salvation). In premillennialism, the church has a limited role in society with respect to social change or social reform, and the church's mission is primarily to evangelize so that individuals may be saved from a world that is doomed to destruction.

In African American churches, millennialism may be expressed in ways not limited to these three perspectives on the nature of the millennium relative to the time of Christ's return. In the eighteenth century, and more so in the nineteenth century, Africans, slave and free, who converted to Christianity were introduced to millennialism in its Puritan postmillennial form. African Americans reworked the New England Puritan religious rhetoric about the future of the United States in order to create their own black millennialism and thereby account for their past experience and secure their future participation in the United States and world history. It is not uncommon to find both Christian millennialism and black millennialism in African American churches. These millennialisms may coexist in tension or in combination.

Black millennialism leans toward Christian postmillennialism in that it regards history as progressive and depicts the millennium as a golden age in human civilization that precedes, and even hastens, the return of Christ. Black millennialism appears in several types: (1) cultural, characterized by belief in transformation of the world through American principles and institutions; (2) racial, espousing belief in black leadership established for God's transformation of the world; and (3) progressive, marked by belief in the power of Christianity to transform the world through evangelism, missions, and social reform.[10] These widely varied types of black millennialism share some common aspirations: (1) belief in an imminent golden age that will start and spread from either the United States or the African continent; (2) belief that history is divinely ordained and controlled by God; (3) belief that the movement of history is progressive; (4) belief that the eradication of racism is of primary importance; (5) belief that the kingdom of God is not identical to Western civilization or Christianity, in view of the injustices against African Americans and the distortion of Christianity to sanction these social injustices; and (6) belief that personal and social change involves human participation in God's plan for transforming the world. These core beliefs of black Christian millennialism are a refinement of themes found in folk sources. In these folk sources, the terms "jubilee," "heaven," "kingdom of God," "millennium," and "golden age" are used, as in black millennialism, to describe possible and actual human experience here on earth.

In contrast to the optimism in postmillennial-oriented black millennialism, some African American believers have been skeptical about the desired golden age. They doubt whether the millennium is an event that actually happens within human history. The views of these skeptics suggest that black millennialism could be aligned with some versions of amillennialism, especially the realist interpretations emphasizing that the millennium is figurative and that the reign of Christ in the millennium is equivalent to the church's present work on behalf of Christ. If the fate of humankind, as these critics suppose, is solely what we make it, and if the outcome of history is left to chance, humanity is without hope in this life. Against the realism of these critics, believers must look to heaven both here on earth and in another world.

HEAVEN AND THE AFTERLIFE

African Americans overwhelmingly believe in the afterlife. A large number believe, as most Americans do, that heaven is open to all persons, regardless of their religious affiliation or level of personal piety, and even if they do not hold membership in any church. Visions of heaven have been shaped by sermons and songs and displayed in funeral practices, not to mention how the experience of oppression in this life may be a major contributing factor in persons' fixation on the next life in heaven.

From the earliest periods in African American history, when certain spirituals were sung, slaves knew that these songs were coded messages about escape and flight to the North.[11] Heaven was not only above, in the sky, but also north of the Mason-Dixon Line or in Canada, where slaveholding was not sanctioned by law. Heaven is a metaphor for community, where one is reunited with loved ones and is recognized and respected. In heaven, needs and desires are met adequately and fully.

In African American churches, funerals are community events. The death of the individual is not only an occasion to honor the life of the deceased but also to celebrate their "homegoing." The common perception that black funerals are different from those of other peoples in America is confirmed by research that documents the distinctives of these events.[12] Black funerals tend to be lengthy services, not to mention the extended period of visitation with the deceased's family before the funeral service begins. Expectations are that the funeral sermon will not only be comforting but also a rousing address that signifies the presence of the Spirit. The funerals involve the entire (or most) of the community to which the deceased or the deceased person's family members belong. The largest gatherings in churches, when seating capacity is reached and surpassed, are at funerals. Sometimes the funerals show excess and exaggeration to dramatize the lifestyle and importance of the deceased person. The funeral is usually followed by the "funeral banquet," sometimes called "the repast," where members of the community provide for as well as share a meal with the family of the deceased person.

Heaven has multiple meanings. Reunions take place in heaven. Loved ones, family, and friends will be together forever. Heaven yokes the living and the deceased together and securely in a community that transcends the separations caused by death. In song, sermon, and testimony, believers speak about heaven as a place where they will again see mother or another cherished relative or friend. Once they are reunited, they will never again be separated. In heaven, there is no hatred, strife, violence, or war. In heaven, persons "lay down their sword and shield and study war no more." Believing that in heaven there is no sorrow, persons have sung: "Soon I will be done with the troubles of the world. No more weeping and a-wailing. I'm going home to live with God." Heaven represents reward, confirmed in God's pronouncement: "Well, done, thou good and faithful servant." Through talk about heaven, we imagine an alternative way of perceiving and locating the self in a broader expanse of time and space. Thus, through heaven, we re-embody ourselves for life in a larger environment than mundane appearances or events. Heaven is home: it reveals our true identity, purpose of life, and place of belonging. Belief in heaven actually inspires persons in their quest for something better in this life as well as in the life to come.

As heaven's opposite, hell is life undefined and without end. It represents estrangement from self, others, and one's environment. Hell is condemnation to and misery of a private, solitary existence, disconnected from other persons and things necessary for sustaining and enhancing one's life. Thus hell is the locus of death—physical death by the body's demise and spiritual death resulting from nonfulfillment, which in either case is torment.

ESCHATOLOGY AND VERIFICATION
OF RELIGIOUS BELIEFS

Although black mythic consciousness is central in black religion, William R. Jones has criticized the use of eschatology in the verification of religious belief.[13] He argues that the postulation of a future state as verification of belief is insufficient evidence. Reasonable belief requires something in the present, something empirical. Criticism of belief is not possible if verification is constantly postponed into a remote, inaccessible future. Reliance on eschatological verification leads to irrationalism, he declares.

In view of the recent calls of African American theologians for African American churches to be more self-critical, a position of critical anti-evidentialism may be an appropriate response to Jones's critique of Christian eschatology. Critical anti-evidentialism is the view that, if a person already has an adequate basis for their beliefs, then they do not need to give reasons in support of those beliefs but may, in the interest of civility and community, respond to objections against the beliefs. Critical anti-evidentialism is cautiously optimistic, open to revision, and tolerant of opposing views. It is not anti-reason or anti-intellectualism. It does, however, resist the reduction of all knowledge to the outcomes produced through empirical method. Critical anti-evidentialism insists that, just as knowledge produced through empirical method has a right to be considered in cultural dialogue, knowledge produced through other means is entitled to be heard in the same public arena.

In the use of eschatology for framing (structuring) hope, believers must construct their theological interpretations with an awareness of both the positive features of eschatology and those peculiarities of eschatology that invite criticism and disbelief of the Christian gospel. Toward that end, the following four features of eschatology may be offered as an explanation for why it is believed and used in African American churches. First, eschatology is *biblical.* The Bible is an important source of theology. Eschatology is a concept that is present in Scripture and is evident in the New Testament, as in Jesus' preaching and Paul's Letters.

Second, eschatology is *hopeful.* Hope is central to eschatology. The kingdom of God is a symbol of destiny (on earth and/or in the afterlife). Hope in or for the kingdom of God may take the form of comfort or solace in the face of death. Also, hope becomes motivation for faith or a ground of faith, an impetus for action.

Third, eschatology is *moral.* Eschatology conceives a vision of the end (*telos*) that functions as a moral norm as well as the goal of history. The kingdom of God is goal and norm; it is not only a symbol of destiny but also a standard by which to judge social practices and behaviors. Eschatology is a way to talk about ethical standards and social goals. It is often used to ground Christian ethics.

Fourth, eschatology is *historical.* Eschatology is a way of interpreting human history, talking about the future, and talking about what God is doing and will accomplish over time. The final event (the eschaton) of history that triggers the end of the world is the second coming of Jesus Christ. The end of the world marks the beginning of something new and better: the kingdom (rule/reign) of God on earth in its fullness, and along with it is eternal life. In short, Christian eschatology reflects a distinctive view of human history, showing the direction toward which human history is moving.

Jones's criticism is not refuted here, nor is the above explanation of eschatology's features exempt from further questioning. Theology is an attempt to say something meaningful about human experience and the world in which this experience takes. Without fail, theology intersects with other forms of discourse about human experience and the physical world. Aside from the dominance of science in the construction of modern culture, theology cannot avoid engagement with science if theology hopes to gain or maintain any legitimacy as truthful speech in our society. The next chapter explores how African American theology may best engage modern science.

Questions for Discussion

1. Presently for black peoples in the United States, what is the meaning of hope? Does the object (the end) justify the efforts (the means) taken to obtain it?
2. If heaven is purely metaphorical, what can persons say matter-of-factly about the physical world?
3. Is postmillennialism in American millennialism or is a contrasting Christian interpretation of the millennium (Rev. 20:1–7) capable of alignment with the core beliefs of black millennialism?
4. Is premillennialism compatible with the core beliefs of black millennialism?

Suggested Reading

Crawford, A. Elaine Brown. *Hope in the Holler: A Womanist Theology*. Louisville, KY: Westminster John Knox Press, 2002.
Sweet, Leonard I. *Black Images of America, 1784–1870*. New York: W. W. Norton & Co., 1976.
Wilmore, Gayraud S. *Last Things First*. Philadelphia: Westminster Press, 1982.

12
Nature and Science

Following James Cone's lead, contemporary black and womanist theology has not dealt with topics in science and religion. Early in the black theology movement, Cone argued that black theology does not concern itself with metaphysics and philosophical speculation.[1] Issues such as the creation of the universe and God's existence and relation to the physical world were labeled as "white questions" and excluded from black theology. Though well intended, the direction taken by Cone and others has overlooked an important aspect of Christian theology as well as the previous history of African American theology, where such topics are explored. This trajectory has been quite unfortunate. Given that all theological claims about reality and what is real do rest upon certain metaphysical assumptions, at some point these assumptions need to be scrutinized. And a reading of science must be part of this assessment of theological claims. African American theology cannot afford to overlook the long history of African American participation in and contributions to science, technology, mathematics, and philosophy.

Since the early developments in black and womanist theology, more primary sources and documentation of African American thought on science and religion are available. The purpose of this chapter is to acquaint the reader with a few of the topics in science and religion that have been approached from the perspectives of African Americans. The topics covered in this chapter include evolutionary biology and its implications, negative and positive, for race; theology of nature and black environmentalism; and creation and divine action.

PEOPLE OF COLOR AND THE DIALOGUE
ON SCIENCE AND RELIGION

African American Christians' attitudes about science are varied, ranging from fear and fascination to cautious acceptance and benign rejection. This posture is taken even though African Americans have made outstanding contributions in the development of modern science.[2] Edward Alexander Bouchet is the first African American in the United States to have earned a PhD degree (Yale, 1876); his doctorate was in physics. In the cognitive neuroscience field, contributions have been made by black scientists such as George Malcolm Langford, Solomon Carter Fuller, and Roy Davage Hudson. Though known primarily for their skill as neurosurgeons, Alexa Canady, Deborah Maxine Hyde, Jesse Balmary Barber, and Benjamin Carson are very knowledgeable about brain and mental function. Overall, in African American communities, rarely, if ever, is science viewed as absolutely authoritative in the realm of religion, even by persons who highly appreciate science. Religious experience is and remains normative in the realm of African American churches.

Notwithstanding their religious experience, there is a long history of African American Christians' positive engagement with science. In 1881, Daniel Alexander Payne, a bishop of the African Methodist Episcopal Church, founded the Bethel Literary and Historical Society in Washington (D.C.). The organization was dissolved in 1915. For most of the time of its operation, the Bethel Literary and Historical Society met weekly and attracted large audiences. These audiences, sometimes numbering in the hundreds, are indicative of the interest of African Americans in knowledge and hearing the emerging intellectual class share their discoveries and insights with the public. In addition to the large audiences at the public events, Negro newspapers, several with national circulation, carried stories about the topics presented and discussed at the society's meetings. The extant minutes of the Bethel Society show clearly that religion and science and science-related topics were of major concern to African Americans. Included in the minutes are the records of the following lectures and discussions. Professor Isaiah Mitchell, who professed to be a Christian evolutionist, presented a paper titled "Has God Made a Mistake in the Creation of Man?" (June 1885). Dr. L. W. Livingston read a paper titled "The Negro in Science" (October 1885). Dr. J. M. Townsend lectured on the topic "The Evolution of Man" (1889). J. G. Weems presented a paper titled "Science and the Beginnings" (1892). Dr. Richard Foster, Professor of Natural History, Howard University, spoke to the Bethel Society (1894). Mr. Francis L. Cardozo, Ms. Laura G. Wilkes, Mr. Alphonzo O. Stafford, and Ms. Charlotte E. Hunter were panelists on a debate about "Animal Rights" (1890). In 1890, Professor Richard Foster, MD, spoke on the topic "Evolution."

WAYS OF RELATING SCIENCE AND RELIGION

The sampling of talks at the Bethel Literary and Historical Society suggests that African Americans shared the same opinion about science. However, African Americans have adopted a variety of postures toward science. African American thinkers have related science and religion in terms of conflict (John Jasper and Charles Satchell Morris), independence (James Cone and Charles Long), dialogue (Barbara Holmes), and integration (Theophilus Steward and Alma Booker).

In the *conflict model*, the objects and aims of religion and science are the same. Religion and science make conflicting and competing claims. Atheists and archcritics of religion argue that science supersedes religion with respect to an accurate view of reality. Someone like John Jasper, known for his sermon "The Sun Do Move," believes that religion supersedes science (mentioned in chap. 4 above).

This is how Jasper reasons that the sun moves.[3] First, he notes that God made the sun stand still for Joshua in order to enable the Hebrews more hours of daylight, which was crucial for them to gain a decisive victory over their enemies (Josh. 10:12–13). Only that which stops is an object that is in motion. Second, Jasper points to God allowing the shadow of the sundial to move backward as a sign of assurance to Hezekiah that God's word, as spoken by Isaiah, would come to pass (2 Kgs. 20:8–10). The forward and then more amazingly the backward movement of the dial implies that the sun moves also. Third, Jasper argues that the earth is stationary. In the Bible, the earth is said to have four corners (e.g., Isa. 11:12). Anything that has four corners is square. Anything with four corners cannot be circular. A square is flat. So the earth, having four corners, is flat and not round. Fourth, eventually the sun will no longer be needed (Rev. 22:5). There will be a new earth, but there will not be a new sun. Jesus will provide light for the new earth. Fifth, Jasper is critical of scientific estimates of the distance between the sun and the earth. He points out conflicting estimates about the distance between these two objects. Any real distance is one that can be crossed or traversed. If this distance between the sun and the earth is real and to be taken seriously, then there must be a record or means of travel over this distance. Last, Jasper points out, from the Bible itself, that there is no disproof of his claim that the sun moves. Therefore, the sun does move.

Jasper is willing to accept what scientists say about the sun, provided that their claims do not challenge truths from the Bible. He thinks that it is disbelief in God that prevents persons from accepting the notion that the earth is stationary and that the sun moves about it. Jasper's goal is to uplift and not to disgrace African Americans. For Jasper, belief in the word of God, as derived from the Bible, is crucial to the uplift of the race. Science is okay, so long as it makes no claim that intrudes upon religion. Jasper's hope is for his personal transformation and the transformation of the world. Hardly anyone in the modern world believes that the earth is flat or that the sun revolves around the earth. Notwithstanding the critiques of the obvious weaknesses of Jasper's sermon, his position has some merits in that he creatively employs commonsense realism in order to envision an all-powerful God, the Waymaker, who is in control of the universe.

Charles Satchell Morris was renowned for his criticism of evolution. Morris's lecture series "Up from a Monkey or Down from God," like Jasper's sermon, presupposes conflict between religion and science.[4] Morris claims that biological evolution started with a guess in that Charles Darwin began with several speculations before he had obtained facts. Evolution offers explanations for the development of biological organisms but does not explain the origin of matter itself. Thus evolution can only say that living organisms change over time. According to Morris, the evolutionists are making a giant leap in postulating the origin of organisms, a leap that cannot be sustained by facts currently in their possession. The only reasonable explanation for life is that God created it. The confession of faith in God as creator is not made by facts but by faith in the revelation of God recorded in the Bible. Creationists have an appropriate basis for their claims about the origin of life, but evolutionists do not, Morris claims.

In the *independence model*, religion and science represent two entirely separate domains. The objects, aims, and methods of religion and science are utterly different. There is no inherent conflict between religion and science because they are separate enterprises. James Cone and Charles Long adhere to the independence model. Cone espouses a kind of fideism, contending that theologians operate under a system of logic that differs from other forms of rational discourse.[5] Contending that black theology does not concern itself with metaphysics and philosophical speculation, James Cone neglected treatment of topics such as the creation of the universe and God's existence and relation to the physical world. Cone labeled these issues as "white questions" and excluded them from his theological work. According to Cone, the more important question for black theology concerns justice: What is God doing to end injustice in the world? He goes on to explain, "White theologians argued about the general status of religious assertions in view of the development of science generally and Darwin's *Origin of the Species* in particular; blacks were more concerned about their status in American society and its relation to the biblical claim that Jesus came to set the captives free."[6]

Charles Long takes a very different approach in order to affirm the independence model. He argues that the domain of religion is chiefly that of symbol and myth. Certain propositions, such as that the world is created, are myth and not science. Long says that symbols objectify aspects of life and enable us to engage and relate to the mysteries and radical otherness in our world.[7] Myth is storytelling by using symbols. According to Long, "myth thinking" is a way of apprehending the world and is found in any society, regardless of what the current state of scientific knowledge happens to be.[8] With regard to creation myths, these stories express humanity's desire for positioning in the universe and belief that God, who symbolizes the ultimate power of the universe, acts purposefully, lovingly, and redemptively toward humankind.[9] After defining religion as he does, Long says that religion and science are separate and nonsubstitutable domains.

In the *dialogue model*, religion and science are both rational systems of thought, and as such, comparisons and contrasts can be made to show how each follows prevalent canons of rationality. Someone like Barbara Holmes adopts the dialogue model of religion and science.[10] Her intention is to emphasize the differences but also mutual influences between theology and science. She says, "[Ian] Barbour's dialogue category influences [my] study and suggests that 'methodological and conceptual parallels' between the disciplines of theology and science have the potential to enlighten both."[11] So, in principle, she distinguishes yet equally values science and religion.

Holmes's understanding and choice of the dialogue model is influenced by her take on quantum physics, which she suspects truly reveals the nature of reality. According to Holmes, for black liberation to be more than wishful thinking, it must be informed by the realities of the universe and humanity's place within the universe. She insists that a certain question is important for the future of liberation theology: "How can we align social constructions of liberation and justice with emerging cosmic and quantum images?" In response, Holmes says, "Perhaps solutions to social problems should be linked to our efforts to ascertain the intrinsic aspects of reality."[12] Given that more than forty years have passed since the Civil Rights movement flourished and that solutions to racial injustice are still being sought, she recommends that we now seek solutions of a different kind, solutions that emerge from scientific studies of the physical world. In *Race and the Cosmos*, Barbara Holmes argues for the use of science in liberation theology. From a sort of moral realism, she argues that equality is natural and should be pursued because, in nature, nothing is absolute; things are in constant change; and the least thing, as in chaos theory, may contribute to significant change (development) on a higher level.

In the *integration model*, religion and science each represent a partial grasp of reality and as such are needed for humans gaining a larger, fuller, and more accurate understanding of the world. An example of the integration model is found in Theophilus Steward's *Genesis Re-Read* (1885), the first African American scholarly theological text, although crude by today's standards. Steward weaves together the languages of science and religion in order to create a plausible explanation of creation.

Alma Booker developed a critique of Morris and a defense of evolution.[13] Though Booker's perspective is described here as an integration model, her position could as easily be identified as an independence model. Alma Booker's critique of Morris's antievolutionism spread to African American churches at the time of the Scopes Trial. Her critique, which like Morris's argument is not based on a sophisticate level of scientific knowledge, is nonetheless a case for how the belief in creation may be reconciled with biological evolution. She argues that evolution could be interpreted as the means by which God chose to create—which eliminates any supposed conflict between religion and science.

While African Americans, like other people of faith, may adopt any of these models, there seems to be a major contrast, maybe even a fundamental tension, between Christian eschatology and scientific cosmology concerning the future of the world. The Christian claim is that the universe has a promising future; that the universe will be transformed, becoming better; and that human beings are included in this transformation. In scientific cosmology, the universe that begins with a big bang (a massive explosion from a point of singularity) will end tragically either with a big chill or a big crunch. The idea of the big chill is that the universe, as it continues to expand, will cool off. The loss of heat and energy will result in a collapse and disappearance of the universe. The idea of the big crunch is that the universe will begin to retract, swallowing up all celestial forms, into another singularity, from which another big bang might occur and produce another universe that may not be anything like the one we presently know.

SCIENCE IN THEOLOGICAL EDUCATION

The rich history of African American perspectives as well as the presence of African Americans in the dialogue between science and religion goes ignored for several reasons. Several reasons explain the absence of African American theologians from the contemporary science and religion dialogue: (1) preoccupation of black and womanist theologians with the topic of liberation, to the exclusion of other topics of concern to African American churches and communities; (2) racial segregation leading to separate forums for discussion (minorities are conspicuously absent from the mostly highly publicized dialogues); (3) a general lack of educational opportunities for basic literacy in the sciences; and (4) neglect of science in the theological curriculum. A long history of inadequate instruction in the sciences at black schools and denial of blacks' achievements in science, technology, and invention conspire to form the erroneous claim that blacks are uninterested in and simply not a part of modern science.

The Science for Seminaries project, funded by the American Association for the Advancement of Science (AAAS) with support from the John Templeton Foundation, has the potential to change the state of affairs in African American theological education. Howard University School of Divinity, a historically black theological school, is one of ten schools selected to participate in this project. The project, at Howard University School of Divinity, is themed "Oh So Human, Yet So Divinely Complex: Science and Theology in the Exploration of Human Identity, Community, and Purpose." Through course offerings and campus events, the divinity faculty's goal is not only to make students more aware of how the natural sciences are relevant to theology, ministry, and spirituality, but to also bring together scientists, theological educators, and clergy for conversations on an important topic in science and religion. African American history is often told as a story of a people's struggle to be recognized as fully human. Today the sciences are raising interesting questions and proposing new ideas about what it means to be human. This focus on the nature and meaning of human life is quite fitting for the School of Divinity, given the sizable number of scientists at Howard University, the resources of the National Human Genome Center at Howard University, and Howard University's historic mission of serving African Americans and other peoples of color.

The Science for Seminaries project at Howard University School of Divinity is broadening the African American churches' social mission to include the promotion of education in the natural sciences. The evolutionary biologist Joseph Graves claims that when creationism reigns in African American churches, the capacity of these churches for positive impact in their communities is diminished. In these communities, according to Graves, the lack of understanding about human biology, sexuality, and reproduction has frustrated efforts to curtail teenage pregnancy and the spread of HIV/AIDS. Just as bad, countless numbers of African American youths have been discouraged from pursuing degrees and careers in biology with an emphasis on evolution. This project relates attitudes about science (especially on evolution) to missions and social justice. The curricular revision will add content and emphasis on (1) critical reflection on the scientific worldview and how it affects our orientation toward life; and (2) the disparities in science, technology, engineering, and math (STEM) education as a major concern for social justice ministry and the best practices of churches, nonprofits, and faith-based groups for addressing these disparities.

SCIENCE AND THE HUMANITY OF BLACK PEOPLE

African American Christians' experiences and perceptions of science are influenced by the kind of exposure, good or bad, that they have to science. Factors in the formation of African Americans' attitudes about contemporary science include the following: the prominent role and influence of science and technology in American society and culture, racial and ethnic minority experience of science and technology, evangelical reactions to modern culture, and the use of technology (especially communications technology). The social and cultural landscape of the United States is adorned with all sorts of machines, gadgets, and creations produced by technology grounded in the natural sciences and mathematics: automobiles, garage door openers, airplanes, computers, cell phones, the iPod, televisions, radios, interior lighting, skyscrapers—and the list goes on. Technology is consumed for the conveniences and pleasures thought to be derived from it. Science is valued, not because of its intrinsic worth, but for the technology that it produces. From the megachurch to the storefront assembly, believers have consumed technology for personal and religious uses.

African Americans' attitudes about science are influenced also by their experience as racial minority. Science and technology have been employed to exploit and oppress African Americans. White racism assumed the status of pseudoscience in the eighteenth century. Phrenology (the reading of skulls) and physiognomy (the reading of facial and bodily features) were used to explain the alleged inferiority of people of African descent and the alleged superiority of people of European descent. Technological innovation, such as the development of the cotton gin, made slavery more profitable to white slaveholders and resulted in increased workload upon African American slaves. During and after slavery, African Americans have been the victims of unethical scientific experimentation. From 1845–1849, J. Marion Sims perfected techniques of vaginal surgery on white women by using African American slave women as his subjects, without these black women's consent. From 1932–1972, the U.S. Department of Public Health (in what is known as the Tuskegee Experiment) conducted experiments infecting African American men with syphilis bacteria, without these black men's knowledge or consent.

The internal religious dynamic that influences African American Christian attitudes about science is their belief in a particular kind of religious experience and the authority that accompanies this experience. This religious experience is purported to be an encounter with God characterized by ecstasy (intense feeling), compatible with similar experiences recorded in the Bible, contingent upon belief in Jesus Christ and adherence to his moral example—ecstasy that results in transformation of the person and possibly the person's situation and environment.

In the case of African Americans, their history is framed within the context of the struggle to be human. As explained by theologian and ethicist Riggins Earl, the moral and religious crisis of chattel slavery and the racial injustices that followed after it were rooted in a body-soul dualism that depicted black as either "soulless bodies" or "bodiless souls." As soulless bodies, black persons are regarded as inferior, not human, or less than human, whose only value is in the commodification of their bodies, as in the goods produced by their labor or the uses of their bodies from which other persons derive the greater benefit. Thus black persons are thought to have no value in their souls but only in whatever can be gained or taken from their body. As bodiless souls, black persons are treated kindly but not justly. They are regarded as human in their souls, but the injustices to which their bodies are exposed remain in force. Liberation thought emerges from the desire of the oppressed to be whole. The oppressed do not want to live as fragmented human persons. The wonderful aspects of their souls must be reconciled with the beauty in their bodies. The affirmation expressive of this desire of wholeness is "I am my body." Very early in the history of the United States, freedom became African Americans' central category for defining their experience and their destiny. Freedom is a byword or deep symbol of their aspirations to be fully human. Hence freedom came to symbolize the opposite condition to be desired over against the bondage of chattel slavery and the resulting system of custom and law that restricted black persons' rights to the fruit of their labor and full participation in the American body politic.

The sciences are raising interesting questions about what it means to be human. In particular, evolutionary biology and neuroscience now seriously challenge the traditional but highly problematic body-soul dualism identified above. Race is now understood as a "social construct," a "surrogate" to biological variation. The sciences support the idea of the human personality as, literally, a unitary, embodied whole, as expressed in that same affirmation "I am my body." Our evolutionary history also undergirds, at the deepest level, the unity of the human species and its organic connection with the entire cosmos.

In addition to concerns about the methods and philosophy of science, African Americans' aversion to science has been fueled by the denial and restriction of opportunity for black people to study and pursue careers in the sciences, the involuntary participation of black people in scientific experiments on themselves, and the distortions and abuses of science against black people with the spread of pseudoscientific theories of black inferiority.[14] For contemporary black theology, these concerns show the inaccuracy of James H. Cone's popularized claim that philosophical and scientific questions are not of ultimate concern to African Americans. More to the truth, experiences of exclusion and negative experiences with science have been as influential as creationism in developing antiscience rhetoric and a disinterest in science among African American churches and communities.

AFRICAN AMERICAN THEOLOGIES OF NATURE

Whatever one's choice of modeling for the relation of science and religion, each field has its own integrity. Scientists are not trained to be theologians; theologians are not trained to do science. Neither are theologians trained to teach science. What the theologian actually does and does best as a theologian is to correlate insights from science with core religious beliefs about God. In this process of correlation, the theologian produces a theology of nature, which then becomes representative of a religious community's beliefs about nature that serves as a medium (vehicle or tool) for relating and integrating religion and science.

A number of recent publications may aid African American theologians seeking to develop a theology of nature. These works include *Black Nature: Four Centuries of African American Nature Poetry* (2009), edited by Camile T. Dungy; and Dianne D. Glave's *Rooted in the Earth: Reclaiming the African American Environmental Heritage* (2010). Womanist theologians, because of womanism's emphasis on loving the earth, are leading the way in contemporary African American theology's construction in the theology of nature. Pioneering womanist works include: Karen Baker-Fletcher's *Sisters of Dust, Sisters of Spirit: Womanist Wordings on God and Creation* (1998) and Barbara Holmes's *Race and the Cosmos: An Invitation to View the World Differently* (2002).

Creation and Divine Action

A complement to the theology of nature is the constructive theological treatments of creation and divine action. Several African American theologians who affirm belief in God as creative transformative power are developing noninterventionist models of divine action that emphasize God's working in and through natural processes. Monica Coleman does this in her adoption of *process theology* to explain how God acts in human communities in order to redeem life. The natural sciences depict a world in flux, in whole and part, becoming something other than what it presently is. Process is the "stuff" of the world and makes it what it is. Based on the best scientific studies to date, process (relationality, interaction, change) is fundamental to the universe. As far as we know, this is the way the world is. Coleman's approach was discussed briefly in chapter 9, on salvation.

Victor Anderson uses pragmatic theology, the concept of *creative exchange*, to explain how God enables persons to overcome evil. Anderson makes panentheism a corollary to his theory of creative exchange. *Panentheism* is the view that the world is contained within Godself but that God transcends or is more than the mere sum of all objects making up the world. God absorbs everything, the good and the bad, in God's divine life. Anderson's theory of creative exchange was discussed in the chapters on God (chap. 5) and suffering (chap. 8).

Karen Baker-Fletcher identifies *open theism* as her framework for interpreting God's activity in the world. Although Baker-Fletcher believes that the future is open, she also believes that God is directing history toward an outcome that elevates good over evil. Coleman's process theism, Anderson's panentheism, and Baker-Fletcher's open theism represent attempts by these theologians to construct plausible interpretations of God's existence and activity in the physical world that is described by modern science.

Creation and Biological Evolution

African American Christian history has not been a simple uncritical acceptance or rejection of evolution. Since the late nineteenth century, opinion about modern science has been divided, ranging from uncritical acceptance to vehement rejection.[15]

In the black church, meaning predominately African American congregations and denominations, there has never been wholesale acceptance of biblical literalism, fundamentalism, or antievolutionism. There is a long alternate tradition of African American religious leaders supporting evolutionary creation. The emerging black intelligentsia of the nineteenth century was composed mostly of ministers, with the majority being male. Many of these male ministers were teachers and played key roles in the growth of ministerial education and in partnering with African American women to establish private academies and colleges. In the early period of the African American press, notable advocates of evolutionary creation included Theophilus Gould Steward, Orishatukeh Faduma, Edward A. Clarke, Shelton Hale Bishop, Charles Harris Wesley, and John H. Frank. Women participated in theological debate as lecturers and essayists. For example, women's commentary on science and religion included Fanny Jackson Coppin's assumption of the compatibility of religion and science in her theory and design of education for African American youth, Frances Ellen Watkins Harper's claims that the truths of Christianity are confirmed by science, and Alma Booker's critique of antievolutionism, a critique that strongly influenced African American churches at the time of the Scopes trial (1925). In the history of African American theology, this tradition of openness to science and evolutionary creation has existed alongside other perspectives and was not perceived as a threat to the black church's moral conservatism, social ethics, and high view of Scripture. The vitality of African American churches resides primarily in religious experience, story, testimony, music, and worship. A theology of nature true to the history of African American churches is not a statement of liberalism or fundamentalism but a theology that affirms the insights of modern science while at the same time maintaining belief in the wonder, mystery, and beauty of life created and sustained by God.

In black theological debate during the late nineteenth century, African American religious thinkers were fashioning a new discourse about science and religion. For contemporary American Christians diametrically opposed in their opinions about science and embroiled in heated battles in America's cultural war, the insights and civility of black intellectuals is both invaluable and desperately needed. For example, Daniel Alexander Payne, the AME (African Methodist Episcopal) bishop and president of Wilberforce University, argued against granting any doctrinal authority to Theophilus Gould Steward's *Genesis Re-Read*. Yet Payne recommended that AME ministers (those with better education) read Steward's book.[16] While Payne was president at Wilberforce, Steward's book was a required textbook in the school's curriculum. Clearly, in the nineteenth century and early twentieth century, African American biblical and theological hermeneutics was not the same as liberalism or fundamentalism, as they are conceived antithetically in mainstream Protestant churches in the United States.

African American theology affirms creation (God's creation of the world and the value of nature) and enriches the theology-and-science dialogue through offering for consideration minority experiences, critique of science, decorum in the science-religion dialogue for persons of faith, and alternative ways of thinking about origins (cosmic and biological). For contemporary American Christians diametrically opposed in their opinions about science and embroiled in heated battles in America's cultural war, the insights and ecumenicity of the historic black denominations are both invaluable and desperately needed. Howard Divinity School's project contributes to the effort of building dialogue between church members (clergy and laity), scientists, and professional theologians in African American communities. In a larger ecumenical context, the project provides African Americans and non-African Americans the opportunity to engage each other on many issues in science and technology that impact their faith.

AFRICAN AMERICAN THEOLOGY'S ENGAGEMENT WITH MODERN SCIENCE

It is imperative that the tradition of theological reflection on nature and science be recovered in African American theology. The thought and perspective of racial and ethnic minorities are rarely considered by studies of issues in religion and science. African Americans and their traditions of religious thought constitute a neglected area of study. The world is ever being shaped and impacted, for better or for worse, by science and technology. No theologian, especially if concerned about the quality of human life, may ignore science.

There are benefits to be gained from African American theologians' participation in the religion-science dialogue. The first is contextualization of the religion-science dialogue and giving voice to the thought and experience of an excluded racial and religious minority. Too often when science and religion meet, the religion part of the equation inevitably refers to mainline Protestant or Catholic Christian traditions. Seldom are the religious experiences of women and racial and ethnic minorities given the opportunity to interface with science. Marginalized though African American theology may be, as an intellectual movement it has great social significance. The greatest growth of Christianity in the world is occurring in the so-called third world and within minority communities within the Western world. A second benefit is exploration of interconnections, points of consonance and dissonance, between African American theology and contemporary science.

The task of theological reflection on human existence is challenging and unfinished. Many Christian assumptions of human uniqueness have been challenged by scientific cosmology (the idea that the earth and humans are not one of a kind or the center of the universe), evolutionary biology (the idea that human species developed through the processes of random variation and natural selection), geology (the idea that the history and age of the earth is longer than the record of biblical history), and religious pluralism (competing truth-claims of the world's religions). In chapter 13, we turn to the challenge that pluralism poses for African American theology.

Questions for Discussion

1. How have African American Christians related the discoveries and insights of the natural sciences to the biblical story of creation?
2. Given the predominance of social justice concerns and the historic theme of education as a pathway to freedom in African American churches, what norms or imperatives in these churches' social teachings encourage openness to and appreciation of the natural sciences?
3. If, across the range of biological variations, humans are mostly the same genetically, how may the concepts of race and ethnicity be reconstructed in meaningful and practical ways that emphasize the unity of humanity?

Suggested Reading

Baker-Fletcher, Karen. *Sisters of Dust, Sisters of Spirit: Womanist Wordings on God and Creation*. Minneapolis: Augsburg Fortress Press, 1998.
Dungy, Camile T., ed. *Black Nature: Four Centuries of African American Nature Poetry*. Athens: University of Georgia Press, 2009.
Glave, Dianne D. *Rooted in the Earth: Reclaiming the African American Environmental Heritage*. Chicago: Lawrence Hill Books, 2010.
Holmes, Barbara A. *Race and the Cosmos: An Invitation to View the World Differently*. Harrisburg, PA: Trinity Press International, 2002.

13
Christian Diversity and Religious Pluralism

The present context and crisis of African American churches is very different from the period that gave birth to the contemporary black and womanist theology movements. Of course, racism is still a problem in the United States. The stable coalition that drove the Civil Rights Movement of the 1960s and dismantled the legal structure of segregation no longer exists. There have always been differences within America and differences within in the black population of the nation. Over the course of history, African American churches have fared better or worse than now with the pluralism in America. At times this pluralism has been enriching, and at other moments it has posed a seemingly insurmountable barrier to unity and cooperation around the common good. Always, the worst of this pluralism is manifest in social and economic inequality. African American churches, called like every Christian assembly to model universal community, have struggled to reach across the divide of race, ethnicity, religion, and culture to achieve this idyllic unity of humanity. In order to appraise the challenges and opportunities of pluralism; this chapter covers the topics of the nature and extent of African American Christian involvement in the ecumenical movement, the impact of migration and immigration on the black church and the historic black denominations, and the nature of religious pluralism and kind of interreligious dialogue in African American communities.

BLACK CHRISTIAN ECUMENISM

The predominately black Christian denominations are circumscribed by race and doctrine and have minimal exchanges with nonblacks and other Christian denominations. The participation of certain black Christian denominations in national and global ecumenical organizations has not resulted in the racial and ethnic diversity of their memberships, although they profess to be open, evangelical, and committed to a nonracist appropriation of the Christian faith. Even in predominately white denominations, blacks tend to cluster in predominately black local congregations.

In *Black Ecumenism*, Mary Sawyer identifies the focus on social justice as the defining feature and motivation for black ecumenism. African American churches cross the denominational divide for consultation and collaboration in the social, political, and economic issues affecting their members. Historic black Christian denominations are the African Methodist Episcopal Church (AME, est. 1816), African Methodist Episcopal Church Zion (AMEZ, est. 1821), Christian Methodist Episcopal Church (CME, est. 1870), National Baptist Convention, U.S.A., Incorporated (NBC, est. 1895), National Baptist Convention of America, Incorporated (NBCA, est. 1915), National Missionary Baptist Convention of America (NMBCA, est. 1988), Progressive National Baptist Convention (PNBC, est. 1961), Full Gospel Baptist Church Fellowship (FGBCF, est. 1994), Church of God in Christ (COGIC, est. 1907), and Pentecostal Assemblies of the World (PAW, est. 1914). There is not one overarching body with binding authority on these black Christian denominations. Since 1978, several of the historic black Christian denominations have participated voluntarily in the Conference of National Black Churches, formerly the Congress of National Black Churches, both of which were preceded by the Fraternal Council of Negro Churches. Another large black ecumenical organization is the National Black Evangelical Association. These ecumenical organizations are not conciliar, formed to achieve uniformity in liturgy, theology, and doctrine. Nevertheless these organizations reinforce an approach to theological interpretation that correlates Christian faith to black experience.

A considerable number of black Christian denominations participate in the larger ecumenical movement. Only the AME, AMEZ, CME, NBC, NBCA, NMBCA, and PNBC are members of the National Council of Churches in the USA. Only the AME, AMEZ,

CME, NBC, NBCA, and PNBC are members of the World Council of Churches. Pentecostals participate, if at all, unofficially in the National and World councils. The extent of most Pentecostal ecumenism is intradenominational, which is vital in light of the severe fragmentation of Pentecostalism.

Black Christian denominations may contribute to the larger ecumenical movement by their exploration of the concepts of race, ethnicity, gender, and other markers of human difference, through reflecting on human being (human existence) not just in sociopolitical contexts but also in a cosmological context. This exploration seeks answers to questions like the following: What is the "unity" of human species across race and ethnic lines? How does evolutionary biology and human genetics uncover broader ways of defining "human"? How do the "heavens" (what we see and observe in space and even under the microscope) reflect the character of the Creator and disclose meanings of human existence beyond that suggested by the human-made physical environment of American cities? For example, how might persons' view of themselves change if they are able to imagine themselves within the cosmos as opposed to the urban or suburban settings that tend to alienate them from nature?

The basic questions of human being—Who am I? How am I connected to others, with others not only representing human persons but everything that is separate from oneself? For what purpose do I exist?—are more than ever of ultimate concern. Christianity is fragmented by differences in belief and practice, not to mention how these Christian faith traditions might align with various strata in the world's human societies. There is an urgent need not only for human beings to recognize their common humanity, but also for Christians to recognize each other and peoples of other religions (or of no religions at all) as fully human.

Though circumscribed by race, black ecumenism remains important for several reasons. First, black ecumenism upholds the prophetic tradition through resistance to racism and other forms of injustice. Several African American churches that achieve or aspire to achieve megachurch status are not very progressive in their advocacy for the poor and oppressed. Though not exercising binding authority among its participating organizations, black ecumenism fosters a sense of social responsibility. Second, black ecumenism gives priority to the concerns of black citizens, who as a minority may be and are often overlooked in other social spaces. Third, black ecumenism leads to sharing of information, personnel, and other resources, since no one black denomination can handle and solve the problems of the black population. Not all blacks belong to the same denomination. Professed and demonstrated concern requires cooperation between the black denominations.

THE BLACK CHURCH IMPACTED BY MIGRATION AND IMMIGRATION

The terms "black church" and "black population" require definition and qualification. Black church refers to Christian congregations and denominations in the United States that are, in the composition of their membership, predominately black (with *black* referring to African Americans and other groups of persons of African descent). Some scholars restrict the term *black church* to the seven historic black Christian denominations: AME, AMEZ, CME, NBC, NBCA, PNBC, and COGIC.[1] Though these include a large percentage of African Americans (possibly as high as 85 percent), the others should not be neglected. The Catholic Church has had a presence in African American communities for as long as and, by some accounts, even longer than the black Protestant churches. Black Catholics number in size larger than a few of the historic black Christian denominations. The term *black church* merely enables us to identify persons who represent, on the basis of race and religion, one segment of American society. The term is thus a sociological concept. A theological use of the term *black church* is contestable, given the diversity in the black population of the United States. The mere concentration of peoples in similarly related organizations does not constitute uniformity in thought and belief.

Demographic shifts have resulted in major variations in the experiences of black people in the United States. Four mass movements have altered the black experience in America. The first was the Great Migration, from roughly 1910 to 1940, when blacks in large numbers left the South and ventured North and West, but mostly North, in search of better social and economic conditions. Within a few decades, the black population that was once concentrated and almost restricted in the South was dispersed over the United States. The Great Migration was synchronous with the accelerated industrialization and urbanization of America. The next mass movement was a Second Great Migration, from 1940 to 1970, with still more blacks leaving the South. Third and fourth movements began in 1970 and are still ongoing. There is now also a Reverse Migration, with blacks leaving the North and West in order to return to the South. Blacks are also immigrating from Africa, the Caribbean, and Central and South America to the United States. The African immigrant population has doubled in each decade. As persons have either migrated or immigrated, they have established new churches where they settled or they have changed the composition of the existing churches receiving them.

Church historian David Daniels raises the question of whether the term *black church*, as it is commonly understood, can long remain the same.[2] The segment of black Christians outside of the historic black denominations is increasing so rapidly that their numbers and influence will impact, in new ways, black life and culture in the United States. The meaning of black church will need to expand to include not only Catholics but also the Orthodox, Pentecostals and charismatics, and African-based and indigenous churches transplanted on American soil.

African immigrant churches, located primarily in major urban areas, carry out a number of important functions. Many immigrants are transnational, maintaining relations with the people and institutions of their homeland. Money and consumer products are sent back home. The churches that they establish reproduce familiar patterns of community and preserve language and culture. The churches also facilitate their adaptation to America. Toward that end, immigrant churches provide several services such as English as Second Language (ESL) classes, job assistance, youth programs and tutoring, child-naming ceremonies, weddings, marriage counseling, and funerals. Immigrant churches perform these and other services all while maintaining a vibrant Christian witness.

The rise in African and African diasporic immigration to the United States represents challenge and opportunity for both the historic black denominations and the immigrant congregations and denominations. One challenge is how the distinction between native and newcomer represents, for the black church, another dialectical tension that impedes black solidarity. For example, when the rate of African immigration was low, African immigrants would join or assimilate into existing black Christian denominations. The increase in immigration has meant that Africans have sustainable numbers for church development and, as a consequence, are organizing their own churches. The presence of these emerging immigrant churches represents a new opportunity for black ecumenism. For both the native and the newcomer, the church is the center of community. With the organization of churches among immigrants, historic black Christian denominations are able to establish formal relations with immigrant churches and denominations. Immigrant churches are both an entry for the historic black denominations into the immigrant community and a doorway for immigrant participation in the larger black Christian community. It may be that black ecumenism in America will still retain its focus on social justice. However, the inclusion of immigrant churches and denominations may facilitate further social interaction, cultural exchange, and sharing of resources among black peoples, not to mention the consultation that could lead to improved worship and ministry.

RELIGIOUS PLURALISM AND INTERRELIGIOUS DIALOGUE

African American religious life is not limited to Christianity. Though the majority of African Americans are Christian, a significant number choose other paths for religious expression. These religious traditions include Islam, Judaism, Buddhism, African and African-derived religions, Native American spirituality, and religious humanism. Islam, Judaism, African and African-derived religions, and religious humanism are rooted historically in the black experience and are as old as, maybe even older than, some black Christian denominations. Predominately black Islamic organizations include Moorish Science Temple, Nation of Islam, American Society of Muslims, Hanafi Muslims, Five Percenters (Nation of Gods and Earths), Ahmadiyya Muslim Community, and the Dar ul-Islam movement. Other African American Muslims are affiliated with various mosques that are in the Sunni tradition. Predominately black Jewish organizations include Beth Israel (Ethiopian Jews), Black Hebrews Israelites (i.e., Church of God and Saints of Christ), Commandment Keepers, Nation of Yahweh, Ethiopian Hebrew Community (splintered from Commandment Keepers), Church of God (Prophet F. S. Cherry). Black Jewish groups are divided into Rabbinic (focusing on Talmud and tradition), Torah Only, and Messianic (professing belief in Jesus as the Messiah and combining elements from Christianity with Judaism). African American Jews also are affiliated (though in very small numbers) with predominately ethnic Jewish movements in the Orthodox, Conservative, and Reform traditions. Yet with all of this religious activity, some persons choose the path of no religion: atheism.

African American theologians have shown openness to African traditional religion. For example, Cecil Cone and Gayraud Wilmore have identified African traditional religion as the historical source for black (African American) religion and culture. As discussed earlier (in chap. 5), Cecil Cone claims that black religion is characterized by belief in the Almighty Sovereign God, a concept that is present in the African concept of the Supreme Being. Other African American theologians are treating African traditional religions as an alternative to Christian doctrinal categories.

Religious pluralism represents a major challenge and opportunity for African Americans. For African Americans who are Christian, the pluralism raises a number of questions about divine revelation and the scope of salvation: Who can be saved? Is God and God's truth revealed only in Jesus Christ? Is salvation only through Jesus Christ? What is the fate of persons who have never heard the gospel?

In 2002, Carlton Pearson's "gospel of inclusion" (universalism) started a firestorm of controversy that exposed the landscape of African American Christian belief about the scope of salvation and attitudes toward other religions. Pearson, who at the time was a prominent Pentecostal leader, claimed that all persons will be saved, that God condemns no one to an eternal burning hell, and that God's love is indicative of the love that we should have for each other.[3] Pearson's position was denounced as heresy by his Pentecostal peers and other African American clergy.

The overwhelmingly vehement rejection of Pearson's universalism showed that African American Christians, as represented by their clergy, are entrenched in the exclusivist understanding of salvation. Exclusivism is the view that there can be only one true religion because revelation and salvation are offered only in Jesus Christ. Some exclusivists, those in the more conservative or fundamentalist camp, argue that there is no Ultimate Reality and common form of salvation affirmed in the world of religions. Other exclusivists, in the moderate camp, may concede that God could reveal truth in other religions, but what God reveals in Jesus Christ about salvation is not found in other religions. In both camps of exclusivism, salvation is through Jesus Christ. The believers' only certainty about and hope for salvation is through the medium by which it comes, and that medium is Jesus Christ.

African American Christians, in particular those in the Catholic Church, lean toward inclusivism. Not to be confused with Pearson's notion of inclusion, this inclusivist view is the position that other religions are possible ways of salvation. From this view, there are manifestations of God's revelation and grace in all religions. It just so happens that the church is the best sacramental expression of salvation. Though open to God's revelation in various religions, this inclusivism regards Jesus Christ as the norm for all religions. In other words, if salvation occurs in other religions, it is measured by and must be compatible with salvation in Christianity. God's truth in Jesus Christ is the Truth that must be mirrored in every perspective that claims to be truthful.[4] All persons, Christians as well as others, will be saved by the truth that they have received and believed.

Pearson's gospel of inclusion is a variant, one of several possible formulations, of pluralism. Rather than being christocentric, focused on Christ, the pluralist perspective is theocentric, focused on an Ultimate Reality that some persons name as God and have understood through Christ. Monica Coleman, for example, makes this shift from a christocentric focus to a theocentric focus in order to deepen her analysis of salvation in Christianity, as well as to broaden the concept of salvation to include the experience of transformation in other religions.[5] Long before Pearson and Coleman, Howard Thurman adopted a pluralist approach. Thurman defined the religious experience as "the conscious and direct exposure of the individual to God," with this experience supervening and impacting the whole of life.[6] According to Thurman, Jesus pointed persons to God and not to himself. In all cases, the Christian pluralist is not rejecting Christ but supposing that the truth in other religions does not need to look like it does in Christianity. Pluralism is the view that all religions affirm an Ultimate Reality and may contribute to the transformation of human life. All persons will be saved, in whatever manner salvation is made available to them.

THE COMMENCEMENT OF DIALOGUE

What is the way forward for ecumenical and interreligious dialogue? In Dwight Hopkins's *Heart and Head*, he proposes six principles for interfaith dialogue.[7] The first principle is to recognize and respect other people's religion. In other words, take seriously the religion and culture of others. Second, acknowledge that people have their own distinct religious language, which differs from yours. Be willing to learn others' language and, above all, to listen to them speak. Third, acknowledge other peoples' survival strategies. Listen to their stories of how they have lived their lives, especially how they overcame adversity and suffering. Notice how their stories are told through using song, music, art, and dance. Fourth, be attentive to how race, ethnicity, and gender impact others' experiences. Fifth, focus on the earth, the "sacred" home for all humankind. Sixth, focus on spirituality, in particular the aspiration for liberation, the yearning of humans to live in freedom.

In addition to Hopkins's recommendations, I suggest a few more emphases toward achieving honest and open dialogue: (1) mutual respect, (2) the centrality of witness or testimony rather than doctrine or dogma, (3) willingness to abandon or modify one's beliefs, (4) viewing the process of dialogue as an experience of faith, and (5) having optimism in the process of dialogue.[8] My first and second emphases are compatible with Hopkins's first, second, and third principles. The main objective of dialogue is *to dialogue*. As long as persons are talking, they are not fighting. And if they are not fighting, they are likely to come closer to understanding, cooperation, and a just and enduring peace.

Questions for Discussion

1. What does (or should) vibrant, relevant religion (especially black Christian faith) look like in the twenty-first century, in our present moment in history?
2. What important truths are conveyed through religions other than Christianity, truths to which the Christian theologian ought to pay attention?
3. Which Christian beliefs complicate or make impossible interreligious dialogue? How can a person engage in interreligious dialogue and interfaith cooperation while clearly having beliefs that conflict with the beliefs of other partners?

Suggested Reading

King, Martin Luther, Jr. *In a Single Garment of Destiny: A Global Vision of Justice*. Edited by Lewis V. Baldwin. Boston: Beacon Press, 2013.
Sawyer, Mary R. *Black Ecumenism: Implementing the Demands of Justice*. Harrisburg, PA: Trinity Press International, 1994.
Thurman, Howard. *Footprints of a Dream: The Story of the Church for the Fellowship of All Peoples*. Eugene, OR: Wipf & Stock, 2009.

Notes

Introduction

1. Rodney Stark and Roger Finke, *The Churching of America, 1776–2005: Winners and Losers in Our Religious Economy*, 2nd ed. (New Brunswick, NJ: Rutgers University Press, 2005).

2. Albert J. Raboteau, *Slave Religion: The "Invisible Institution" in the Antebellum South* (New York: Oxford University Press, 2004), 148.

3. Ibid., 128.

4. William D. Wright, *Crisis of the Black Intellectual* (Chicago: Third World Press, 2007).

5. W. E. B (William Edward Burghardt) Du Bois, *The Suppression of the African Slave-Trade to the United States of America, 1638–1870* (New York: Longmans, Green, & Co., 1896).

6. From 2009 to 2013, John J. Thatamanil directed the American Academy of Religion/Henry Luce Summer Seminars on Theologies of Religious Pluralism and Comparative Theology, attended by more than fifty theological educators with womanist theologians Monica A. Coleman and Melanie L. Harris participating in this group. At the same time, the major publications in comparative theology included: Francis X. Clooney's *Comparative Theology: Deep Learning across Religious Borders* (Malden, MA: Wiley-Blackwell, 2010) and *The New Comparative Theology: Interreligious Insights from the Next Generation* (New York: T & T Clark International, 2010), Michelle Voss Roberts' *Dualities: A Theology of Difference* (Louisville, KY: Westminster John Knox Press, 2010), and Hugh Nicholson's *Comparative Theology and the Problem of Religious Rivalry* (New York: Oxford University Press, 2011). The project and publications on comparative theology demonstrate the challenge of pluralism yet the promise of conducting theological study in religions and/or with sources that are not exclusively Christian. Comparative theology compares Christian theology to other religions on topics such as ultimate reality, divine agency and presence, worship, moral norms, and the origin and fate of the universe and humankind with attention to how each religion construes its appeals to revelation, faith, sacred texts, or religious experience. Comparative theology presupposes that theology in any religion is enhanced by recognition of how theology is practiced in other religions.

7. Cano listed ten loci, divided into primary sources (Scripture, Christ and the apostles, Catholic Church, councils, pope, saints, theologians, and canonists) and secondary sources (reason, philosophy and law, and history).

8. Hortense J. Spillers, "Crisis of the Negro Intellectual: A Post-Date," *Boundary 2*, 21, no. 3 (Autumn 1994): 66 n. 2.

9. On the centrality of divine encounter in Christianity, see Adolf von Harnack's *The History of Dogma*, vol. 1 (New York: Dover Publications, 1961), 16, 72.

10. Huston Smith, *The World's Religions: Our Great Wisdom Traditions* (San Francisco: HarperSanFrancisco, 1991), 365–83. Smith defines and contrasts historical religions and primal religions, considering the latter with potential to enliven the former. According to Smith, historical religions are distinguished by their sacred texts and cumulative traditions. The term *historical religions* applies to Hinduism, Buddhism, Confucianism, Taoism, Islam, Judaism, and Christianity. The historical religions are younger (with the earliest emerging about four thousand years ago) than the primal religions (with some reaching back three million years). Though most of the primal religions have or are disappearing, Smith claims that the primal religions may reveal aspects of deep consciousness and "hold insights and virtues that urbanized, industrialized civilizations have allowed to fall by the wayside" (366).

11. Robert Neville, *Religion in Late Modernity* (Albany, NY: SUNY Press, 2002), 94, here quoting Plotinus.

12. U.S. Constitution, Article 1, section 2, clause 3. The Three-Fifths Clause was negated by Amendment 14, section 2.

13. Karl Jaspers, *The Origin and Goal of History*, translated from German by Michael Bullock (New Haven, CT: Yale University Press, 1953), 1–21.

14. Ursula W. Goodenough, "What Science Can and Cannot Offer to a Religious Narrative," *Zygon: Journal of Religion and Science* 29 (September 1994): 321–30.

15. Barbara A. Holmes, *Race and the Cosmos: An Invitation to View the World Differently* (Harrisburg, PA: Trinity Press International, 2002), 10, 105–6, 160–61.

16. Barbara A. Holmes, *Liberation and the Cosmos: Conversations with the Elders* (Minneapolis: Fortress Press, 2008), xi, 12–15, 18–19.

17. Charles H. Long, review of *The Sacred and the Profane*, by Mircea Eliade, *Journal of Religion* 40, no. 1 (January 1960): 50.

Chapter 1: History and Historical Study

1. Riggins R. Earl, *Dark Symbols, Obscure Signs: God, Self, and Community in the Slave Mind* (Maryknoll, NY: Orbis Books, 1993).

2. Here I borrow the term *genealogy* from Michel Foucault, who finds cultural "artifacts," something in which the culture is manifest and that can be examined

(inspected and scrutinized) in a number of ways, and asks what meaning these artifacts have for us today.

3. Joseph R. Washington, *Black Religion: The Negro and Christianity in the United States* (Boston: Beacon Press, 1964), 30–31, 40–41, 297; J. R. Washington, *Politics of God* (Boston: Beacon Press, 1967), 154–55.

4. James H. Cone, *For My People: Black Theology and the Black Church* (Maryknoll, NY: Orbis Books, 1984), 19, 24.

5. Monica A. Coleman, *Ain't I a Womanist Too? Third-Wave Womanist Religious Thought* (Minneapolis: Fortress Press, 2013), 13–19.

6. Gayraud S. Wilmore, "A Revolution Unfulfilled, but Not Invalidated," in *A Black Theology of Liberation*, by James H. Cone, Twentieth Anniversary Edition (Maryknoll, NY: Orbis Books, 1990), 147.

7. Frederick L. Ware, *Methodologies of Black Theology* (Eugene, OR: Wipf & Stock, 2008), 8, 12–13.

8. The pioneer theorist on collective memory is Maurice Halbwachs. Though not using the term, African American historian William D. Wright critiques what is in effect the use of collective memory in African American historiography.

9. The perspectives of Cyprian Davis and Eva Martin are summarized in M. Shawn Copeland's "Method in Emerging Black Catholic Theology," in *Taking Down Our Harps: Black Catholics in the United States*, ed. Diana L. Hayes and Cyprian Davis (Maryknoll, NY: Orbis Books, 1998), 137–38.

10. See Wilson J. Moses, "The Lost World of the Negro, 1895–1919: Black Literary and Intellectual Life before the 'Renaissance,'" *Black American Literature Forum* 21, nos. 1–2 (Spring–Summer 1987): 61–84. Moses also illustrates the problem of collective memory in the twentieth century and later scholars' suppression and ridicule of the nineteenth-century black middle class, which tended to stress Victorian values and the practical expression of religion as opposed to emotionalism and the revival/camp meeting style of religion. According to Moses, the black middle class represents one of several streams of black intellectual life and should not be ignored outright.

11. Charlotte Heth, ed., *Native American Dance: Ceremonies and Social Traditions* (Washington, DC: National Museum of the American Indian, Smithsonian Institution, with Starwood Publishing, 1993).

12. Sibyl R. Heim, "The Shakers," *CORD News* 2, no. 1 (April 1970): 27–39. Heim cites several eyewitness accounts of the Shakers' dances, including the "round" dance, which is performed in a circle.

Chapter 2: Sources

1. James H. Cone, *For My People*, 117; Paul Tillich, *Systematic Theology*, vol. 1 (Chicago: University of Chicago Press, 1951), 10, 15, 60, 62, 64.

2. Anthony B. Pinn, *Terror and Triumph: The Nature of Black Religion* (Minneapolis: Fortress Press, 2003), 157–59.

3. C. Eric Lincoln, *The Black Church Experience in Religion* (Garden City, NY: Anchor Press, 1977), 3.

4. Cecil W. Cone, *The Identity Crisis in Black Theology* (Nashville: African Methodist Episcopal Church, 1975), 18.

5. Ibid., 6.

6. Ibid., 5.

7. Ibid., 23.

8. Charles H. Long, *Significations: Signs, Symbols, and Images in the Interpretation of Religion* (Aurora, CO: Davies Group Publishers, 1999), 7.

9. Ibid.

10. Paul Tillich, *Theology of Culture*, ed. Robert C. Kimball (New York: Oxford University Press, 1959), 6–7.

11. Paul Tillich, *What Is Religion?*, ed. James Luther Adams (New York: Harper & Row, 1969), 138.

12. Long, *Significations*, 188–197; Long, "African American Religion in the United States: A Bibliographic Essay," in *The African American Experience: An Historiographical and Bibliographical Guide*, ed. Arvarh E. Strickland and Robert E. Weems (Westport, CT: Greenwood Press, 2001), 378–79.

13. James H. Cone, *A Black Theology of Liberation* (1990), 38; J. Cone, *God of the Oppressed*, (San Francisco: Harper & Row, 1975), 81–82.

14. Jonathan Tran, "The New Black Theology: Retrieving Ancient Sources to Challenge Racism," *Christian Century*, February 8, 2012, 24–25, 27.

Chapter 3: Methods

1. J. Cone, *God of the Oppressed*, 16–17; J. Cone, *A Black Theology of Liberation* (1990), xix, 4–5, 21–23.

2. M. Shawn Copeland, "Method in Emerging Black Catholic Theology," in Hayes and Davis, *Taking Down Our Harps*, 128–32.

3. Jamie T. Phelps, "Sources of Theology: African American Catholic Theology," in *Black and Catholic: The Challenge and Gift of Black Folk; Contributions of African American Experience and Thought to Catholic Theology*, ed. Jamie T. Phelps (Milwaukee: Marquette University Press, 1997), 165–67.

4. W. E. B. Du Bois, *The Souls of Black Folk* (Greenwich, CT: Fawcett Publications, 1961), 17.

5. J. Cone, *God of the Oppressed*, 2.

6. Victor Anderson, *Creative Exchange: A Constructive Theology of African American Religious Experience* (Minneapolis: Fortress Press, 2008), 4, 30–31.

7. Alistair Kee, *The Rise and Demise of Black Theology*, enlarged ed. (London: SCM Press, 2008).

8. Anthony B. Pinn, "Review of *The Rise and Demise of Black Theology*, by Alistair Kee," *Journal of Contemporary Religion* 22, no. 1 (January 2007): 126–28.

9. Victor Anderson, foreword to *The Rise and Demise of Black Theology*, by Alistair Kee (2008), vii–xii, giving a positive assessment of Kee's book.

10. Long, *Significations*, 7, 179–81.

11. Anderson, *Creative Exchange*, 4, 30–31.

12. Long, *Significations*, 116, 153, 179–83; J. Cone, *God of the Oppressed*, 144.

13. Charles H. Long, "Passage and Prayer: The Origin of Religion in the Atlantic World," in *The Courage to Hope: From Black Suffering to Human Redemption*, ed. Quinton Hosford Dixie and Cornel West (Boston: Beacon Press, 1999), 17.

14. Ibid., 7–12, 14.

15. Henry M. Turner, "The Outrage of the Supreme Court: A Letter from Henry M. Turner," in *Readings in African-American History*, 3rd ed., ed. Thomas R. Frazier (Belmont, CA: Wadsworth Thompson Learning, 2001), 180–81.

16. Maria W. Stewart, "An Address Delivered Before the Afric-American Female Intelligence Society," in *With Pen and Voice: A Critical Anthology of Nineteenth-Century African-American Women*, ed. Shirley Wilson Logan (Carbondale: Southern Illinois University Press, 1995), 13; Martin Luther King Jr., "The Violence of Desperate Men," from *Stride toward Freedom*, in *The African-American Archive: The History of the Black Experience through Documents*, ed. Kai Wright (New York: Black God & Leventhal Publishers, 2001), 535.

17. Zora Neale Hurston, "Religion," in *African-American Humanism: An Anthology*, ed. Norm R. Allen (Amherst, NY: Prometheus Books, 1991), 153–54; Alice Walker, *In Search of Our Mothers' Gardens* (New York: Harcourt Brace Jovanovich, 1983), 265.

18. Long, *Significations*, 176–79.

19. Ibid., 175–76.

20. Paul Cuffe, "Back to Africa," and James Forteen and Russell Perrott, "It Is Not Asked for By Us," in *African-American Archive*, 128–33.

21. Wendy W. Walters, "One of Dese Mornins, Bright and Fair / Take My Wings and Cleave de Air: The Legend of the Flying Africans and Diasporic Consciousness," *Mellus* 22, no. 3 (Fall 1997): 3–27.

22. Thomas L. Webber, *Deep Like the Rivers: Education in the Slave Quarter Community, 1831–1865* (New York: W. W. Norton & Co., 1978), 63–70, 80–101, 131–48.

23. David Walker, "Our Wretchedness in Consequence of the Preachers of the Religion of Jesus Christ," from *Appeal to the Colored Citizens of the World*, in *Readings in African-American History*, 94–100; Frederick Douglass, "Appendix" to *Narrative of the Life of Frederick Douglass, An American Slave*, in *African-American Humanism*, 109–15; David Walker, "I Ask You, O My Brethren!, Are We Men?", from Walker's *Appeal*, Frederick Douglass, "I Have Come to Tell You Something about Slavery—What I Know of It, as I Have Felt It," and

Frederick Douglass, "What Is American Slavery?", in *African-American Archive*, 142–50, 197–98, 213–14.

24. Frances Ellen Watkins Harper, "Duty to Dependent Races," in *With Pen and Voice*, 40–41.

25. Francis J. Grimké, "Excerpts from a Thanksgiving Sermon," in *Negro Orators and Their Orations*, ed. Cater G. Woodson (Washington, DC: Associates Publishers, 1925), 705.

26. Benjamin Banneker, "I Freely and Cheerfully Acknowledge, that I am of the African Race," Letter to and Reply from President Thomas Jefferson, in *African-American Archive*, 102–5.

27. Stewart, "An Address Delivered Before the Afric-American Female Intelligence Society," in *With Pen and Voice*, 12–16.

28. Wilson J. Moses, *The Golden Age of Black Nationalism, 1850–1925* (Hamden, CT: Archon Books, 1978), 85–86.

29. Frances Ellen Watkins Harper, "Woman's Political Future," in *With Pen and Voice*, 43–46; Maria Stewart, "There are No Chains So Galling as the Chains of Ignorance," Anna Julia Cooper, "A Black Woman of the South," and W. E. B. DuBois, "The Talented Tenth," in *African-American Archive*, 184–87, 419–20, 535.

30. Diana L. Hayes, "Through the Eyes of Faith: The Seventh Principle of the Nguzo," in *Taking Down Our Harps: Black Catholics in the United States*, ed. Diana L. Hayes and Cyprian Davis (Maryknoll, NY: Orbis Books, 1998), 61.

31. Langston Hughes, "Salvation," in *African-American Humanism*, 119–21.

32. Victor Anderson, *Beyond Ontological Blackness: An Essay on African American Religious and Cultural Criticism* (New York: Continuum, 1995), 93, 99, 109–10.

33. Will Coleman, "Coming through 'Ligion: Metaphor in Non-Christian and Christian Experiences of the Spirit(s) in African American Slave Narratives," and Cheryl J. Sanders, "Liberation Ethics in the Ex-Slave Interviews," in *Cut Loose Your Stammering Tongue: Black Theology in the Slave Narratives*, ed. Dwight N. Hopkins and George C. L. Cummings (Maryknoll, NY: Orbis Books, 1991), 47–66, 67–102.

34. George C. L. Cummings, "Slave Narratives, Black Theology of Liberation (USA), and the Future," in *Cut Loose Your Stammering Tongue*, 103–36.

35. Monica A. Coleman, "Must I Be a Womanist?" *Journal of Feminist Studies in Religion* 22, no. 1 (2006): 85–96.

36. Anna Julia Haywood Cooper, "Womanhood a Vital Element in the Regeneration and Progress of a Race," in *With Pen and Voice*, 53–74.

37. Delores S. Williams, "Womanist Theology: Black Women's Voices," in *Black Theology: A Documentary History*, vol. 2, *1980–1992*, ed. James H. Cone and Gayraud S. Wilmore (Maryknoll, NY: Orbis Books, 1993), 269–71.

38. Ware, *Methodologies of Black Theology*, 44–55, 84, 87–89, 94.

39. Ibid., 99.

40. Tillich, *Systematic Theology*, 1:46.

41. Ibid., 50: the norm of Christian theology is the "New Being in Jesus as the Christ."

Chapter 4: Epistemology

1. In addition to suspicions that African American theology is not an academic discipline, African American theologians must also contend with the claims of critics who argue that African American theology is not Christian. For an example of an argument that black theology is not genuinely Christian, see H. Wayne House's "An Investigation of Black Liberation Theology," *Bibliotheca Sacra* 139, no. 554 (April 1982): 159–74.

2. Frederick L. Ware, "The Epistemic Publicity of Academic Black Theology," in *Religious Studies, Theology, and the University: Conflicting Maps, Changing Terrain*, ed. Delwin Brown and Linell Cady (Albany: State University of New York Press, 2002), 187–89.

3. Ware, *Methodologies of Black Theology*, 58–59, 89–90, 134; see also 46–47.

4. Ibid., 124–28.

5. Ibid., 128–29.

6. James H. Cone, *Black Theology and Black Power* (Maryknoll, NY: Orbis Books, 1989), 27; J. Cone, "God Is Black," in *Lift Every Voice: Constructing Christian Theology from the Underside*, ed. Susan Brooks Thistlethwaite and Mary Potter Engel (San Francisco, CA: Harper & Row, 1990), 83.

7. Ware, "Epistemic Publicity," 192–93.

8. William R. Jones, *Is God a White Racist? A Preamble to Black Theology* (Garden City, NY: Anchor Press, 1973), 18–20, 114–16.

9. See Michael E. Dyson's "Beyond Essentialism: Expanding African-American Cultural Criticism," introduction to *Reflecting Black: African-American Cultural Criticism* (Minneapolis: University of Minnesota Press, 1993); Cornel West's *Keeping Faith: Philosophy and Race in America* (New York: Routledge, 1993), 19; West, *Beyond Eurocentrism and Multiculturalism*, vol. 2, *Prophetic Reflections: Notes on Race and Power in America* (Monroe, ME: Common Courage Press, 1993), 80; West, *Race Matters* (Boston: Beacon Press, 1993), 21–32.

10. For instances of the kinds of sayings and proverbs that ground and further this commonsense realism, see J. Mason Brewer, "Old-Time Negro Proverbs," in *Mother Wit from the Laughing Barrel: Readings in the Interpretation of Afro-American Folklore*, ed. Alan Dundes (Jackson: University Press of Mississippi, 1990), 246–50; Brewer, *American Negro Folklore* (Chicago: Quadrangle Books, 1968); Harold Courlander, *A Treasury of Afro-American Folklore: The Oral Literature, Traditions, Recollections, Legends, Tales, Songs, Religious Beliefs, Customs, Sayings, and Humor of Peoples of African American Descent in the Americas* (New York: Crown Publishers, 1976; reprint, New York: Marlowe & Co., 1996).

11. Sojourner Truth, "Ain't I a Woman?," http://www.feminist.com/resources/artspeech/genwom/sojour.htm.

12. Frederick Douglass, *North Star* (1852?); "She . . . never learned to read or write," http://www.sojournertruth.org/Library/Archive/LegacyOfFaith.htm. For a study of Sojourner Truth's style of speaking, see Suzanne P. Fitch and Roseann Manzuik, *Sojourner Truth as Orator: Wit, Story, and Song* (Westport, CT: Greenwood Press, 1997).

13. John Jasper's sermon is recollected in Frank Leslie's *Popular Monthly* 52 (New York: Frank Leslie Publishing House, 1901): 303–5; Edwin Archer Randolph, *The Life of Rev. John Jasper* (Richmond, VA: R. T. Hill & Co., 1884), chap. 5; William E. Hatcher, *John Jasper: The Unmatched Negro Philosopher and Preacher* (New York: Fleming H. Revell Co., 1908), 133–49, http://baptisthistory homepage.com/jasper.sun.do.move.html.

14. Lewis R. Gordon, *An Introduction to Africana Philosophy* (New York: Cambridge University Press, 2008), 136. Gordon, an African American philosopher, characterizes William Jones's philosophy as a form of existentialism.

15. For identification and critique of the humanistic dimensions of Alice Walker's womanism, see Cheryl Sanders, "Christian Ethics and Theology in Womanist Perspective," in J. Cone and Wilmore, *Black Theology*, 2:336–44.

16. William R. Jones, "Religious Humanism: Its Problems and Prospects in Black Religion and Culture," *Journal of the Interdenominational Theological Center* 7 (Spring 1980): 169–86.

17. William R. Jones, "Functional Ultimacy as Authority in Religious Humanism," *Religious Humanism* 12 (1978): 29–31.

18. Anthony Pinn, *Why, Lord? Suffering and Evil in Black Theology* (New York: Continuum, 1995), 141.

19. In *Writing God's Obituary: How a Good Methodist Became a Better Atheist* (Amherst, NY: Prometheus Books, 2014), Anthony Pinn chronicles his journey, as a black religious humanist, to the position of atheism. Religious humanism is significantly different from the new atheism. The new atheists are hostile to religion, voicing not only their rejection of it but also engaging in activities to eradicate religion from society; religious humanists may value religions for their positive contributions to society yet still not believe in the religions' tenets about the supernatural.

20. Cornel West, *Beyond Eurocentrism and Multiculturalism*, vol. 1, *Prophetic Thought in Postmodern Times* (Monroe, ME: Common Courage Press, 1993), 37, 43.

21. Victor Anderson, *Pragmatic Theology: Negotiating the Intersections of an American Philosophy of Religion and Public Theology* (Albany, NY: SUNY Press, 1998).

22. Victor Anderson, "Contour of an American Public Theology," *Journal of Theology* (2000): 49–68, http://livedtheology.org/wp-content/uploads/2012/10/v_anderson.pdf.

23. Rufus Burrow, *Personalism: A Critical Introduction* (St. Louis: Chalice Press, 1999), 85, 89. In addition to the works of Martin Luther King Jr. and

J. Deotis Roberts, Burrow claims that womanist theology is, in some respects, an expression of personalism.

24. Martin Luther King Jr., "Pilgrimage to Nonviolence," in *A Testament of Hope: The Essential Writings of Martin Luther King, Jr.*, ed. James M. Washington (San Francisco: Harper & Row, 1986), 35–40.

25. Burrow, *Personalism*, 77–78, 221–22.

26. Ibid., 81–85.

27. Memphis State University, now the University of Memphis, is the school from which most African Americans are receiving the PhD degree in philosophy. For statistical information on African Americans in philosophy, see Tina F. Botts, Liam Kofi Bright, Myisha Cherry, Guntur Mallarangeng, and Quayshawn Spencer, "What Is the State of Blacks in Philosophy?," *Critical Philosophy of Race* 2, no. 2 (2014): 224–42.

28. Henry J. Young, *Hope in Process: A Theology of Social Pluralism* (Minneapolis: Fortress Press, 1990); Theodore Walker, *Mothership Connections: A Black Atlantic Synthesis of Neoclassical Metaphysics and Black Theology* (Albany, NY: SUNY Press, 2004); Monica Coleman, *Making a Way Out of No Way: A Womanist Theology* (Minneapolis: Fortress Press, 2008).

29. Theodore Walker, "Theological Resources for a Black Neoclassical Social Ethics," *Journal of Religious Thought* 45, no. 2 (Winter–Spring 1989): 21–39.

30. Monica A. Coleman, "Process Thought and Womanist Theology: Black Women's Science Fiction as a Resource for Process Theology," paper presented at the Center for Process Studies Seminar, Claremont School of Theology, April 29, 2003, http://www.ctr4process.org/sites/default/files/pdfs/26_2%20 Coleman%20-%20PT%20and%20Womanist%20theology.pdf.

31. Ibid., 17–18.

32. Karen Baker-Fletcher, *Dancing with God: The Trinity from a Womanist Perspective* (St. Louis: Chalice Press, 2006), 2, 5, 24, 49.

33. Kelly Brown Douglas, *Sexuality and the Black Church* (Maryknoll, NY: Orbis Books, 1999), 12.

34. Ibid., 123–26.

35. Hilary Putnam, "Meaning and Reference," *Journal of Philosophy* 70, no. 19 (1973): 704–6, 710–11.

36. William R. Jones, "Toward an Interim Assessment of Black Theology," *Christian Century* 89 (May 21, 1975): 515.

Chapter 5: God

1. Benjamin E. Mays, *The Negro's God as Reflected in His Literature* (Boston: Chapman & Grimes, 1938), vii.

2. C. Cone, *Identity Crisis*, 26–36, 39. These same elements are fundamental to black religion, according to Cecil Cone.

3. Long, "Passage and Prayer," in Dixie and West, *Courage to Hope*, 17.

4. Charles H. Long, "The West African High God: History and Religious Experience," *History of Religion* 3, no. 2 (1964): 332–33, 335.

5. U.S. Religions Landscape Survey, *Religious Affiliation: Diverse and Dynamic* (Washington, DC: Pew Research Center, 2008).

6. Mays, *The Negro's God*, 255.

7. Ibid., 14.

8. Ibid., 14, 48–49, 218–220.

9. C. Cone, *Identity Crisis*, 40–41.

10. Ibid., 42–48, 139–41.

11. Henry H. Mitchell, *Black Belief: Folk Beliefs of Blacks in America and West Africa* (New York: Harper & Row, 1975), 109–11, 126–36.

12. Long, *Significations*, 197.

13. Henry H. Mitchell and Nicholas Cooper-Lewter, *Soul Theology: The Heart of American Black Culture* (San Francisco: Harper & Row, 1986), 14–21, 29–35, 43–48, 55–59, 66–71, 79–85.

14. Mitchell, *Black Belief*, 125.

15. Major J. Jones, *The Color of God: The Concept of God in Afro-American Thought* (Macon, GA: Mercer University Press, 1987), 47.

16. Ibid., 49.

17. Baker-Fletcher, *Dancing with God*, 19, 47.

18. Ibid., 58–62.

19. M. Jones, *Color of God*, 110–11.

20. Long, *Significations*, 179–81.

21. Amos Yong, *The Spirit Poured Out on All Flesh: Pentecostalism and the Possibility of Global Theology* (Grand Rapids: Baker Academic, 2005), 206; Estrelda Alexander, ed., *Black Fire Reader: A Documentary Resource on African American Pentecostalism* (Eugene, OR: Cascade Books, 2013), 115, 118.

22. E. Alexander, *Black Fire Reader*, 119.

23. Ibid., 101.

24. Yong, *Spirit Poured Out*, 209–10.

25. For a summary and analysis of William R. Jones's argument against black liberation theism and his statement of humanocentric theism, see Ware, *Methodologies of Black Theology*, 87–97.

26. J. Cone, *God of the Oppressed*, 191–94.

27. Baker-Fletcher, *Dancing with God*, 5. Open theism, a movement in evangelical Protestant Christian theology, maintains that classical statements of God's attributes of immutability, impassibility, and timelessness are incompatible with the conception of God in the Bible. Open theists argue that God is personal and open to the prayers, decisions, and actions of human beings. God has foreknowledge of the future but is capable of acting in response to humans in their present situation. The future is not determinative of human action in the present because the future does not yet exist, but God knows what it will be.

28. Ibid., 5.

29. Ibid., 29–30.

30. Ibid., 38, 140, 153.

31. Ibid., 17.

32. Ibid., 17, 161.

33. Ibid., 9.

34. Ibid., 18, 29, 37–38, 79, 110, 139, 150, 153, 163.

35. Ibid., 56.

36. Ibid., 47, 154.

37. Alice Walker, *Our Mothers' Gardens*, 265.

38. Long, *Significations*, 193–97.

39. Anderson, *Creative Exchange*, 16, 130, 134, 144.

40. Dwight N. Hopkins, "Black Theology on God: The Divine in Black Popular Religion," in *The Ties That Bind: African American and Hispanic American/Latino/a Theologies in Dialogue*, ed. Anthony B. Pinn and Benjamín Valentín (New York: Continuum, 2001), 100.

41. Ibid., 105.

42. Ibid., 106.

43. Ibid., 107–11.

44. Mays, *The Negro's God*, 249–50.

45. King, *Testament of Hope*, 40, 41–42, 508–9. King's last public telling of his encounter with God was in his sermon "Why Jesus Called a Man a Fool," preached at Mt. Pisgah Missionary Baptist Church, in Chicago on August 27, 1967. http://mlk-kpp01.stanford.edu/kingweb/publications/sermons/670827.000_Why_Jesus_Called_a_Man_a_Fool.html

Chapter 6: Human Being

1. Earl, *Dark Symbols, Obscure Signs*, 5.

2. K. Douglas, *Sexuality and the Black Church*, 59.

3. Pinn, *Terror and Triumph*, 142.

4. Stephanie Y. Mitchem, "Embodiment in African American Theology," in *The Oxford Handbook of African American Theology*, ed. Katie G. Cannon and Anthony B. Pinn (New York: Oxford University Press, 2014), 308.

5. King argues for this position in his "Letter from a Birmingham Jail" and in one of his signature sermons, "A Knock at Midnight." See King, *Testament of Hope*, 289–302, 497–504.

6. Long, *Significations*, 7.

7. Anderson, *Creative Exchange*, 4, 30–31.

8. Holmes, *Race and the Cosmos*, 158.

9. King's multiple deliveries of this sermon are under the titles "What Is Man?" (1954 & 1963), "The Measure of a Man" (1959), and "Who Are We?"

(1966). Martin Luther King Jr., *Measure of a Man* (Philadelphia: Christian Education Press, 1959), 7–31; M. L. King Jr., "What Is Man?," *The Papers of Martin Luther King, Jr.*, vol. 6, *Advocate of the Social Gospel, September 1948-March 1963*, eds. Clayborne Carson, Susan Clayborne, Susan Englander, Troy Jackson, and Gerald L. Smith (Berkeley: University of California Press, 2007), 174–79.

10. King, *Where Do We Go from Here: Chaos or Community?* (New York: Harper & Row, 1967; Boston: Beacon Press, 1968), 98–99.

11. Ibid., 98.

12. Ibid.

13. C. Cone, *Identity Crisis*, 21–23.

14. Charles H. Long, "African American Religion in the United States of America: An Interpretative Essay," *Nova Religio: The Journal of Alternative and Emergent Religions* 7, No. 1 (July 2003): 21.

15. Ibid., 20.

16. Mitchell and Cooper-Lewter, *Soul Theology*, 95–102, 112–15, 127–32, 141–47.

17. Long, review of *The Sacred and the Profane*, 50.

18. Ibid.

19. National Conference of Black Churchmen, "Black Power" statement, in *Black Theology: A Documentary History*, vol. 1, *1966–1979*, ed. James S. Cone and Gayraud S. Wilmore, 2nd ed. (Maryknoll, NY: Orbis Books, 1993), 555–62; as a full-page ad in the *New York Times*, Sunday, July 31, 1966, http://www.episcopalarchives.org/Afro-Anglican_history/exhibit/pdf/blackpowerstatement.pdf.

20. Using the spiritual narrative of Charles H. Mason, I illustrate this feature of self-transcendence in African American churches: Frederick L. Ware, "Can Religious Experience Be Reduced to Brain Activity? The Place and Significance of Pentecostal Narrative," in *Science and the Spirit: Pentecostal Engagements*, ed. James K. A. Smith and Amos Yong (Bloomington: Indiana University Press, 2010), 117–32.

21. For autobiographical information on Dabney, see E. J. Dabney, *What It Means to Pray Through* (1945; reprint, Memphis, TN: Church of God in Christ Publishing Board, 1987). A biography and information on Dabney's ministry appear in LaVerne Haney, "Praying Through: The Spiritual Narrative of Mother E. J. Dabney," *Journal of the Interdenominational Theological Center* 22, no. 2 (Spring 1995): 231–40.

Chapter 7: Religious Experience

1. Long, *Significations*, 9.

2. Carlyle F. Stewart, *Black Spirituality and Black Consciousness: Soul Force, Culture, and Freedom in the African-American Experience* (Trenton, NJ: Africa World Press, 1999), 20–21.

3. Ibid., 17–18.

4. Howard Thurman, *The Creative Encounter: An Interpretation of Religion and Social Witness* (Richmond, IN: Friends United Press, 1954), 20.

5. Ibid., 41, 90.

6. Ibid., 115.

7. Ibid., 65.

8. Ibid., 67, 71, 80–81.

9. Ibid., 72–74.

10. Ibid., 75–76, 87.

11. Ibid., 77–78.

12. Ibid., 130–134.

13. Carlyle F. Stewart, *Soul Survivors: An African American Spirituality* (Louisville, KY: Westminster John Knox Press, 1997), 17–19.

14. Stewart, *Black Spirituality*, 27–56, 67–69.

15. C. Eric Lincoln and Lawrence H. Mamiya, *The Black Church in the African American Experience* (Durham, NC: Duke University Press, 1990), 6.

16. Charles S. Johnson, introduction to *God Struck Me Dead*, ed. Clifton H. Johnson (Philadelphia: Pilgrim Press, 1969), xxvii.

17. Jon Alexander, *American Personal Religious Accounts, 1600–1980: Toward an Inner History of America's Faiths* (Lewiston, NY: Edwin Mellen Press, 1983), 9–11.

18. Jon Alexander, "Job Considered as a Conversion Account," *Spirituality Today* 42, no. 2 (Summer 1990): 128–29.

19. Mary Mason, compiler, *History and Life Work of Elder C. H. Mason, Chief Apostle, and His Co-Laborers* (Memphis, TN: Howe Printing Dept., 1920; reprint, Memphis, TN: Church of God in Christ Publishing House, 1924, 1987); E. J. Dabney, *What It Means to Pray Through*; Frances Burnett Kelley, *Here I Am, Send Me: The Dramatic Story of Presiding Bishop J. O. Patterson [Sr.], Challenging and Bold Leader of the Church of God in Christ* (Memphis, TN: Church of God in Christ Publishing House, 1970).

20. Mason's story is described as a narrative of self-transcendence by Ware, "Can Religious Experience Be Reduced to Brain Activity?," 117–32.

21. Gerald L. Davis, in *The Performed Word*, film produced by G. L. Davis with Paul Grindrod, 59-minute color film (Memphis, TN: Center for Southern Folklore, 1982), http://www.folkstreams.net/film,194.

22. W. E. B. Du Bois, *The Souls of Black Folk: Essays and Sketches* (Chicago: A. C. McClurg & Co., 1903), 135.

23. James H. Cone, *Speaking the Truth: Ecumenism, Liberation, and Black Theology* (Grand Rapids: Wm. B. Eerdmans Publishing Co., 1986), 22.

24. Ibid., 21–22, 26–27.

25. Phelps, "Black Spirituality," in *Taking Down our Harps*, 190.

26. Barbara A. Holmes, *Joy Unspeakable: Contemplative Practices of the Black Church* (Minneapolis: Augsburg Fortress Press, 2004), 29–31.

27. Thurman, *The Creative Encounter*, 10.

28. Cone, *Speaking the Truth*, 20, 34.

29. Thurman, *Creative Encounter*, 34–36, 86–87.

Chapter 8: Suffering

1. Thomas M. Shapiro, *The Hidden Cost of Being African American: How Wealth Perpetuates Inequality* (New York: Oxford University Press, 2004).

2. Alexander Crummell, "The Destined Superiority of the Negro," in *Preaching with Sacred Fire: An Anthology of African American Sermons, 1750 to the Present*, ed. Martha J. Simmons and Frank A. Thomas (W. W. Norton & Co., 2010), 132–33.

3. Delores S. Williams, *Sisters in the Wilderness: The Challenge of Womanist God-Talk* (Maryknoll, NY: Orbis Books, 1995), 167.

4. Ibid., 200.

5. Pinn, *Why, Lord? Suffering and Evil*, 10–11, 16–18.

6. Baker-Fletcher, *Dancing with God*, 126.

7. Ibid., 156–58.

8. Anderson, *Creative Exchange*, 83.

9. Ibid., 102.

10. Ibid., 103.

11. Henry N. Wieman, *The Source of Human Good* (Carbondale: Southern Illinois University Press, 1946; reprint, Eugene, OR: Wipf & Stock, 2008), 20, 45, 124.

12. Anderson, *Creative Exchange*, 17.

13. Ibid., 11–12.

14. Ibid., 81.

15. King, "Suffering and Faith," in *Testament of Hope*, 41–42.

16. Ibid., 42.

17. Martin Luther King Jr., *Strength to Love* (Philadelphia: Fortress Press, 1981), 92–93.

18. J. Cone, *God of the Oppressed*, 191–94.

Chapter 9: Salvation

1. J. Cone, *For My People*, 81–82.

2. Coleman, *Making a Way Out of No Way*, 97.

3. J. Cone, *A Black Theology of Liberation* (1990), 106–8.

4. Dwight N. Hopkins, *Heart and Head: Black Theology—Past Present, and Future* (New York: Palgrave Macmillan, 2002), 130–31, 134–37.

5. J. Cone, *A Black Theology of Liberation* (1990), 104.

6. J. Cone, *God of the Oppressed*, 108–15.

7. Ibid., 115–37.

8. Jacquelyn Grant, *White Women's Christ and Black Women's Jesus: Feminist Christology and Womanist Response* (Atlanta: Scholars Press, 1989), 217.

9. Jamie Phelps, "Inculturating Jesus," in Hayes and Davis, *Taking Down Our Harps*, 79.

10. Ibid., 82.

11. Lewis V. Baldwin, "Deliverance to the Captives: Images of Jesus in the Slave Community," in *Reading Communities, Reading Scripture: Essays in Honor of Daniel Patte*, ed. Gary A. Phillips and Nicole Wilkinson Duran (Harrisburg, PA: Trinity Press International, 2002), 243.

12. Phelps, "Inculturating Jesus," 87.

13. Jonathan Tran, "The New Black Theology: Retrieving Ancient Sources to Challenge Racism," *Christian Century* 129, no. 3 (February 8, 2012): 24–27, esp. 25.

14. Josiah Royce, *The Problem of Christianity* (Washington, DC: Catholic University of America Press, 2001), 104.

15. George Lakoff and Mark Johnson, *Metaphors We Live By* (Chicago: University of Chicago Press, 2003), 30–32, 144–45.

16. J. Cone, *A Black Theology of Liberation*, 93–94, 101–3.

17. Pinn, *Terror and Triumph*, 157–59, 235 n. 26.

18. Anthony B. Pinn, "Black Is, Black Ain't: Victor Anderson, African American Theological Thought, and Identity," *Dialog: A Journal of Theology* 43, no. 1 (Spring 2004), 60.

19. Baker-Fletcher, *Dancing with God*, 47, 154.

20. Ibid., 38, 140, 153.

21. Coleman, *Making a Way Out of No Way*, 94–100.

22. Stephanie Y. Mitchem, *Name It and Claim It? Prosperity Preaching in the Black Church* (Cleveland: Pilgrim Press, 2007), 30–36.

23. Olin P. Moyd, *Redemption in Black Theology* (Valley Forge, PA: Judson Press, 1979), 7.

24. Ibid., 23–24, 28.

25. Ibid., 99–100.

Chapter 10: Moral Life and Community

1. Christine P. Gambino, Edward N. Trevelyan, and John Thomas Fitzwater, "The Foreign-Born African Population from Africa: 2008–2012," American Community Survey Brief of the U.S. Census Bureau (Washington, DC: U.S. Department of Commerce, Economics and Statistics Administration, October 2014).

2. Eugene Robinson, *Disintegration: The Splintering of Black America* (New York: Doubleday, 2010).

3. Quoted from Moses, *Golden Age of Black Nationalism*, 40.

4. Ibid., 85–86, quoting Frederick Douglass.

5. Ibid., 75.

6. W. E. B. Du Bois, *Conservation of the Races*, Occasional Papers 2 (Washington, DC: American Negro Academy, 1897), 6, http://www.webdubois.org/dbConsrvOfRaces.html.

7. Moses, *Golden Age of Black Nationalism*, 96.

8. Wilson J. Moses, *Alexander Crummell: A Study of Civilization and Discontent* (New York: Oxford University Press, 1989), 292.

9. Walter Fluker, *They Looked for a City: A Comparative Analysis of the Ideal of Community in the Thought of Howard Thurman and Martin Luther King, Jr.* (Lanham, MD: University Press of America, 1989), 117, 137. Certainly, as King appropriated the term for the development of his personalist philosophy and public theology, this is what he thought beloved community meant.

10. Royce, *Problem of Christianity*, 81.

11. Tommie Shelby, *We Who Are Dark: The Philosophical Foundations of Black Solidarity* (Cambridge, MA: Belknap Press of Harvard University Press, 2007), 207–9.

12. Ibid., 233, 247.

13. Ibid., 137–39, 150–51, 201–2, 206, 216, 241–42, 244, 249.

14. Ibid., 141–44, 146.

15. W. E. B. Du Bois, *The Philadelphia Negro: A Social Study* (Philadelphia: University of Pennsylvania; Boston: Ginn & Co, 1899), 201.

16. Hopkins, *Heart and Head*, 130, 132, 134–35.

17. Ibid., 129.

18. Ibid.

19. Ronald B. Neal, "Beyond Fundamentalism: Reconstructing African American Religious Thought," *Journal of Race, Ethnicity, and Religion* 1, no. 8 (July 2010), 19, http://www.raceandreligion.com/JRER/Volume_1_%282010%29_files/Neal%201%2008.pdf.

20. Cornel West, *Democracy Matters: Winning the Fight against Imperialism* (New York: Penguin, 2005), 175–78.

21. King, "A Knock at Midnight," in *Testament of Hope*, 497–504.

22. Orishatukeh Faduma, *The Defects of the Negro Church*, Occasional Papers 10 (Washington, DC: American Negro Academy, 1904): 1–17, http://archive.org/stream/thedefectsofthen31261gut/31261.txt.

23. Lewis V. Baldwin, *The Voice of Conscience: The Church in the Mind of Martin Luther King, Jr.* (New York: Oxford University Press, 2010), 246–49.

24. West, *Prophetic Thought*, 23–26.

25. James H. Cone, *My Soul Looks Back* (Nashville: Abingdon, 1982), 88–92.

26. James H. Cone, "The White Church and Black Power," in J. Cone and Wilmore, *Black Theology*, vol. 1, *1966–1979*, 67–68.

27. Stewart, *Soul Survivors*, 20.

28. Peter J. Paris, *The Spirituality of African Peoples: The Search for a Common Moral Discourse* (Minneapolis: Fortress Press, 1994), 136–54.

29. Mitchell and Cooper-Lewter, *Soul Theology*, 141–47.

30. King, *Where Do We Go from Here?*, 70–71, 80–81, 83.
31. Ibid., 186.
32. Ibid., 98.
33. Ibid.
34. Ibid., 187.
35. Ibid., 189.
36. Ibid., 190.
37. Robert M. Franklin, *Crisis in the Village: Restoring Hope in African American Communities* (Minneapolis: Fortress Press, 2007), 217–37.
38. Stephen G. Ray, *Do No Harm: Social Sin and Christian Responsibility* (Minneapolis: Fortress Press, 2003), 33–34.
39. Ibid., 129–34.
40. Victor Anderson, *Beyond Ontological Blackness*, 13, 81, 110.
41. Hopkins, *Being Human*, 171–80.
42. Courlander, *Treasury of Afro-American Folklore*, 429–31, 438–40.
43. Stewart, *Soul Survivors*, 26–30.
44. These basic positions on violence are discussed in detail by Ware, *Methodologies of Black Theology*, 60, 74, 109.

Chapter 11: Hope

1. A. Elaine Brown Crawford, *Hope in the Holler: A Womanist Theology* (Louisville, KY: Westminster John Knox Press, 2002), 82, 112.
2. Ibid., 103, 107, 109.
3. Ibid., xii, 82.
4. Long, "Passage and Prayer," 17–18; Long, *Significations*, 184.
5. Long, "African American Religion," 371–72.
6. David Walker, *Appeal to the Coloured Citizens of the World*, http://www.docsouth.unc.edu/nc/walker/walker.html.
7. Gayraud S. Wilmore, *Pragmatic Spirituality: The Christian Faith through Africentric Lens* (New York: New York University Press, 2004), 176–77.
8. Ibid., 175.
9. C. Cone, *Identity Crisis*, 63.
10. These types are described by Timothy E. Fulop, "The Future Golden Day of the Race: Millennialism and Black Americans in the Nadir, 1877–1901," *Harvard Theological Review* 84, no. 1 (1991): 75–99.
11. Lewis V. Baldwin, "'A Home in Dat Rock': Afro-American Folk Sources and Slave Visions of Heaven and Hell," *Journal of Religious Thought* 41, no. 1 (1984): 55; James H. Cone, *The Spirituals and the Blues: An Interpretation* (New York: Seabury Press, 1972), 79–82.
12. Karla F. C. Holloway, *Passed On: African American Mourning Stories, A Memorial* (Durham, NC: Duke University Press, 2002).
13. W. Jones, *Is God a White Racist?*, 18–20, 114–16.

Chapter 12: Nature and Science

1. J. Cone, *A Black Theology of Liberation* (1990), xiv, 8, 36, 38, 75; J. Cone, *God of the Oppressed*, 54–55; J. Cone, *For My People*, 29, 41–42, 115.

2. For information on African Americans' contributions to modern science, see Charles W. Carey Jr., *African Americans in Science: An Encyclopedia of People and Progress* (Santa Barbara, CA: ABC-CLIO, 2008).

3. Hatcher, *John Jasper*, 134–49.

4. Charles Satchell Morris, "Up from a Monkey or Down from God: A Talk on Evolution," *Pittsburgh Courier*, July 18, 1925, 16.

5. J. Cone, *God of the Oppressed*, 191–94.

6. Ibid., 54.

7. Charles H. Long, *Alpha: The Myths of Creation* (New York: G. Braziller, 1963), 9, 18, 23.

8. Ibid., 16.

9. Ibid., 18, 159, 161.

10. In addition to dialogue, other relations emphasize conflict, separation, and integration. For description of these types of relations, see Ian G. Barbour, *Religion and Science: Historical and Contemporary Issues*, rev. ed. (San Francisco: HarperSanFrancisco, 1997), 77–105; Barbour, *When Science Meets Religion: Enemies, Strangers, or Partners?* (San Francisco: HarperSanFrancisco, 2000), 7–38.

11. Holmes, *Race and the Cosmos*, 54.

12. Ibid., 40.

13. Alma Booker, "Is Evolution Based on a Guess?," *Pittsburgh Courier*, August 8, 1925, 5.

14. Harriet A. Washington, *Medical Apartheid: The Dark History of Medical Experimentation on Black Americans from Colonial Times to the Present* (New York: Doubleday, 2008); George Bishop, "The Religious Worldview and American Belief about Human Origins," *Public Perspective* 9, no. 5 (1998): 39–44.

15. An example of varied opinion about modern science in the history of the black church is treated by Jeffrey P. Moran, "Reading Race into the Scopes Trial: African American Elites, Science, and Fundamentalism," *Journal of American History* 90, no. 3 (December 2003): 891–911; Moran, "The Scopes Trial and Southern Fundamentalism in Black and White: Race, Region, and Religion," *Journal of Southern History* 70, no. 1 (February 2004): 95–120.

16. Daniel Alexander Payne, *Recollection of Seventy Years* (Nashville: Publishing House of the A. M. E. Sunday School Union, 1888), 239.

Chapter 13: Christian Diversity and Religious Pluralism

1. Lincoln and Mamiya, *The Black Church*, 1.

2. David D. Daniels, "African Immigrant Churches in the United States and the Study of Black Church History," in *African Immigrant Religions in America*,

ed. Jacob K. Olupona and Regina Gemignani (New York: New York University Press, 2007), 47–60.

3. Carlton Pearson, *The Gospel of Inclusion: Reaching Beyond Religious Fundamentalism to the True Love of God and Self* (New York: Atria Books, 2009).

4. J. Cone, *God of the Oppressed*, 33.

5. Coleman, *Making a Way Out of No Way*, 41.

6. Thurman, *Creative Encounter*, 20.

7. Hopkins, *Heart and Head*, 114–24.

8. These aspects are adapted from Raimon Panikkar's theory in *The Intrareligious Dialogue*, rev. ed. (Mahwah, NJ: Paulist Press, 1999), 50, 61–70, 168–69.

Select Bibliography

Alexander, Esterlda Y. *Black Fire: One Hundred Years of African American Pentecostalism*. Downers Grove, IL: IVP Academic, 2011.

———, ed. *Black Fire Reader: A Documentary Resource on African American Pentecostalism*. Eugene, OR: Cascade Books, 2013.

Alexander, Jon. *American Personal Religious Accounts, 1600–1980: Toward an Inner History of America's Faiths*. Lewiston, NY: Edwin Mellen Press, 1983.

———. "Job Considered as a Conversion Account." *Spirituality Today* 42, no. 2 (Summer 1990): 126–40.

Allen, Norm R., ed. *African-American Humanism: An Anthology*. Amherst, NY: Prometheus Books, 1991.

Anderson, Victor. *Beyond Ontological Blackness: An Essay on African American Religious and Cultural Criticism*. New York: Continuum, 1995.

———. "Contour of an American Public Theology." *Journal of Theology* (2000): 49–68.

———. *Creative Exchange: A Constructive Theology of African American Religious Experience*. Minneapolis: Fortress Press, 2008.

———. *Pragmatic Theology: Negotiating the Intersections of an American Philosophy of Religion and Public Theology*. Albany: State University of New York Press, 1998.

ANET. See Pritchard

Baker-Fletcher, Karen. *Dancing with God: The Trinity from a Womanist Perspective*. St. Louis: Chalice Press, 2006.

———. *Sisters of Dust, Sisters of Spirit: Womanist Wordings on God and Creation*. Minneapolis: Augsburg Fortress Press, 1998.

Baldwin, Lewis V. "Deliverance to the Captives: Images of Jesus in the Slave Community." In *Reading Communities, Reading Scripture: Essays in Honor of Daniel Patte*, edited by Gary A. Phillips and Nicole Wilkinson Duran, 235–48. Harrisburg, PA: Trinity Press International, 2002.

———. "'A Home in Dat Rock': Afro-American Folk Sources and Slave Visions of Heaven and Hell." *Journal of Religious Thought* 41, no. 1 (1984): 38–57.

———. *The Voice of Conscience: The Church in the Mind of Martin Luther King, Jr.* New York: Oxford University Press, 2010.

Barbour, Ian G. *Religion and Science: Historical and Contemporary Issues*. Rev. ed. San Francisco: HarperSanFrancisco, 1997.

————. *When Science Meets Religion: Enemies, Strangers, or Partners?* San Francisco: HarperSanFrancisco, 2000.

Baumfree, Isabella. *See* Sojourner Truth

Bishop, George. "The Religious Worldview and American Belief about Human Origins." *Public Perspective* 9, no. 5 (1998): 39–44.

Booker, Alma. "Is Evolution Based on a Guess?" *Pittsburgh Courier*, August 8, 1925, 5.

Bostic, Joy R. *African American Female Mysticism: Nineteenth-Century Religious Activism.* New York: Palgrave Macmillan, 2013.

Botts, Tina F., Liam Kofi Bright, Myisha Cherry, Guntur Mallarangeng, and Quayshawn Spencer. "What Is the State of Blacks in Philosophy?" *Critical Philosophy of Race* 2, no. 2 (2014): 224–42.

Brewer, J. Mason. *American Negro Folklore.* Chicago: Quadrangle Books, 1968.

————. "Old-Time Negro Proverbs." In *Mother Wit from the Laughing Barrel: Readings in the Interpretation of Afro-American Folklore,* edited by Alan Dundes, 246–50. Jackson: University Press of Mississippi, 1990.

Burrow, Rufus. *God and Human Dignity: The Personalism, Theology, and Ethics of Martin Luther King, Jr.* Notre Dame, IN: University of Notre Dame Press, 2006.

————. *Personalism: A Critical Introduction.* St. Louis: Chalice Press, 1999.

Cannon, Katie G., Alison P. Gise Johnson, and Angela D. Sims. "Living It Out: Womanist Works in Word." *Journal of Feminist Studies in Religion* 21, no. 2 (Fall 2005): 135–46.

Cannon, Katie G., and Anthony B. Pinn, eds. *The Oxford Handbook of African American Theology.* New York: Oxford University Press, 2014.

Carey, Charles W. *African Americans in Science: An Encyclopedia of People and Progress.* Santa Barbara, CA: ABC-CLIO, 2008.

Chapman, Mark L. *Christianity on Trial: African-American Religious Thought before and after Black Power.* Maryknoll, NY: Orbis Books, 1996.

Coleman, Monica A., ed. *Ain't I a Womanist Too? Third-Wave Womanist Religious Thought.* Minneapolis: Fortress Press, 2013.

————. *Making a Way out of No Way: A Womanist Theology.* Minneapolis: Fortress Press, 2008.

————. "Must I Be a Womanist?" *Journal of Feminist Studies in Religion* 22, no. 1 (2006): 85–96.

————. "Process Thought and Womanist Theology: Black Women's Science Fiction as a Resource for Process Theology." Paper presented at the Center for Process Studies Seminar, Claremont School of Theology, April 29, 2003. http://www.ctr4process.org/sites/default/files/pdfs/26_2%20Coleman%20 -%20PT%20and%20Womanist%20theology.pdf.

Cone, Cecil W. *The Identity Crisis in Black Theology.* Nashville: African Methodist Episcopal Church, 1975.

Cone, James H. *Black Theology and Black Power*. Maryknoll, NY: Orbis Books, 1989.

————. *A Black Theology of Liberation*. Philadelphia: Lippincott, 1970. Twentieth Anniversary Edition. Maryknoll, NY: Orbis Books, 1990.

————. *The Cross and the Lynching Tree*. Maryknoll, NY: Orbis Books, 2011.

————. *For My People: Black Theology and the Black Church*. Maryknoll, NY: Orbis Books, 1984.

————. "God Is Black." In *Lift Every Voice: Constructing Christian Theology from the Underside*, edited by Susan Brooks Thistlethwaite and Mary Potter Engel, 81–94. San Francisco: Harper & Row, 1990.

————. *God of the Oppressed*. San Francisco: Harper & Row, 1975.

————. *Martin & Malcolm & America: A Dream or a Nightmare*. Maryknoll, NY: Orbis Books, 1991.

————. *My Soul Looks Back*. Nashville: Abingdon, 1982.

————. *Speaking the Truth: Ecumenism, Liberation, and Black Theology*. Grand Rapids: Wm. B. Eerdmans Publishing Co., 1986.

————. *The Spirituals and the Blues: An Interpretation*. New York: Seabury Press, 1972.

Cone, James H., and Gayraud S. Wilmore, eds. *Black Theology: A Documentary History*. Vol. 1, *1966–1979*. 2nd ed. Maryknoll, NY: Orbis Books, 1993.

————, eds. *Black Theology: A Documentary History*. Vol. 2, *1980–1992*. Maryknoll, NY: Orbis Books, 1993.

Courlander, Harold, ed. *A Treasury of Afro-American Folklore: The Oral Literature, Traditions, Recollections, Legends, Tales, Songs, Religious Beliefs, Customs, Sayings, and Humor of Peoples of African Descent in the Americas*. New York: Crown Publishers, 1976. Reprint, New York: Marlowe & Co., 1996.

Crawford, A. Elaine Brown. *Hope in the Holler: A Womanist Theology*. Louisville, KY: Westminster John Knox Press, 2002.

Dabney, Elizabeth J. *What It Means to Pray Through*. Philadelphia: E. J. Dabney, 1945. Reprint, Memphis, TN: Church of God in Christ Publishing House, 1987.

Davis, Gerald L., with Paul Grindrod, producers. *The Performed Word*. 59-minute color film. Memphis, TN: Center for Southern Folklore, 1982. http://www.folkstreams.net/film,194.

Dixie, Quinton Hosford, and Cornel West, eds. *The Courage to Hope: From Black Suffering to Human Redemption*. Boston: Beacon Press, 1999.

Douglas, Kelly Brown. *The Black Christ*. Maryknoll, NY: Orbis Books, 1993.

————. *Sexuality and the Black Church: A Womanist Perspective*. Maryknoll, NY: Orbis Books, 1999.

Douglass, Frederick. "To Our Oppressed Countrymen." *North Star* (December 3, 1847). http://chnm.gmu.edu/loudountah/resources_files/byrne_douglass.pdf.

Du Bois, W. E. B. *Conservation of the Races*. Occasional Papers 2. Washington, DC: American Negro Academy, 1897. http://www.webdubois.org/dbConsrv OfRaces.html.

―――. *The Philadelphia Negro: A Social Study*. Philadelphia: University of Pennsylvania; Boston: Ginn & Co, 1899.

―――. *The Souls of Black Folk: Essays and Sketches*. Chicago: A. C. McClurg & Co., 1903.

Dungy, Camile T., ed. *Black Nature: Four Centuries of African American Nature Poetry*. Athens: University of Georgia Press, 2009.

Dyson, Michael E. *Reflecting Black: African-American Cultural Criticism*. Minneapolis: University of Minnesota Press, 1993.

Earl, Riggins R. *Dark Symbols, Obscure Signs: God, Self, and Community in the Slave Mind*. Maryknoll, NY: Orbis Books, 1993.

Evans, James H. *We Have Been Believers: An African American Systematic Theology*. 2nd ed. Minneapolis: Fortress Press, 2012.

Faduma, Orishatukeh. *The Defects of the Negro Church*. Occasional Papers 10. Washington, DC: American Negro Academy, 1904. http://archive.org/ stream/thedefectsofthen31261gut/31261.txt.

Fitch, Suzanne P., and Roseann Manzuik. *Sojourner Truth as Orator: Wit, Story, and Song*. Westport, CT: Greenwood Press, 1997.

Floyd-Thomas, Stacey M., ed. *Deeper Shades of Purple: Womanism in Religion and Society*. New York: New York University Press, 2006.

Fluker, Walter E. *Ethical Leadership: The Quest for Character, Civility, and Community*. Minneapolis: Fortress Press, 2009.

―――. *They Looked for a City: A Comparative Analysis of the Ideal of Community in the Thought of Howard Thurman and Martin Luther King, Jr.* Lanham, MD: University Press of America, 1989.

Franklin, Robert M. *Crisis in the Village: Restoring Hope in African American Communities*. Minneapolis: Fortress Press, 2007.

Frazier, Thomas R., ed. *Readings in African-American History*. 3rd ed. Belmont, CA: Wadsworth Thompson Learning, 2001.

Fulop, Timothy E. "The Future Golden Day of the Race: Millennialism and Black Americans in the Nadir, 1877–1901." *Harvard Theological Review* 84, no. 1 (1991): 75–99.

Gambino, Christine P., Edward N. Trevelyan, and John Thomas Fitzwater. "The Foreign-Born Population from Africa: 2008–2012." American Community Survey Brief of the U.S. Census Bureau. Washington, DC: U.S. Department of Commerce, Economics and Statistics Administration, October 2014.

Glave, Dianne D. *Rooted in the Earth: Reclaiming the African American Environmental Heritage*. Chicago: Lawrence Hill Books, 2010.

Goodenough, Ursula W. "What Science Can and Cannot Offer to a Religious Narrative." *Zygon: Journal of Religion and Science* 29 (September 1994): 321–30.

Gordon, Lewis R. *An Introduction to Africana Philosophy*. New York: Cambridge University Press, 2008.

Grant, Jacquelyn. *White Women's Christ and Black Women's Jesus: Feminist Christology and Womanist Response*. Atlanta: Scholars Press, 1989.

Greer, Christina M. *Black Ethnics: Race, Immigration, and the Pursuit of the American Dream*. New York: Oxford University Press, 2013.

Haney, LaVerne. "Praying Through: The Spiritual Narrative of Mother E. J. Dabney." *Journal of the Interdenominational Theological Center* 22, no. 2 (Spring 1995): 231–40.

Harnack, Adolf von. *The History of Dogma*. Vol. 1. Translated from the 3rd German ed., by Neil Buchanan. New York: Dover Publications, 1961.

Harrison, Milmon F. *Righteous Riches: The Word of Faith Movement in Contemporary African American Religion*. New York: Oxford University Press, 2005.

Hatcher, William E. *John Jasper: The Unmatched Negro Philosopher and Preacher*. New York: Fleming H. Revell Co., 1908. http://baptisthistoryhomepage.com/jasper.sun.do.move.html.

Hayes, Diana L. *And Still We Rise: An Introduction to Black Liberation Theology*. Mahwah, NJ: Paulist Press, 1996.

———. *Forged in the Fiery Furnace: African American Spirituality*. Maryknoll, NY: Orbis Books, 2012.

Hayes, Diana L., and Cyprian Davis, eds. *Taking Down Our Harps: Black Catholics in the United States*. Maryknoll, NY: Orbis Books, 1998.

Heim, Sibyl R. "The Shakers." *CORD News* 2, no. 1 (April 1970): 27–39.

Hendricks, Obery M. *The Politics of Jesus: Rediscovering the True Revolutionary Nature of Jesus' Teachings and How They Have Been Corrupted*. New York: Three Leaves Press, 2007.

Heth, Charlotte. *Native American Dance: Ceremonies and Social Traditions*. Washington, DC: National Museum of the American Indian, Smithsonian Institution, with Starwood Publishing, 1993.

Holloway, Karla F. C. *Passed On: African American Mourning Stories, A Memorial*. Durham, NC: Duke University Press, 2002.

Holmes, Barbara A. *Joy Unspeakable: Contemplative Practices of the Black Church*. Minneapolis: Fortress Press, 2004.

———. *Liberation and the Cosmos: Conversations with the Elders*. Minneapolis: Fortress Press, 2008.

———. *Race and the Cosmos: An Invitation to View the World Differently*. Harrisburg, PA: Trinity Press International, 2002.

Hopkins, Dwight N. *Being Human: Race, Culture, and Religion*. Minneapolis: Fortress Press, 2005.

———. "Black Theology on God: The Divine in Black Popular Religion." In *The Ties That Bind: African American and Hispanic American/Latino/a Theologies in Dialogue*, edited by Anthony B. Pinn and Benjamin Valentin, 99–112. New York: Continuum, 2001.

————. *Heart and Head: Black Theology—Past, Present, and Future.* New York: Palgrave Macmillan, 2002.

————. *Introducing Black Theology of Liberation.* Maryknoll, NY: Orbis Books, 1999.

————. *Shoes That Fit Our Feet: Sources for a Constructive Black Theology.* Maryknoll, NY: Orbis Books, 1993.

Hopkins, Dwight N., and Edward P. Antonio, eds. *The Cambridge Companion to Black Theology.* New York: Cambridge University Press, 2012.

Hopkins, Dwight N., and George C. L. Cummings, eds. *Cut Loose Your Stammering Tongue: Black Theology in the Slave Narratives.* Maryknoll, NY: Orbis Books, 1991.

House, H. Wayne. "An Investigation of Black Liberation Theology." *Bibliotheca Sacra* 139, no. 554 (April 1982): 159–74.

Jaspers, Karl. *The Origin and Goal of History.* Translated from German by Michael Bullock. New Haven, CT: Yale University Press, 1953.

Johnson, Clifton H., ed. *God Struck Me Dead: Religious Conversion Experiences and Autobiographies of Ex-Slaves.* Philadelphia: Pilgrim Press, 1969.

Johnson, Paul E., ed. *African-American Christianity: Essays in History.* Berkeley: University of California Press, 1994.

Jones, Major J. *The Color of God: The Concept of God in Afro-American Thought.* Macon, GA: Mercer University Press, 1987.

Jones, William R. "Functional Ultimacy as Authority in Religious Humanism." *Religious Humanism* 12 (1978): 28–32.

————. *Is God a White Racist? A Preamble to Black Theology.* Garden City, NY: Anchor Press, 1973. Reprint, Boston, MA: Beacon Press, 1998.

————. "Religious Humanism: Its Problems and Prospects in Black Religion and Culture." *Journal of the Interdenominational Theological Center* 7 (Spring 1980): 169–86.

————. "Toward an Interim Assessment of Black Theology." *Christian Century* 89 (May 21, 1975): 513–17.

Kee, Alistair. *The Rise and Demise of Black Theology.* Enlarged ed. London: SCM Press, 2008.

King, Martin Luther, Jr. *Measure of a Man.* Philadelphia: Christian Education Press, 1959.

————. *The Papers of Martin Luther King, Jr.* Vol. 6, *Advocate of the Social Gospel, September 1948–March 1963.* Edited by Clayborne Carson, Susan Clayborne, Susan Englander, Troy Jackson, and Gerald L. Smith. Berkeley: University of California Press, 2007.

————. *In a Single Garment of Destiny: A Global Vision of Justice.* Edited by Lewis V. Baldwin. Boston: Beacon Press, 2014.

————. *Strength to Love.* Philadelphia: Fortress Press, 1981.

————. *A Testament of Hope: The Essential Writings of Martin Luther King, Jr.* Edited by James M. Washington. San Francisco: Harper & Row, 1986.

————. *Where Do We Go from Here: Chaos or Community?* New York: Harper & Row, 1967. Boston: Beacon Press, 1968.

Lakoff, George, and Mark Johnson. *Metaphors We Live By.* Chicago: University of Chicago Press, 2003.

Lincoln, C. Eric. *The Black Church Experience in Religion.* Garden City, NY: Anchor Press, 1977.

Lincoln, C. Eric, and Lawrence H. Mamiya. *The Black Church in the African-American Experience.* Durham, NC: Duke University Press, 1990.

Logan, Shirley Wilson, ed. *With Pen and Voice: A Critical Anthology of Nineteenth-Century African-American Women.* Carbondale: Southern Illinois University Press, 1995.

Long, Charles H. "African American Religion in the United States: A Bibliographic Essay." In *The African American Experience: An Historiographical and Bibliographical Guide,* edited by Arvarh E. Strickland and Robert E. Weems, 368–94. Westport, CT: Greenwood Press, 2001.

————. "African American Religion in the United States of America: An Interpretative Essay." *Nova Religio: The Journal of Alternative and Emergent Religions* 7, no. 1 (July 2003): 11–27.

————. *Alpha: The Myths of Creation.* New York: G. Braziller, 1963.

————. Review of *The Sacred and the Profane,* by Mircea Eliade. *Journal of Religion* 40, no. 1 (January 1960): 49–50.

————. *Significations: Signs, Symbols, and Images in the Interpretation of Religion.* Aurora, CO: Davies Group Publishers, 1999.

————. "The West African High God: History and Religious Experience." *History of Religion* 3, no. 2 (1964): 328–42.

————. "What Is Africa to Me? Reflection, Discernment, and Anticipation." *Journal of Africana Religions* 1, no. 1 (2013): 91–108.

Maffly-Kipp, Laurie F. *Setting Down the Sacred Past: African-American Race Histories.* Cambridge, MA: Belknap Press of Harvard University Press, 2010.

Mason, Mary, compiler. *History and Life Work of Elder C. H. Mason, Chief Apostle, and His Co-Laborers.* Memphis, TN: Howe Printing Dept., 1920. Reprint, Memphis, TN: Church of God in Christ Publishing House, 1924, 1987.

Mays, Benjamin E. *The Negro's God as Reflected in His Literature.* Boston, MA: Chapman & Grimes, 1938.

McGrath, Alister E. *Christian Theology: An Introduction.* 5th ed. Malden, MA: Wiley-Blackwell, 2010.

————, ed. *Christian Theology Reader.* 4th ed. Malden, MA: Wiley-Blackwell, 2011.

Mitchell, Henry H. *Black Belief: Folk Beliefs of Blacks in America and West Africa.* New York: Harper & Row, 1975.

Mitchell, Henry H., and Nicholas Cooper-Lewter. *Soul Theology: The Heart of American Black Culture.* San Francisco: Harper & Row, 1986.

Mitchem, Stephanie Y. *Introducing Womanist Theology*. Maryknoll, NY: Orbis Books, 2002.

———. *Name It and Claim It? Prosperity Preaching in the Black Church*. Cleveland: Pilgrim Press, 2007.

Moran, Jeffrey P. "Reading Race into the Scopes Trial: African American Elites, Science, and Fundamentalism." *Journal of American History* 90, no. 3 (December 2003): 891–911.

———. "The Scopes Trial and Southern Fundamentalism in Black and White: Race, Region, and Religion." *Journal of Southern History* 70, no. 1 (February 2004): 95–120.

Morris, Charles Satchell. "Up from a Monkey or Down from God: A Talk on Evolution." *Pittsburgh Courier*, July 18, 1925, 16.

Moses, Wilson J. *Alexander Crummell: A Study of Civilization and Discontent*. New York: Oxford University Press, 1989.

———. *The Golden Age of Black Nationalism, 1850–1925*. Hamden, CT: Archon Books, 1978.

———. "The Lost World of the Negro, 1895–1919: Black Literary and Intellectual Life before the 'Renaissance.'" *Black American Literature Forum* 21, nos. 1–2 (Spring–Summer 1987): 61–84.

Moyd, Olin P. *Redemption in Black Theology*. Valley Forge, PA: Judson Press, 1979.

Mwakikagile, Godfrey. *Relations between Africans, African Americans, and Afro-Caribbeans: Tensions, Indifference and Harmony*. Dar es Salaam, Tanzania: New Africa Press, 2007.

Neal, Ronald B. "Beyond Fundamentalism: Reconstructing African American Religious Thought." *Journal of Race, Ethnicity, and Religion* 1, no. 8 (July 2010): 1–37. http://www.raceandreligion.com/JRER/Volume_1_%282010%29_files/Neal%201%2008.pdf.

Neville, Robert. *Religion in Late Modernity*. Albany: State University of New York Press, 2002.

Olupona, Jacob K., and Regina Gemignani, eds. *African Immigrant Religions in America*. New York: New York University Press, 2007.

Panikkar, Raimon. *The Intrareligious Dialogue*. Rev. ed. Mahwah, NJ: Paulist Press, 1999.

Paris, Peter J. *The Social Teaching of the Black Churches*. Philadelphia: Fortress Press, 1985.

———. *The Spirituality of African Peoples: The Search for a Common Moral Discourse*. Minneapolis: Fortress Press, 1994.

Payne, Daniel Alexander. *Recollection of Seventy Years*. Nashville: Publishing House of the A. M. E. Sunday School Union, 1888.

Pearson, Carlton. *The Gospel of Inclusion: Reaching beyond Religious Fundamentalism to the True Love of God and Self*. New York: Atria Books, 2009.

Phelps, Jamie T., ed. *Black and Catholic: The Challenge and Gift of Black Folk: Contributions of African American Experience and Thought to Catholic Theology*. Milwaukee: Marquette University Press, 1997.

Pinn, Anthony B. "'Black Is, Black Ain't': Victor Anderson, African American Theological Thought, and Identity." *Dialog: A Journal of Theology* 43, no. 1 (Spring 2004): 54–62.

———. *Embodiment and the New Shape of Black Theological Thought*. New York: New York University Press, 2010.

———, ed. *Moral Evil and Redemptive Suffering: A History of Theodicy in African-American Religious Thought*. Gainesville: University Press of Florida, 2002.

———. Review of *The Rise and Demise of Black Theology*, by Alister Kee. *Journal of Contemporary Religion* 22, no. 1 (January 2007): 126–28.

———. *Terror and Triumph: The Nature of Black Religion*. Minneapolis: Fortress Press, 2003.

———. *What Is African American Religion?* Minneapolis: Fortress Press, 2011.

———. *Why, Lord? Suffering and Evil in Black Theology*. New York: Continuum, 1995.

———. *Writing God's Obituary: How a Good Methodist Became a Better Atheist*. Amherst, NY: Prometheus Books, 2014.

Pritchard, James B., ed. *Ancient Near Eastern Texts Relating to the Old Testament*. Princeton, NJ: Princeton University Press, 1950. 3rd ed. 1969.

Putnam, Hilary. "Meaning and Reference." *Journal of Philosophy* 70, no. 19 (1973): 699–711.

Raboteau, Albert J. *Slave Religion: The "Invisible Institution" in the Antebellum South*. New York: Oxford University Press, 1978. Updated ed. 2004.

Ray, Stephen G. *Do No Harm: Social Sin and Christian Responsibility*. Minneapolis: Fortress Press, 2003.

Roberts, James Deotis. *Liberation and Reconciliation: A Black Theology*. Rev. ed. Maryknoll, NY: Orbis Books, 1994.

Robinson, Eugene. *Disintegration: The Splintering of Black America*. New York: Doubleday, 2010.

Royce, Josiah. *The Problem of Christianity*. Washington, DC: Catholic University of America Press, 2001.

Sanders, Cheryl J. *Empowerment Ethics for a Liberated People*. Minneapolis: Fortress Press, 1995.

Sawyer, Mary R. *Black Ecumenism: Implementing the Demands of Justice*. Harrisburg, PA: Trinity Press International, 1994.

Shapiro, Thomas M. *The Hidden Cost of Being African American: How Wealth Perpetuates Inequality*. New York: Oxford University Press, 2004.

Shelby, Tommie. *We Who Are Dark: The Philosophical Foundations of Black Solidarity*. Cambridge, MA: Belknap Press of Harvard University Press, 2007.

Simmons, Martha J., and Frank A. Thomas, eds. *Preaching with Sacred Fire: An Anthology of African American Sermons, 1750 to the Present.* New York: W. W. Norton & Co., 2010.

Smith, Huston. *The World's Religions: Our Great Wisdom Traditions.* San Francisco: HarperSanFrancisco, 1991.

Smythe, Victor N., and Howard Dodson, eds. *African-American Religion: Research Problems and Resources for the 1990s.* New York: New York Public Library, 1992.

Sojourner Truth. "Ain't I a Woman?" http://www.feminist.com/resources/artspeech/genwom/sojour.htm.

Spillers, Hortense J. "Crisis of the Negro Intellectual: A Post-Date." *Boundary 2* 21, no. 3 (Autumn 1994): 66–116.

Stark, Rodney, and Roger Finke. *The Churching of America, 1776–2005: Winners and Losers in Our Religious Economy.* 2nd ed. New Brunswick, NJ: Rutgers University Press, 2005.

Stewart, Carlyle Fielding. *Black Spirituality and Black Consciousness: Soul Force, Culture, and Freedom in the African-American Experience.* Trenton, NJ: Africa World Press, 1999.

———. *Soul Survivors: An African American Spirituality.* Louisville, KY: Westminster John Knox Press, 1997.

Sweet, Leonard I. *Black Images of America, 1784–1870.* New York: W. W. Norton & Co., 1976.

Terrell, JoAnne Marie. *Power in the Blood? The Cross in the African American Experience.* Maryknoll, NY: Orbis Books, 1998. Reprint, Eugene, OR: Wipf & Stock, 2005.

Thurman, Howard. *The Creative Encounter: An Interpretation of Religion and Social Witness.* Richmond, IN: Friends United Press, 1954.

———. *Footprints of a Dream: The Story of the Church for the Fellowship of All Peoples.* Eugene, OR: Wipf & Stock, 2009.

———. *Jesus and the Disinherited.* Boston: Beacon Press, 1996.

Tillich, Paul. *Systematic Theology.* Vol. 1. Chicago: University of Chicago Press, 1951.

———. *Theology of Culture.* Edited by Robert C. Kimball. New York: Oxford University Press, 1959.

———. *What Is Religion?* Edited by James Luther Adams. New York: Harper & Row, 1969.

Tran, Jonathan. "The New Black Theology: Retrieving Ancient Sources to Challenge Racism." *Christian Century* 129, no. 3 (February 8, 2012): 24–27.

U.S. Religions Landscape Survey. *Religious Affiliation: Diverse and Dynamic.* Washington, DC: Pew Research Center, 2008.

Walker, Alice. *In Search of Our Mothers' Gardens.* New York: Harcourt Brace Jovanovich, 1983.

Walker, David. *Appeal to the Coloured Citizens of the World.* http://www.doc south.unc.edu/nc/walker/walker.html

Walker, Theodore. *Mothership Connections: A Black Atlantic Synthesis of Neoclassical Metaphysics and Black Theology.* Albany: State University of New York Press, 2004.

———. "Theological Resources for a Black Neoclassical Social Ethics." *Journal of Religious Thought* 45, no. 2 (Winter–Spring 1989): 21–39.

Walters, Wendy W. "One of Dese Mornins, Bright and Fair, / Take My Wings and Cleave de Air: The Legend of the Flying Africans and Diasporic Consciousness." *Mellus* 22, no. 3 (Fall 1997): 3–27.

Walton, Jonathan L. *Watch This! The Ethics and Aesthetics of Black Televangelism.* New York: New York University Press, 2009.

Ware, Frederick L. "Black Theology." In *Global Dictionary of Theology: A Resource for the Worldwide Church*, edited by William Dyrness and Veli-Matti Kärkkäinen, 111–18. Downers Grove, IL: InterVarsity Press, 2008.

———. "Can Religious Experience Be Reduced to Brain Activity? The Place and Significance of Pentecostal Narrative." In *Science and the Spirit: Pentecostal Engagements*, edited by James K. A. Smith and Amos Yong, 117–32. Bloomington: Indiana University Press.

———. "The Epistemic Publicity of Academic Black Theology." In *Religious Studies, Theology, and the University: Conflicting Maps, Changing Terrain*, edited by Delwin Brown and Linell Cady, 187–98. Albany: State University of New York Press, 2002.

———. "Methodologies of African American Theology." In *The Oxford Handbook of African American Theology*, edited by Anthony B. Pinn and Katie G. Cannon, 124–35. New York: Oxford University Press, 2014.

———. *Methodologies of Black Theology.* Cleveland: Pilgrim Press, 2002. Reprint, Eugene, OR: Wipf & Stock, 2008.

Warnock, Raphael G. *The Divided Mind of the Black Church: Theology, Piety, and Public Witness.* New York: New York University Press, 2014.

Washington, Harriet A. *Medical Apartheid: The Dark History of Medical Experimentation on Black Americans from Colonial Times to the Present.* New York: Doubleday, 2008.

Washington, Joseph R. *Black Religion: The Negro and Christianity in the United States.* Boston: Beacon Press, 1964.

———. *Politics of God.* Boston: Beacon Press, 1967.

Webber, Thomas L. *Deep Like the Rivers: Education in the Slave Quarter Community, 1831–1865.* New York: W. W. Norton & Co., 1978.

West, Cornel. *Beyond Eurocentrism and Multiculturalism.* Vol. 1, *Prophetic Thought in Postmodern Times.* Monroe, ME: Common Courage Press, 1993.

———. *Beyond Eurocentrism and Multiculturalism.* Vol. 2, *Prophetic Reflections: Notes on Race and Power in America.* Monroe, ME: Common Courage Press, 1993.

———. *Democracy Matters: Winning the Fight against Imperialism*. New York: Penguin, 2005.

———. *Keeping Faith: Philosophy and Race in America*. New York: Routledge, 1993.

———. *Race Matters*. Boston: Beacon Press, 1993.

Whelchel, Love Henry, Jr. *Hell without Fire: Conversion in Slave Religion*. Nashville: Abingdon Press, 2002.

Wieman, Henry N. *The Source of Human Good*. Carbondale: Southern Illinois University Press, 1946. Reprint, Eugene, OR: Wipf & Stock, 2008.

Williams, Delores S. *Sisters in the Wilderness: The Challenge of Womanist God-Talk*. Maryknoll, NY: Orbis Books, 1995.

Wilmore, Gayraud S. *Black Religion and Black Radicalism: An Interpretation of the Religious History of African Americans*. 3rd ed., revised and enlarged. Maryknoll, NY: Orbis Books, 1998.

———. *Last Things First*. Philadelphia: Westminster Press, 1982.

———. *Pragmatic Spirituality: The Christian Faith through an Africentric Lens*. New York: New York University Press, 2004.

Woodson, Carter G., ed. *Negro Orators and Their Orations*. Washington, DC: Associated Publishers, 1925. Reprint, New York: Russell & Russell, 1969.

Wright, Kai, ed. *The African-American Archive: The History of the Black Experience through Documents*. New York: Black Dog & Leventhal Publishers, 2001.

Wright, William D. *Black History and Black Identity: A Call for a New Historiography*. Santa Barbara, CA: ABC-CLIO, 2002.

———. *Crisis of the Black Intellectual*. Chicago: Third World Press, 2007.

———. *Critical Reflections on Black History*. Westport, CT: Praeger, 2002.

Yancy, George, ed. *Christology and Whiteness: What Would Jesus Do?* New York: Routledge, 2012.

Yong, Amos. *The Spirit Poured Out on All Flesh: Pentecostalism and the Possibility of Global Theology*. Grand Rapids: Baker Academic, 2005.

Young, Henry J. *Hope in Process: A Theology of Social Pluralism*. Minneapolis: Fortress Press, 1990.

Name Index

Equiano, Olaudah (Gustavus Vassa),
   63
Evans, James, 67–68

Faduma, Orishatukeh, 163, 193
Farley, Edward, 60, 112
Foster, George Burman, 80
Foster, Richard, 183
Foucault, Michel, 84, 208n2
Frank, John H., 193
Franklin, Robert, 167
Fuller, Solomon Carter, 182

Gerhard, Johann, 6, 7
Gilkes, Cheryl Townsend, 68, 81
Glave, Dianne D., 191
Gordon, Lewis R., 214n14
Grant, Jacqueline, 58, 68, 144, 145
Graves, Joseph, 188
Grimke, Francis, 64

Halbwachs, Maurice, 209n8
Haley, Alex, 63
Hamer, Fannie Lou, 68, 168
Harnack, Adolf von, 8
Harper, Frances Ellen Watkins, 64,
   65, 193
Harris, Melanie L., 207n6
Hartshorne, Charles, 82
Hayes, Diana L., 65
Heim, Sibyl R., 209n12
Holmes, Barbara, 15, 114, 128, 183,
   185–86, 191
Hopkins, Dwight, 29, 68, 102–3,
   145, 162, 166, 168, 204–5
House, H. Wayne, 213n1
Hudson, Roy Davage, 182
Hughes, Langston, 66
Hunter, Charlotte E., 183
Hurston, Zora, 62, 102, 168
Husserl, Edmund, 81
Hyde, Deborah Maxine, 182

James, William, 80
Jasper, John, 77, 78, 183–84

Jaspers, Karl, 15
Jefferson, Thomas, 64
Jennings, Willie J., 51, 145
Jones, Absalom, 13–14
Jones, Major, 68, 169
Jones, William, 68, 74, 75–77,
   78–79, 86–87, 98–99, 100–101,
   136–37, 169, 171, 178–79, 180,
   214n14

Kee, Alistair, 60
King, Martin Luther, Jr., 62, 80–81,
   104, 111, 114–15, 132, 135–36,
   142, 160, 161, 163–64, 166–67,
   168, 169, 214n23, 217n45, 222n9

Langford, George Malcolm, 182
Lee, Jarena, 68, 168
Lincoln, C. Eric, 68, 81, 124
Livingstone, L. W., 183
Lombard, Peter, 6
Long, Charles H., 16, 44, 45, 48, 49,
   61–62, 68, 81, 93, 97, 102, 111–12,
   115, 117, 122, 173, 183, 185
Luther, Martin, 9

Mamiya, Lawrence, 124
Martin, Eva Regina, 32
Mason, Charles H., 125
Matthews, Shailer, 80
Mays, Benjamin E., 91–92, 93, 94,
   99–100, 104
Melanchthon, Philipp, 6, 7
Mitchell, Henry, 68, 81, 95, 96, 117,
   165
Mitchell, Isaiah, 182–83
Mitchem, Stephanie, 110
Morris, Charles Satchell, 183, 184,
   186
Morrison, Toni, 63
Moses, Wilson J., 209n10
Moyd, Olin, 68, 154, 171

Nicholson, Hugh, 207n6
Niebuhr, Reinhold, 80

Subject Index

"abandoned minority," 159
abolitionism, 2
abundance, 152
the academy
  black theology in, 29, 85–86
  development of disciplines in, 86
  guilds of, 52, 85
Accessible Archives, 53–54
adoption, 152
aesthetics, 52
Africa
  and black culture in the U.S.,
    63–64
  before contact with Europeans,
    173
  flying to, 63
  as place of destiny, 63
  as symbol, 45, 49, 62–64
  tourism to, 63
African American Christianity. See
    also black religion
  "Apostolic" churches in, 97–98
  caricature of, 92
  contributions of, 5, 17–18, 86,
    165, 194, 199
  core beliefs of, 96, 117, 176
  pluralism and, 197–205
  as political association, 44–45
  as "true," 64, 65
African American Odyssey Collec-
    tion, 53
African Americans
  dehumanization of, 107, 108–10
  discouraged from sciences, 188
  diversity among, 77, 158–59
  as exemplars, 132, 168

humanity of, 188–91
migrations of, 158, 200–201
prioritizing concerns of, 199
rights of, as free blacks, 109
self-understanding of, 15
special "errand" of, 104
uniqueness of, 165
African American spirituality, 121–29
  emotion in, 126–28
  functions of, 123–24
  intellect in, 127–28
  as practice of freedom, 165
African American theology
  authorities of, 73–74
  black religion as subject matter of,
    44–47
  definition of, 3–5, 16–17, 31
  development of, 86–87
  diversity and, 4
  as epistemically public, 73, 76
  freedom as theme in, 12–17,
    50–51
  loci theologici of, 11–12
  monotheism and, 93–94
  origins of, 24–27
  oversimplification of, 71
  production and publication of,
    73–74, 85–86
  suspicion of, 213n1
  wholeness as theme of, 25
African American women, 68–69,
    78, 145, 167. See also womanist
    theology
  experiments on, 189
  hope of, 172
  literature of, 83

243

Printed in the USA
CPSIA information can be obtained
at www.ICGtesting.com
LVHW091959060823
754477LV00003B/318